THE BUSINESS ENVIRONMENTAL HANDBOOK

By Martin D. Westerman

Edited by Melody Joachims

OASIS PRESS
BOOKS & SOFTWARE

The Oasis Press® / PSI Research
Grants Pass, Oregon

061093

Published by The Oasis Press

The Business Environmental Handbook

© 1993 by Martin D. Westerman

This publication is designed to provide accurate and authoritative information in regard to the subject matter covered. It is sold with the understanding that the publisher is not engaged in rendering legal, accounting, or other professional service. If legal advice or other expert assistance is required, the services of a competent professional person should be sought.

> —*from a declaration of principles jointly adopted by a committee of the American Bar Association and a committee of publishers*

Editorial Assistance: Rosanno Alejandro
Page Design & Formatting: Melody Joachims
Project Assistance: Debbie Johnson, Jan Olsson
Cartography: James E. Joachims

Please direct any comments, questions, or suggestions regarding this book to The Oasis Press, Editorial Department, at the address below.

PSI Research
300 North Valley Drive
Grants Pass, OR 97526
(503) 479-9464
(800) 228-2275

The Oasis Press® is a Registered Trademark of Publishing Services, Inc., an Oregon corporation doing business as PSI Research.

Library of Congress Cataloging-in-Publication Data
Westerman, Marty.
    The business environmental handbook / by Martin D. Westerman ; edited by Melody Joachims.
        p.   cm. -- (PSI successful business library)
    Includes index.
    ISBN 1-55571-163-4 (paper) : $19.95. -- ISBN 1-55571-304-1 (binder) : $39.95
        1. Industrial management--Environmental aspects--United States.
    2. United States--Industries--Environmental aspects.
    3. Environmental protection--United States.   4. Factory and trade waste--United States--Management.   5. United States--Industries--Energy conservation.   I. Joachims, Melody.   II. Title.
    III. Series.
    HD69.P6W47   1993   92-50429
    658.4 ' 08--dc20   CIP

Printed in the United States of America
First edition

 Printed on recycled paper.

To my wife, our parents, brothers, sisters, and children.

Preface

Whether or not you believe the earth's environment is in trouble, you still need to be wary of the environmental tide of trends, public opinion, and laws that are sweeping North America. This tide is transforming the commercial world almost daily. To stay in business, you must adjust accordingly.

This book is designed to help you meet that challenge, to guide you to both an environment-friendly *and* an environment-profitable business.

It can be done. The words *environment* and *profits* do not need to be diametrically opposed to each other. In the short run, environmental changes can pose costs for businesses and affect your market. In the long run, however, environmental changes can pay dividends far into the future.

With this book, you will be able to create a comprehensive environmental plan for your business. It covers the basic A-to-Z of environmental issues: how to manage hazardous materials; reduce solid waste; make more efficient uses of water, energy, and transportation resources; improve landscaping and structural design; and generally, streamline your operations to achieve a competitive edge in the global marketplace.

You will discover how your choices of office and industrial equipment and systems directly affect your bottom line. You will learn how these choices also affect your structural designs, procurement, inventory, distribution and transportation networks, and waste treatment and disposal, as well as the health of your employees, land development and settlement patterns, and plant and animal species. The power and water you consume also affect electric and water utility decisions to expand current sources of supply, or develop new ones.

Environmental pressure is the wave in the global marketplace that forces us to operate more efficiently and profitably, use fewer resources, generate less waste, and cut costs. As new environmental demands appear, new products and jobs are created to satisfy them. This, in turn, stimulates the economy.

You can either ride this environmental wave to prosperity and efficiency, or you can allow it to sweep you away. It's your choice.

Martin Westerman

Seattle, 1993

Table of Contents

Worksheets in this Book

Worksheets in this Book (continued)

Samples in this Book

Illustrations, Charts, and Tables

Acknowledgments

Every book is a team effort. I take this opportunity to thank my "team" for the knowledge they shared with me:

Lawrence Ashley, Jim Ball, Misha Bawkage, Sue Bogert, Jim Bowman, Jack Brautigan, Mary Brown, Scott Chaplin, Doug Coburn, Ralph Earl, Nadine Edelstein, Bob Friks, Rebecca Glasscock, Steve Goldstein, Michele Hadley, Mark Hauser, Bill Hedgebeth, Rick Heede, Ray Hoffman, Phd, Sego Jackson, George Jorgensen, Susan Julick, Dan Kennedy, Mary Knackstedt, Dave Kolan, Dave Lattimer, Tod Littman, Mitch Mamagewa, Jerri McDermott, Larry McKerick, Suellen Mele, Frederica Merrell, Chaz Miller, John Morrill, Mike Nelson, Renne Nicholas, Carol O'Dahl, Eileen Parkin, Rob Penney, Bruce Perlson, Cynthia Putnam, Rick Renner, Betty Seldner, Moshe Shaller, Larry Sherwood, Randy Smith, Gifford Stack, Ron Ward, Sharon Wilson, Dave Wirth, Carl Woest-Wind, Azita Yazdani, Bill Younger, ACE[3], American Solar Energy Society, BPA, EMHI, InContext, Holden Village, SnoCo PUD

How to Use this Book

The Business Environmental Handbook is designed to help your business create a comprehensive environmental plan that can reduce your operating costs, comply with government requirements, and, most importantly, protect the environment around you. By following the directions in this guide, you will not only gain an understanding of the importance of an environmental plan for your company, but you will also be able to create a plan that best fits your company's needs.

How this Book is Organized

Chapters 1–3 provide an overview of the issues affecting business and the environment, and what you should do initially. Read these chapters first, then you can skip to the chapters and areas that are more important to your company at this time. For example, if your biggest concern is water use, then skip to Chapter 8.

Chapters 4–9 each focus on a particular area, such as energy conservation, recycling, or water use. Each chapter is in itself a standalone program — which your company can adopt alone, in combination with other programs, or as part of an overall plan incorporating all the areas discussed.

For example, your company may only be interested in recycling and transportation programs at this time; not all companies have to deal with hazardous waste, so you may want to skip that chapter entirely. This unique book will allow you to do that, helping you create a plan that can grow with your company.

Worksheets can be found at the end of their respective chapters. These worksheets will help you gather the information you need to create your environmental plan. Read the chapter leading to the worksheets in its entirety before attempting to complete the worksheets.

Efficiency Measures are found throughout the book. Use these handy tools as checklists to help you keep a record of your programs.

Coordinators/Committees are part of the action plan for each respective program. You can create a committee and coordinator for each specific program or you can create one committee that can discuss several areas, such as recycling, water use, and energy conservation.

Appendices are provided at the back of the book, listing valuable resources you can contact for additional information.

A **Glossary** is also included to explain the technical terms you will need to understand when creating your program.

Chapter 1

Issues and Options: Why Change?

Your business cannot avoid making an environmental impact. Its space has already been carved out of the land, its structures already built, its processes, resource demands, and effluents already established. In one stroke, however, you can minimize your environmental impact and benefit your business: How? — use your energy, water, and other resources more efficiently, and take advantage of "green" opportunities.

Twenty years ago, most of today's environmental laws were not even proposed. Endangered species and resource conservation were the pursuits of eccentrics. The population in general ate rainforest beef burgers from Styrofoam® clamshells and drove passenger cars whose average fuel efficiency was 12 to 14 miles per gallon. Few people "managed" their hazardous materials or bought "recycled-content" products.

Today, these are crucial issues with dramatic consequences. If your company handles hazardous materials, it may have to comply with up to 41 different local, state, and federal laws — see Appendix A. Compliance costs money. To avoid that cost, your company must reduce its reliance on hazardous materials. This reduces its exposure to regulation — and its costs in every area, from purchasing and production to waste disposal.

In fact, wherever a business can reduce its needs for energy, water, and materials, it can cut its exposure to competition, future costs of resources, and capital.

That is the purpose of this book — to help you achieve greater efficiency and be more competitive through environment-friendly improvements.

You can't attain this goal all at once. You must set achievable goals and move toward them in manageable steps in which all participants can share each accomplishment. Every new success builds confidence and creates anticipation for tackling the next step. Every step will have some cost, but every step will also pay you back.

Installing low-flow shower heads and faucet aerators can pay back in three months with reduced energy and water consumption. A lighting retrofit can cut energy use enough to return your investment in a year. Heating, air conditioning, or process flow improvements can pay back with water and energy savings in less than three years. A reduction in materials input can pay off in one year through avoided purchasing costs and disposal fees.

Whether you are handling underground storage tanks, water efficiency improvements, or recycling, you follow the same steps:

1. Create a commitment for the program from top management. Encourage employees to participate. Announce your intentions with a mission statement.
2. Eliminate obvious wastes by implementing low cost/no cost measures.
3. Perform an audit and develop a baseline index of how, where, and what quantity of resources your company uses.
4. Based on the audit, create a plan of action for implementing moderate and high-cost environmental actions, outlining costs, benefits, financing options, priorities, and schedule action.
5. Market your green image to suppliers, customers, and the public. See Appendix B for more information on green marketing.

How efficiently your company runs, and how to manage its revenues are ultimately up to you. Regulatory pressures, the cost-effectiveness of the proposed improvement, your available budget, and your corporate culture will all be factors in deciding whether or not to make the investment. You may find the current benefits don't provide as much benefit as investing the money now for future use.

Remember, the healthier and more efficient you make your business now, the more resources you will have to reinvest and devote to helping save the planet tomorrow.

By re-examining your business processes, you can reduce material that is harmful to the environment and save money, too. In many instances, you can even increase your profits by implementing environment-friendly programs.

Environment-friendly and Profitable

For years, circuit board manufacturers from California to Massachusetts used CFC-based (chlorofluorocarbon) solvents to clean solder flux from their boards. When scientists discovered the link between CFCs and ozone depletion and the federal government announced a ban on releasing CFCs into the atmosphere, these companies scrambled to find a new, environmentally-safe solvent.

They couldn't simply drop CFCs cold. They had to review their board assembly processes to find where they used CFCs and where they could make changes. In looking at the "big picture," they made an amazing discovery — in many operations, they could reduce or eliminate flux entirely. That presented them with several opportunities to save time and money:

- Reduce purchases and inventories of flux and cleaning solvents and eliminate CFCs;
- Eliminate hazardous material recordkeeping for CFCs;
- Eliminate assembly steps and costs; and
- Eliminate costs for CFC-related hazardous waste handling and disposal.

This example illustrates the point of this book: Your business can be both environment-friendly and profitable. By re-examining your business processes, you can eliminate or reduce material that is harmful to the environment and save money, too. In many instances, you can even increase your profits by implementing environment-friendly programs.

Here are two more examples:

Source Reduction

Typically, 60 to 70% of business office waste is paper and cardboard. What is the most popular solution for this problem? An office recycling program.

But wait! Before one company jumped into recycling, an employee took time to examine the flow of paperwork through her company's offices. She discovered that waste could be reduced or eliminated by better using office resources that were already in place. Among her suggestions:

- Use more electronic mail (E-mail), less paper.
- Create a cross-reference filing system to avoid having duplicate copies in separate files.
- Don't send copies to people who don't use them.
- Make two-sided photocopies.

By acting on these and other ideas, the company cut paper purchases by 35% and saved over $25,000 on procurement and labor costs during its first year alone.

Source reduction programs can save your company time and money at least six ways:

1. Less purchases made.
2. Lower inventory costs.
3. Less inventory-related taxes.
4. More efficient uses of labor.
5. More streamlined paper and materials flows.
6. Reduced waste disposal costs.

The key to source reduction is to realize that a single saving at the head of the pipe will pay you back all the way down the line to the end.

For more source and waste-reduction details, see Chapter 6.

Energy Conservation

If you operate from a home or small office, you may not think of your lights as a source of revenue or cost avoidance. Now, consider a change from incandescent bulbs and fixtures to compact fluorescents or halogens.

The drawback to these new technologies is, they can cost as much as twelve times more than standard ones. Where is the advantage to you?

The compacts last ten to twelve times longer. Besides reducing the damage to the environment caused by the release of CO_2, you save money in the following ways:

1. Ten to twelve fewer trips down the light bulb aisle of your grocery or hardware store. The time you save is money in your pocket, and time you can use to pursue other opportunities.
2. Less labor — ten to twelve fewer light bulb changes.
3. Less trash — nine to eleven fewer non-recyclable light bulbs to throw away.
4. Lower energy costs, since you get the same bulb brightness for 80% less wattage.

For more energy conservation details, see Chapter 7.

Debunking the Myths

There are two myths which must be dealt with immediately, so they won't hamper further progress.

Myth #1

Environmentalism will kill consumers' desires for goods and services and put the brakes on the engine that drives the world's economies.

Truth #1

Even in an environmentally sound future, businesses will have ample opportunities to succeed. People of the future will still need food, shelter, clothing, furnishings, means of communication, and transportation — just as people do now. They will also want reading materials and entertainment, they will travel and have hobbies, and they will collect items that interest them.

In fact, as you read on, you will see how many businesses are thriving now with environmentally sound practices. The only question for the future is how today's supplies, demands, and business cultures will evolve to satisfy new consumers of goods and services.

Myth #2

Environmental pressures will drive companies out of business. The pressures come in two shapes: (1) regulations that require costly compliance efforts and paperwork; and (2) having to bear the costs of "externalities." Externalities include:

- Treatment and disposal of wastes; and
- Protection of employees, the public, wild habitats, and resources.

Until recently, these were never considered part of commercial products or services, and instead were passed on to the consumer or the general public.

Truth #2

When presented with environmental pressures, the leading companies in America get pro-active, incorporate the new values into their operations, and continue to flourish. The list includes giants, such as 3M, AT&T, Hyatt, and McDonald's; mid-sized companies such as Ben & Jerry's, Real Goods, The Body Shop, and Puget Power; and small enterprises in every city and town in North America.

Their accomplishments include:

- More efficient uses of energy and water through new structural and process designs, equipment, monitoring and control systems, drought-tolerant landscaping or xeriscaping (also known as zeriscaping), and irrigation equipment and techniques.
- Reductions of hazardous materials use and hazardous waste outputs through production process improvements.
- Better management of supply inputs and waste disposal by restructuring procurement and usage procedures to cut purchasing, inventory, and disposal costs.

Placing a Value on Externalities

Today's environmental concerns create a demand for environmentally friendly products, services, and business practices. As businesses realize their health depends upon the health of the environment, they are taking a new look at how to value externalities, such as:

- Keeping the air people breathe clean;
- Protecting the earth's atmosphere, land, and water;
- Conserving the earth's plant and animal life; and
- Managing the garbage produced by business operations.

Few creatures on this planet can survive without air. As the value of life cannot be quantified, the value of the air on which it depends is priceless. Valued in terms of survival, a price cannot be put on the other externalities, either.

Yet until recently, businesses around the world have had access to plants, animals, minerals, land, water, and air for free or at a small cost, and assumed they were inexhaustible resources. That belief gave little incentive to conserve and protect them.

Research now indicates that these resources are finite, and so are their capacities to recover from damage. Assigning more value to the resources is

"A biological system's health is defined as its capacity for self-renewal."

Aldo Leopold
The Sand County Almanac

the best way to protect them from over-exploitation. This leads to the question of how to value the resources. For example:

- Is clean air valued more than air with smog, which results from using vehicles and factories to maintain our lifestyles and economies?
- Are wetlands — their species and the surface water they cleanse —valued more than shoreline developments and the business and traffic these developments attract?
- Are forested areas and their biodiversity valued more than timber and the building materials and pulp papers made from the timber?

Life on earth depends on air, water, biodiversity, and other natural factors. That is why it is difficult or impossible to place a dollar value on these resources. Before beginning or continuing development, ask these key questions:

- What quantity of clean air is needed for a biosphere to survive — that is, a particular population of humans, plants, and animals inhabiting a particular portion of earth?
- What natural resources are needed to supply the biosphere with clean air?
- How many acre feet of potable water does this biosphere require to maintain its entire food chain?
- What natural resources are needed to supply the water?
- What other factors, such as food and medicinal plant supplies are important and what quantities are required for survival?

After obtaining answers to the above questions, ask:

- What level of development will still allow these resources to remain healthy and insure the biosphere's survival?

None of these questions has a simple answer. Every one is debated daily in some form by people on this continent.

Commercial resistance against adding value to resources results from a status quo based on centuries of practice. In fits and starts, however, the resource revaluing process is already underway. The key questions revolve around which entities will pay:

- Higher prices for resources?
- To create and use new processes and procedures that demand fewer resources and generate less pollutants?
- To reduce and control current exhausts and effluents?
- To clean already-contaminated areas?
- To comply with and enforce environmental laws?

Some companies have answered these questions by packing up their factories and fleeing from areas where resources are highly valued and anti-pollution laws are strict, to areas where they are less valued and pollution laws are lax. As pro-environment laws and litigants gather momentum worldwide, however, these "hopping factories" can count on less and less uncontested time in each new location.

"In every deliberation we must consider the impact of our decisions on the next seven generations . . ."

Great Law of the Iroquois Nation

Other companies have invested in environmental changes which make procedures and processes more efficient, cut costs, and generate fewer pollutants and less waste. The initial price may seem high, but it pays them long-term dividends, including:

- Lower operating costs;
- Reduced exposure to penalties and liability;
- Lower employee medical and insurance costs;
- Competitive advantages over enterprises which haven't made environmental investments; and
- Enhanced public image and employee self-esteem.

How Valuing Externalities Works: Some Simple Examples

Most often, the cost burden of revaluing an externality is shared by all parties involved.

Example 1

John is a non-smoker. He arrives at his favorite restaurant, and the maitre d' seats him in the smokers' section. He demands to have his table changed.

Why? He values smoke-free air.

John, and others like him, have now put a price on air — the price of his meal check and his repeat business.

The increased value John and other non-smokers have assigned to air has spawned changes and new businesses in a wide range of areas, including:

- Creation of smoking and non-smoking sections in public and private spaces nationwide;
- Regulation of smoking and non-smoking spaces by government agencies;
- Design and construction of these spaces, including ventilation, signage, furnishings, lighting, and partitions;
- A quit-smoking industry of training centers, therapists, and products;
- Research on issues of health, human factors, and design;
- Litigation on issues related to health and space;
- Manufacture of equipment for ventilation, smoke detection, cleaning, and disinfection;
- Advertising;
- Medical procedures to correct smoking-related diseases;
- Services to clean smoky clothing, bedding, rugs, and spaces;
- Diversification by cigarette makers into other business areas, and by tobacco growers into other crops; and
- Special offerings for non-smokers by hospitality, rental car, insurance, and other industries.

Example 2

Barbara's company will be assembling delicate components for mainframe computers. Her company needs a "clean room" for the purpose. Why? To create these products, they need highly-filtered, electrically-neutral air. If they don't have a clean room, their products will be damaged before they even leave the plant.

Now, the price put on clean air is the sum of the cost of the clean room, plus the value of all the products produced with it.

Just as in Example 1, businesses have also developed to satisfy new demands for clean air in spaces where commercial processes are performed.

Business success results from spotting trends and capitalizing on them with products and services. Environmental challenges present ample opportunities on which to capitalize, in terms of streamlining operations and avoiding costs, and of supplying new commercial demands. There is no reason any business cannot be both environment-friendly, and environment-profitable.

Remember, no environmental change occurs suddenly. Each one evolves by degrees. Momentum for the change builds, public debate develops, then conversions, retrofits, shifts, and new regulations become the operating rules.

It is human nature to fight for the status quo, particularly if you operate profitably in it. You resist change at your peril, however. Companies that invest in resistance, rather than capitalizing on change, will repeatedly be caught off guard when change comes and will expose themselves to fines and other liabilities. The beverage industry is a good example of this.

Resistance Case Study: "Bottle Bills" and the Beverage Industry

In the mid-1960s, beer and soft drink producers started switching from refillable bottles (R-bottles) to cans and non-returnable (NR) bottles. Though R-bottles represented a one-time investment that could be re-used up to 14 times, trucks that carried empty R-bottles back to the plant generated no revenue, and plants used six times as much water to rewash R-bottles as to wash new cans and NR bottles. On a revenue basis, bottlers could make more profit selling 10,000 NR units than reselling 1,000 R units ten times.

The public appeared to embrace the convenience of the new one-way packages. Now they could simply throw out the empty containers because they had no deposit value. By the early 1970s, however, the public was complaining about one-way container litter on streets and highways. Nationwide, a movement grew to recreate deposits that would once again make cans and bottles valuable enough for people to collect and return.

The beverage industry protested that its products should not be singled out for such treatment. Every other industry made litterable products, and they should be included in any deposit plan, too. Grocers and packagers joined in, suggesting that people be taught to "dispose of litter appropriately" in the garbage.

The controversy built to fever pitch, and the industries spent between $1.00 and $50.00 per voter fighting bottle bills in states across the nation. During one legislative season in 1982, for example, they spent $4.5 million fighting deposits in California alone.

Despite the industry's protests, ten states passed mandatory deposit legislation and forced their bottlers and grocers back into returnable containers.

The beverage and container industries learned from their defeats and their victories. They could win against deposit advocates by helping establish and support statewide litter control and recycling programs, which collected a variety of metals, glass, papers, and other items. Why collect less than 10% of a state's litter stream with a deposit law, when you can get twice to ten times as much voluntarily with a recycling program?

With the help of an aluminum industry that placed a premium value on collecting its empty cans, the beverage and related industries brought recycling into America's mainstream. Where beverage containers are collected in curbside recycling programs, they account for less than 20% by weight of materials collected, but generate up to 73% of total scrap revenue, according to a July 1991 study by Gershman, Brickner & Bratton for the National Soft Drink Association. The Can Manufacturers Association, a packaging industry trade group based in Washington, D.C., estimates that Americans have recycled 415 billion aluminum cans alone since 1970, and that the can recycling rate was over 60% nationwide in 1991.

Did it pay beverage, packaging, and grocery interests to spend as much as they did fighting container deposit proposals? There is no way to know what the right amount to spend was, but the act of protesting and losing apparently led them to research and implement alternative solutions. The members of these industries continue to be leaders in recycling today.

You resist change at your peril. Companies that invest in resistance, rather than capitalizing on change, will repeatedly be caught off guard when change comes and will expose themselves to fines and other liabilities.

Developing Trends

As new issues and regulations face businesses in the '90s, your best avenue is to stay abreast of developing trends and incorporate them before they become controversial. Key trends to be aware of are discussed below.

Priority Shifts

In a 1991 survey of corporate shareholders, Sy Syms School of Business professor Marc Epstein found that shareholders ranked plant cleanup and stopping environmental pollution as 1 and 2 in importance. Higher dividends ranked 3. Shareholders also favored modifying corporate structures to become pro-active rather than crisis-reactive and creating incentives for ethical, environmental, and socially responsible behavior on the part of employees.

In a 1992 nationwide survey of 497 small businesses, the Kessler Exchange found that 62% were acting to make their businesses environmentally friendly because they thought it was "the right thing to do," not because of local, state, or federal mandates. Another 8% acted due to mandates, and 29% acted because of both.

Responsibilities Shift Upstream

The public and laws are moving responsibilities for externalities toward suppliers and manufacturers.

Any business that uses packaging, for example, may soon be obliged to link it with an appropriate recovery, reuse, or recycling system before introducing any new product in it. In cities that host trade shows, convention centers are beginning to include the contract requirement that exhibitors must reduce, reuse, or recycle all packaging materials they bring to the show. Some plan to prohibit any disposal of packaging materials within city limits.

In hazardous materials, laws since the early 1980s have made it cheaper to invest in new processes, environmental controls, and waste site remediation than to pay fines. Any entity that contributes hazardous waste to contaminating a site can be held liable for that action and for its cleanup without time limit.[1]

Laws also require users and manufacturers of hazardous materials to control the effects of these products, and to inform and protect their employees and the public from harm.[2] Ban dates have been set, and some bans are already in effect on a growing number of toxics and hazardous materials.

Water and Energy Supplier Shifts

It is cheaper for energy and water suppliers to make efficient use of existing capacity, than to find and develop new sources. Thus, they happily urge and assist their commercial and industrial customers toward greater efficiency.

Energy utilities now encourage customers to make structural improvements, use more efficient office and industrial equipment, and satisfy power needs through co-generation, heat recapture, and alternative energy technologies, such as on-site solar, wind, and waste-generated methane. Water suppliers urge customers to retrofit plumbing and improve processes to boost efficiencies. Both suppliers hope to satisfy as much future demand growth as they can with efficiency measures today. Their methods include:

- Rate restructuring — raising rates, fees, and charges and reducing or eliminating volume discounts;
- Providing efficiency audits for customers, and in some cases, supplying equipment, arranging retrofits and financing; and
- Producing educational materials.

A growing number of homeowners and small businesses are combining conservation and generating options to disconnect themselves from energy grids supplied by oil-, coal- or nuclear-powered and hydroelectric generating plants. At last count, a California-based company estimated that one in every 2,000 American households is now "off the grid."[3]

Waste Management Shifts

Solid waste and disposal entities also want to make better use of existing capacity. Current landfills are closing and new ones are hard to find, permit, and more costly than ever to operate. Thus, utilities and disposal contractors alike now encourage companies to streamline procurement and production systems, generate less waste, and find more appropriate ways to deal with that waste.

Their methods include:

- Raising dump fees at transfer stations and landfills;
- Adopting new priorities for waste management, such as:
  - Source reduction and inventory control;
  - Treatment and reuse;
  - Materials exchange;
  - Recycling and composting;
- Banning citizens and businesses from mixing landscape trimmings with garbage — separation is now required in more than 30 states;
- Creating advance disposal fees — fees paid at the time of purchase which subsidize the subsequent disposal costs; and
- Creating laws and tax incentives to stimulate markets for products that contain recycled materials and subsidize industries that use them in manufacturing.

Transportation Shifts

A company's worst pollution headache may be its commuting employees. Urban air pollution is bad enough that the federal government has required the 100 worst-polluted cities to create and implement air quality improvement plans within this decade. Nationwide, this means more telecommuting (working at home from telephone, computer, or both), a restructuring of land development, highway design and use patterns, public transit, and commuting.

That restructuring may force companies to rethink where they place offices and facilities, how to set work schedules, how to plan warehousing and distribution networks, and other factors.

The cheapest real estate may no longer be desirable. It may be so distant from employees, they would unacceptably impact air quality just by commuting to work.

Vehicle gas mileage and pollutant output, carbon and energy taxes, route planning, proximity of facilities and offices to the workforce, availability of public transit, bicycle lanes, car- and vanpools all are becoming factors in business decisions.

Property Rights Changes

Environmental battles are being waged over private property rights. The specific questions at issue are:

- Does the owner's right include damaging the property?
- What constitutes damage?
- Does the public have a right to intervene and stop, control, or reverse the alleged damage, and at whose expense?

The federal government will be steadily increasing its fees for such land uses as grazing, resource extraction, irrigation, timber harvesting, leases, and sales. Until recently, these resources were not so highly valued and usage fees were far below market value, which encouraged large scale exploitation and little or no mitigation of the environmental damage. The new trend is to value these publicly-owned resources at market rates, which will force more conservative use, protect the lands, change business revenue structures, and possibly result in higher commodities prices.

Regional Planning and Building Code Shifts

Expect building codes to increasingly require energy and water efficient equipment and designs for new construction and efficiency retrofits in remodeling. In sunny climates, codes may require incorporating solar panels into external surfaces; in water short areas, they may require drought-tolerant landscaping and "grey water" systems that recover used water for outdoor irrigation. Codes generally set limits on how much energy can be used per square foot for illumination, and some now require that builders provide space in new construction where recyclable materials can be stored and handled.

Noise pollution is already covered by federal law[4] and it has become a local policy issue in urban residential areas near factories, highways, and airports. "Light pollution" may show up as a problem as people decide they want to see the stars in the night sky again.

On a larger scale, regional planning is moving away from urban sprawl and toward commercial clustering honeycombed with, or surrounded by concentric areas of residential and agricultural development, mixed with green spaces and wildlife corridors. This development will also impact where businesses locate and how they operate .

When presented with environmental pressures, the leading companies in America get pro-active, incorporate the new values into their operations, and continue to flourish.

Businesses that Change with the Times

Listed below are examples of companies that have changed their processes and implemented new programs in response to growing concern for the environment.

Fast Food Companies

The two fast food giants, McDonald's and Burger King, conduct ongoing source reduction, reuse, and recycling programs that have reduced their waste output by tens of thousands of tons since they began in the late 1970s. These include several initiatives, including cuts in case and consumer packaging, use of non-disposable fountain systems, and food waste composting programs. Extra benefits: avoided costs for purchasing and disposal, less storage space requirements, and less transportation, which cuts air pollution, and hazardous materials use and waste.

Airlines

United Airlines, one of the top United States air carriers, has complete recycling facilities at its Newark, Chicago, Denver, and Seattle hubs. Newark alone, which handles only 29 flights a day, needs just two days of effort to reclaim more than a ton of aluminum cans and four tons of cardboard each month, earning United Airlines more than $2,000 a month. American, Delta, Northwest, and USAir have begun similar programs at their key airports.

Commercial Buildings

In the summer of 1989, LaSalle Partners real estate group installed silver reflectors in all 2'x4' fluorescent fixtures in their 175,000 square foot Chicago headquarters building. The change enabled them to remove two of the four lamps in each fixture and cut their operating costs by $70,000 per year. The project was lease financed at a cost of $130,000, required no up-front capitalization, and reduced electrical load in the building by 160 kilo-watts, which also eliminated the need to add $500,000-worth of new electrical switch gear.

In 1991 the National Audubon Society moved its headquarters into New York City's 1891 vintage Schermerhorn building after completing a notable renovation. In the renovation, architects and designers used tools such as the U.S. Department of Energy's DOE-2 building energy audit software to assess energy, daylighting, lighting, and mechanical opportunities and created internal recycling and compost collection systems. The renovated building's energy consumption (30,000 British thermal units per square foot) is the lowest figure ever achieved in the United States for a commercial retrofit and enables the building to operate 50% below the energy efficiency standards set by New York State's tough energy code. Paybacks in avoided costs on most of the efficiency investments are five years or less.

Recreational Equipment Companies

REI, an outdoor clothing and equipment company in Washington State, constantly re-evaluates its business practices to be sure they are consistent with the company's goal to be a good environmental citizen. REI returns all cardboard shipping boxes to its distribution center for reuse or recycling; recycles wood pallets as wood mulch or repairs them for resale; recycles office paper, glass, and aluminum; and uses only recyclable materials for packing. These and many other initiatives give REI a highly marketable green image.

Newspapers

By 1994, some 80% of U.S. newspaper editions will contain recycled pulp fiber. Twelve states have mandated this after researchers found that the quality of recycled newsprint is as good as or better than newsprint from virgin pulp wood. Other raw materials for paper, such as the grass kenaf and hemp, are also on the horizon and may someday replace wood.

Electric Utilities

Pacific Gas & Electric (PG&E) of San Ramon, California expects to satisfy only 25% of its demand growth through the end of this decade with capacity expansion. The rest will come from customer energy efficiency.

In 1990 PG&E initiated the Advanced Customer Technology Test (ACT^2) program for maximum energy efficiency. Applied to residential, commercial, industrial, and agricultural projects, ACT^2 creates new configurations and technologies to dramatically improve energy use. PG&E is already proving that energy efficiency works. Its 20,000 square foot research headquarters is combining new glazing, design daylighting, new lighting and structural systems, and energy efficient office equipment to yield total energy savings 78 to 92% below standard building systems.

Resource Companies

For nearly two decades, 3M Company has been building environmentally sound processes into product design and manufacturing, investing in pollution control equipment for older plants, forfeiting rather than selling federal pollution-reduction credits, and cleaning up its operations before state and federal regulations force it to do so. The company's Environmental Marketing Claims Review Committee ensures that all its new and existing products meet environmental claims, symbols, slogans, and firm standards for accuracy, appropriateness, and clarity before they are used.

Camp Complexes

In 1990, Brandeis-Bardin Institute, a Southern California summer camp complex, replaced the shower heads in its 120 showers with low-flow aerator units, and put one- and two-liter displacer bottles in its 30 tank-style toilets. That action helped Brandeis-Bardin cut its water demand by more than 325,000 gallons. During the same summer, the 500-guest per week facility put two tons of food waste out for compost per week and recycled one-fourth to one-half ton of packaging materials.

Snack Food Companies

Frito Lay recycles its cartons, diverting 56 million pounds of cardboard a year from landfills. They also recycle more than 20 million pounds of corn and potato waste as cattle feed, recycle used oil and solvents, and implemented a water conservation program with the goal of cutting demand by one billion gallons by the end of 1993. Most of its manufacturing plants burn natural gas as the primary fuel — one cogenerates power for sale back to the local utility's power grid; another uses waste heat from cooking operations to heat the plant. All this saves the equivalent of more than a million gallons of oil a year.

Manage the Environmental Issues Before They Manage You

The point of this chapter is issues management. For most businesses, this is a matter of developing strategies to meet the competition, set pricing, and fine-tune products.

Equally important is keeping abreast of environmental issue life cycles. You may ask yourself why the Endangered Species Act has seemingly caught so many resource companies by surprise; why the new federal nutrition guidelines are catching the meat and dairy industries off-guard; and why the Alar scare caught the apple industry unawares.

The answer is simple: They, like the beverage and packaging industries noted above, are not pro-actively handling the life cycles of the environmental issues that affect them. Instead, they are fighting these developments and suffering dramatic consequences.

Why let environmental issues catch your company off-guard? Stay informed and keep your company ahead of the game.

Regulators and business people rarely speak the same language, because regulators rarely grasp the entrepreneurial spirit. As an owner, manager, or entrepreneur today, you have a choice. You can stay in front of the wave, and make your decisions and shifts as the issues develop, or you can chase the wave, and be forced to make your moves in a regulatory environment, where people who don't understand your business present you with lists of unattractive alternatives that are expensive and dissatisfying.

Chapter 2

How to Begin

Your goal with this book is to create a more efficient business. You can streamline your operation, avoid future costs, and become a tougher, more successful competitor. Current environmental events can help you.

First, your energy, water, and disposal suppliers will provide you with incentives that include:

- Free or low-cost consultations to help make your operations more efficient;
- Low-cost and free equipment to help you improve water and energy efficiency;
- Low- or no-interest loans and rebates for efficiency investments and retrofits; and
- Alternative modes of service, such as restructuring rates based on demand changes for energy and water or dividing your disposal pickups into garbage, recyclable, and compostable materials.

Second, through tax incentives and regulations, local, state, and federal governments are helping the private sector create new markets for recycled-content products. The demands they are stimulating will help make recycled-product prices competitive with virgin products.

Third, new "eco-friendly" products appear all the time:

- Water-based solvents, adhesives, cleaners, and paints;
- Energy and water efficient equipment and technologies;
- Top quality recycled-materials products; and
- Biodegradable and recyclable packaging and packing materials.

As you take your steps toward making your business more efficient, you can employ many of these new options and products.

Do not try to do everything at once. The more limited the goals you set, the more likely you will be to succeed, and to take another step. Any one thing is enough, outside those you may be required to do by law. Once you have begun, however, you will probably want to do more.

Investments in environmental items begin paying off immediately and continue returning the initial investment over the long-term. A building-wide energy conservation retrofit can pay for itself in savings within two years, then continue to pay dividends for years after in avoided costs for equipment and labor. Your partners, investors, and stockholders will applaud these actions.

In each case, ask, "Where can we get the best leverage for the invested people, time, and capital, and reduce our exposure to liability?" If you don't feel comfortable calculating the opportunity costs yourself, find an expert to help. Here are some scenarios you may encounter:

Sample Environmental Action Items

- **You own an office building.** Will it pay you dividends in energy cost savings to retrofit your lighting, heating, and cooling systems with more efficient units? In most cases, the answer is yes. Paybacks of the initial investment in avoided costs can be as fast as six months. The first step is to get an energy audit from your utility company, or a licensed auditor. This will put you on the road to reducing your future costs for energy, cutting lamp purchasing costs and replacement labor in half, and substantially reducing waste.

- **You work out of a home office.** Is it more cost effective for you to heat or cool your entire home during the day, or just the space where you work? Answer — just your workspace. Save whole-house heating or cooling for when the whole family is home or you are entertaining.

- **Your company has landscaped grounds.** Should you lay pipe for a grey water system — one that uses the facility's clean waste water — to irrigate your plants? For example, Olympia Brewing Company of Tumwater, Washington, uses cooling water from its brewing operations to water its lush grounds. Or should you change your turf and plants to those which are compatible with your climate and need little or no extra water as they do throughout the southwest United States? Either option can be cost effective. Talk with piping specialists and your water utility about advantages of the grey water system, and with a horticulturist about plants that will save you water and money.

Make Everyone Your Partner

Whatever environmental programs you want to do, plan on the following:

- Encourage everyone to be co-owners of the environmental changes. You need their support to succeed. Make it part of your mission statement and your corporate culture. It's not a matter of simply explaining it to your board, staff, and employees, nor of imposing the program from the top, but of developing program ownership by all participants through suggestions and participation. This also avoids political problems and in-fighting.
- Redesign programs and schedules, if necessary, to accommodate environmental changes. Offer "perks," such as close-in parking for employees who carpool, free monthly transit passes for those who bus, and showers and sheltered bike racks for those who bicycle.
- Encourage employees to be alert about wastes in procurement, processes, energy and water use, and to suggest environmental improvements. Provide grounds space to experiment with food service composting to create mulch for your xeriscape.

Remember, policy starts at the top. The way to declare that policy is in a statement of mission and corporate belief. The best statement sets forth simple, clear ideas that all company employees can support. The statement from the Weyerhaeuser Paper Company in the margin of this page is a good example. Another good example is provided on page 22 from 3M Company.

Before you begin, consider the strengths and limitations discussed below.

"We support the well-being of the communities where we do business, will be responsible stewards of natural resources and will work to continually improve the environmental friendliness of our processes and products."

Weyerhaeuser Paper Company

Strengths and Limitations of Your Suppliers

Even now, many suppliers may not be up-to-date with changes on the environmental front. The markets, manufacturing and supply networks for conservation equipment, and products made of recycled materials are still being developed, and their acceptance by suppliers will come as they prove themselves.

Prices for the new "ecological" items are often higher than those for standard equipment and products made from virgin materials, because they are not widely known or distributed yet. A single 2,500-sheet box of recycled computer printer paper may cost up to $4.00 more than a box of paper made from virgin fibers.[1] As the recycled materials market develops, however, prices will even out.

Prices for new energy and water conservation equipment are more competitive. These are designed to the same specifications and install the same way as the standard items. If tradespeople or suppliers try to dissuade you from using certain items, make sure they can back up their objections with experiences and references.

You may have to research these things to enlighten yourself, your tradespeople, and your suppliers; once you get the new products, test whether or not they do work better than the old ones. Approach this as a partnership of exploration with these two groups, and it will be a win-win situation.

Strengths and Limitations of Your Locality

Most of the items and equipment mentioned in this book are readily available. Whatever you can't find locally, you can often order from catalogs — see listing in Appendix D. If you order by mail, factor delivery times into your schedule.

Recycling

The materials recyclers will take depends on your locality. In some areas, they may only take cardboard and aluminum. In others, everything. Many small towns have well-developed programs, many big cities don't.

Nationwide in the early 1990s, public response to recycling programs has taken local governments by surprise, and their contract waste haulers have amassed materials that are flooding recyclables markets, depressing scrap prices, and forcing industries in some cases to dump collected recyclable materials.

These supply gluts are adjustments the market must make as a consumer base develops, demand is created, and new plants and distribution networks are built. To learn about resources in your area, call your municipal or county solid waste department or your contract trash hauler, and check the Yellow Pages listings under "Recycling."

Composting

The scale on which you plan to implement composting will depend on how much space and equipment you'll need and whether your locality offers composting programs for yard wastes and other organic or "wet" materials. See Chapter 4 and Appendix D for further reading and resources.

Energy and Water Conservation

Your local utilities are often great resources for energy and water conservation programs. Increasingly, power and water companies provide free literature, run comparisons of your past years' bills, and do on-site surveys to help get you started on conservation. Many water companies provide conservation kits that include toilet tank displacer bags, shower flow restricter discs, and pamphlets on conserving water.

If your utility doesn't do efficiency audits, ask for referrals to experts from them, from your electrical and plumbing suppliers, or check in the Yellow Pages.

Many utilities also offer rebates and low- or zero-interest loan programs for customers that do conservation work. If you devise a way to generate electric power at your facility, the electric utility is obligated to buy your excess energy. All these options can help offset the costs of your improvements.

Hazardous Materials and Toxics

If your company does not have a hazardous materials department or specialist, contact your municipal or county solid waste, ecology, or environmental department for details on local regulations, requirements, documentation, and disposal. You can also call or write your regional Environmental Protection Agency (EPA) office for advice and reference materials. See Appendix E for a listing of EPA regional offices.

Strengths and Limitations of Your Facility

You may see endless possibilities for improving your facility or facilities, but there are limitations, such as:

- How much indoor and outdoor space you have;
- The designs, structures, and site placements of your buildings;
- Your equipment, vegetation, climate, and surroundings; and
- Your programs, personnel, and budget.

Whatever your circumstances, most conservation upgrades are so beneficial, your directors, managers, and employees should find them too good to refuse. Just follow this simple rule: take every change one step at a time.

Strengths and Limitations of Your Staff and Employees

The world's most successful companies keep their people well-trained, informed, and encouraged to take responsibility, so everyone, top to bottom, feels they have a stake in making things work.

Your staff and employees will support any program in direct proportion to the effort and enthusiasm that management puts into it. Any time you start or expand an environmental program, your success will depend on planning, equipping, and briefing your people before and during implementation. If necessary, give them opportunities to discuss and rehearse the new routines as they are developed.

On a regular basis, update your people on your progress in a way that gives them the feeling that they have been partners in the accomplishments. Even if they complain along the way, they will be eager to take some credit once they realize how successful the new efforts are.

Anticipating and Dealing with Resistance

The environment is a "good guys" issue, but your board of directors or colleagues may veto conservation, tracking, and materials management efforts if they appear to be costly or require unusual changes.

You can avoid the problem if you start with low cost/no cost measures that have clear paybacks for the invested time and money, are limited in scope, and require little or no sacrifices from your partners, investors, staff, or employees.

Point out that the possibilities are amazing. Products only imagined by science fiction writers a few decades ago are realities today, such as cellular phones, FAX machines, electronic mail, super-insulated building materials, and new lighting products. As you invest in conservation programs, you will find you save so much time and energy out front, and achieve such long-term savings and dividends, that the programs pay for themselves several times over in convenience and avoided costs.

Sample Corporate Environmental Policy

3M Corporate Environmental Policy
Adopted by the Board of Directors
February 10, 1975

3M will continue to recognize and exercise its responsibility to:

- Solve its own environmental pollution and conservation problems.
- Prevent pollution at the source wherever and whenever possible.
- Develop products that will have a minimal effect on the environment.
- Conserve natural resources through the use of reclamation and other appropriate methods.
- Assure that its facilities and products meet and sustain the regulation of all federal, state, and local environmental agencies.
- Assist, wherever possible, governmental agencies and other official organizations engaged in environmental activities.

Chapter 3

Manage Your Materials Flow

The basic lesson of this chapter is:

Less Input = Less Waste Output.

This formula applies to everything in your business, from office supplies to raw materials for manufacturing products. Just by efficiently managing your materials flow, you can reduce waste and disposal costs by at least 30% and as much as 70%.

Here are the findings of solid waste management agencies nationwide:[1]

- Source reduction and reuse — using fewer materials or reusing materials to get the same job done — can cut waste output by 10 to 30%.
- Recycling — using durable goods that can be repaired and reused, recycling fluid and solid materials, and trading materials between departments and industries through such networks as industrial materials exchanges — can further reduce throw-aways by 20 to 40%.
- Composting — transforming organic materials such as landscape trimmings and food scraps into topsoil — can cut garbage output and costs by another 10%.

Each time you reduce your waste output, you also reduce your costs for waste disposal.

Incorporating the five environmental R's into your business practices and procedures is the key to successfully managing your materials flow and reducing your disposal costs.

"There are five environmental R's now. You do the first four; Rethink, Reduce, Reuse, Recycle, and you get the fifth — Results."

The New Environmental Litany

The Five R's

The five R's are Rethink, Reduce, Reuse, Recycle, and Results. By using the first four to manage your materials flow, you will achieve the fifth.

Rethink

The days of "garbage" may be numbered. Many solid waste experts want to change its name entirely to America's "municipal supply of discards" (MSD). The new name gives it new value.

For more than a century, materials have been recycled profitably: steel, copper, and rags; then rubber tires and glass; and since the 1960s, newsprint, corrugated cardboard, aluminum, and other scrap metals. Since the late 1970s, more than 2,300 cities and towns have begun their own residential and commercial recycling programs. In more than 30 states, landscape trimmings are banned from being mixed with regular garbage for disposal. Trimmings must be separated out for composting.

Even though in many cases municipal programs are not profitable, supporters assert that recycling enables America to shift suppliers of raw materials from virgin sources to our own back yards. Recycling makes people conscious of resources they consume and throw away. Likewise, programs for composting landscape waste cut municipal disposal costs, reduce burdens on landfills, and create a product that improves soils for growing.[2]

Coupled with recycling — and in some cases composting — source reduction enables businesses to create more cost-effective systems of materials management. According to 1990 EPA figures, the 195.7 million tons of MSD produced in the United States yearly includes:

Paper & paperboard	37.5%
Wood	6.3%
Food	6.7%
Yard	17.9%
Metals	8.3%
Plastics	8.3%
Glass	6.7%
Other (leather, mattresses, construction, medical)	8.3%

Up to 90% of these (65% manufactured materials, 25% compostable materials) or up to 176 million tons a year can potentially be reclaimed for remanufacturing into new products or composted into soil amendments. According to the EPA, the United States currently recovers about 17%, or 33.3 million tons of its MSD a year. The chart on the following page shows the break down by weight.[3]

Item	Percentage Recycled
Paper & paperboard	63%
Food and yard	12%
Metals	11%
Plastics	1%
Glass	8%
Other (leather, mattresses, construction, medical)	5%

Before going further, there is another myth which must be dealt with:

Myth

Ninety percent of all MSD can be recycled.

Truth

Technically, almost everything is recyclable. The plastics industry, for example, claims that all plastics are recyclable, but they actually recycled only 2.9% of the available plastics they produced in 1991.[4] That is the question here: What can actually be recycled from the the 90% of MSD that can potentially be recovered? Assuming optimum recovery at every step, the formula for reckoning that is as follows:[5]

Category of Potential	% Possible
1. Recyclable materials	90
2. Recyclable materials that can be captured	90
3. Participation rate in recycling programs	90
4. Processing efficiency of manufacturer	90
5. Production/distribution efficiency of manufacturer	90

% of potentially recoverable MSD that can be recycled into reusable materials and delivered to market, assuming 90% efficiency at each step:

$.90 \times .90 \times .90 \times .90 \times .90 = 59\%$

So, even with the best of circumstances and conditions, we can expect to reclaim about two-thirds of our materials for manufacturing into recycled-content products. This is not a judgement on how viable or profitable recycling is, simply a tally of potential recovery rates. And on a life cycle basis, 59% efficiency is good.

Now, how much MSD does your company produce?

The figures below can be applied across the board — to individuals, on-the-road salespeople, those who work out of a home office or shop, or to groups of people working in companies. They are based upon average, per-employee waste rate survey data compiled by several agencies:[6]

Business Type	Generation Rate Lbs/Employee/Mo.
Wholesale	230
Retail	180
Food/Lodging	230
Office	50
Education (per student)	20
Other Services	170

During the average American's 70-year lifetime, he or she throws away up to 600 times his or her own weight in goods (this figure comes from plotting population growth against solid waste growth in the United States). That means that a 125-pound average American will leave this country a 75,000-pound legacy of garbage. You now have a choice — you can leave this country with a legacy of trash 600 times your own weight, or consider putting that trash on a diet. That means rethinking your day-to-day activities. The Rethink Questionnaire on pages 32–33 will help you identify areas where you can make changes.

As you rethink your activities, you may discover item after item you can eliminate or change, some dramatic, some ordinary.

Consider these developments as you begin making changes:

- Municipalities are running out of landfill space. New sites are difficult to find, get permitted, and build because new landfill standards are difficult to satisfy. City and county solid waste utilities are refusing to handle hazardous wastes without test data and permits. They are afraid their old landfills may be declared hazardous waste sites, and they and other contributors will have to pay to clean them up.

  Waste disposal utilities are raising their rates. This penalizes waste producers, and rewards waste reducers, recyclers, and composters. In fact, local, state, and federal governments are shooting for as much as a 60% recovery of paper, metals, and glass by the end of the '90s.

- To move the materials recovery process along, governments have tried banning materials from use (such as food service Styrofoam) and from landfills. They have created "recycled content" procurement policies, which give buyer price preferences to recycled-materials products over virgin. Some buyers even request that these be recycled and reused in future products they purchase.

- Governments also promote source reduction, reuse and recycling, and several governments are now considering some form of advanced disposal fees (ADFs), which the buyer of a product pays on purchase or when the used item, such as a car battery or tires, is exchanged for a new item. This fee helps offset disposal costs for that product after it has finished its useful life. More than 2,000 local governments in the United States and Canada now conduct residential and commercial recycling programs. The city of Toronto, Ontario has even begun recycling disposable diapers.

Reduce

As stated earlier, source reduction is the key to reducing your waste output. The steps below will help you get your source reduction program started.

Step 1: Create Commitment from the Top

A program in which all levels of your company participate is the most likely to succeed. Announce your intention to become resource-efficient with a public declaration from management at a staff or general meeting. Invite input from everyone at the company, and work out a simple statement that you can post for everyone to see. The statement must answer two questions: "Why are we doing this?" and "What do we expect to accomplish?"

If they understand the answers to these questions, and you celebrate or reward their achievements, people in your company will participate in the program. Keep them informed of progress and challenges through memos, bulletin boards, E-mail, or newsletters.

The statement can be broad and simple, or targeted and specific. A targeted sample, the Materials Efficiency Mission Statement, is provided on page 34.

Step 2: Tour Your Business

Tour your workplace and ask yourself this question: "What does my business throw away, and why?"

The fastest way to learn what is and is not valued in your operation is to look in your wastebaskets.

Your wastebaskets, debris piles, and dumpsters will tell you what is and is not valued in your operation, and what has been thrown out because people didn't know what else to do with it. These items can either be:

- Eliminated, saving you procurement, inventory, disposal, and associated labor and tax costs;

- Revalued through recycling or exchange programs or redesigned for more efficient use. Both options will increase your operational efficiency, decrease your labor and trash hauling costs, and eliminate your exposure to disposal liability; or

- Reoriented — incorporated for use in other processes or departments where they can be used and disposed of more effectively by employees who know what to do with the items when they are used up.

Now ask:

- "How can my suppliers make less waste for me?" Can they provide your products in larger sizes or quantities with less or without packaging? Can they reduce the amount of product and packaging waste they now provide? Open discussions with them on these points.

- "How can our business make less waste for our customers?" Is there a recycling or reuse program in place that can handle your packaging in each place that sells your product? Or must buyers just throw your packaging away? If you produce or package goods, you are potentially producing waste for them, too. Can you cut box weights and reduce or change packing materials?

Finally, keep in mind that when you buy a product, you also buy its packaging. The product is the package. On the average, packaging accounts for 50% of your garbage costs. Is the packaging necessary? Can you get the product without packaging? Can you get the product with packaging you can send back to the supplier or manufacturer for reuse or with materials you can recycle? Also, any disposable product or package you buy, you will eventually throw out. Basically, you are just renting garbage for a temporary utility it will offer you while it is clean.

In Chapter 1, you read about the results achieved by a variety of companies, from fast food and airline companies to circuit board manufacturers. Now, here are some more results in source reduction:

- Campbell Soup Company of Camden, New Jersey, redesigned its Le Menu packaging, dropping its weight by more than 50% and reducing landfill waste by an estimated 8 million pounds.
- Proctor & Gamble Co. eliminated the cartons from its Secret and Sure deodorants, saving 6 million pounds of paper pulp and keeping 80 million cartons out of landfills.
- Before it partnered with the Environmental Defense Fund, McDonald's had already eliminated nearly 12 million pounds of excess packaging from its business. Some of the many changes: adding three more pounds of frozen potatoes to its 36 pound french fries carton, removing corrugated dividers from cup packaging, and employing a fountain soft drink system that uses no disposable packaging.

Step 3: Do the Basic Low Cost/No Cost Measures

There are simple steps every business can take to start reducing the amounts of materials it consumes. These are included in the Basic Source Reduction Measures on pages 35–36.

Packing Materials

The case packaging materials for the world's products, corrugated and flat cardboard, are generally recyclable, and a growing number of companies collect them for that purpose.

To protect the products inside from damage in shipment and storage, however, every industry uses packing materials. The most-used, Styrofoam peanuts and blocks, and sheets of bubble-pack, are rarely reused or recycled and not biodegradable.

There are other options, as the Packing Materials Chart on page 37 indicates. Use them instead of plastic whenever possible.

As you make the shift to reusable materials, work with your suppliers, staff, and employees on the process. Take it gradually. It is important to start decreasing your impact on this planet, but people's habits take time to change.

Reuse

Every business realizes different savings from reusing fixtures, fluid, and solid materials. For example, one may purchase used office equipment from a salvage supplier, another may reuse packing materials for specific products. One company's by-products, surpluses, and wastes can often become another company's raw materials and furnishings.

IMEX programs provide excellent opportunities for reusing materials.

Thirty states have now set up information networks which match businesses that are offering materials with businesses that want them. These networks are usually called Industrial Materials Exchange (IMEX) programs, and they can be contacted through your local or state department of solid waste. See Appendix F for a partial listing. Some are sponsored by local or state governments as free services, some are run for profit, some non-profit. Some serve regional clientele, some only local; some issue catalogs, others put their information on-line.

Construction materials exchanges are also being developed to provide contractors with low-cost surplus goods and to donate materials to public projects.

Packaging and other materials can be reused in a number of ways. Here are several examples:

- The University of Washington molecular biology laboratory in Seattle, Washington, receives its experimental enzymes in Styrofoam coolers packed in cardboard from such suppliers as Sigma, Amersham, and New England Biolabs. All this material was thrown away until the university expressed a strong desire to reduce waste by reusing the packaging. The three suppliers agreed, as appearance of packaging makes no difference in quality of enzymes. The suppliers now include return shipping labels and pay the return postage for the packaging.

- Lee Soap, Inc., of Denver, Colorado, which grew from start-up in the 1960s into a multi-million dollar manufacturer in the 1980s, began business using reclaimed food service cans and tubs for its liquid and dry soaps. Customers joked in the '60s about the low-budget operation, then as the '70s progressed, congratulated the owners on their visionary environmental thinking.

- As the U.S. microbrewing industry opened for business in the mid-1970s, most brewpubs and start-up craft beer breweries began on shoestring budgets. Rather than purchase expensive, new computerized equipment from beer industry suppliers, these entrepreneurs ingeniously gathered and converted used stainless steel dairy tanks, piping, and controls for their purposes.

- Some industrial process companies generate sodium hydroxide as waste, while some buy it to neutralize their acid waste streams. Through an IMEX program, these industries can now be brought together. The first set of companies avoids high hazardous waste disposal costs, the second reduces or avoids procurement costs.

The Reuse Checklist on page 36 provides a few basic reuse options to help you get started.

Recycle

Before you enter the realm of recycling, be sure you are handling the front end of your business and:

1. Rethink flows of materials, reduce and reuse them, and get results in quantity reductions and dollar savings — four of the "five R's."
2. Sell off or donate your surpluses, or trade them through materials exchanges.
3. Work with your suppliers and customers to reduce materials and waste throughout your production and distribution channels.

Once you are dealing successfully with the inputs, you are ready to tackle the outputs with recycling which is explained in the next chapter.

Before we go further, however, let's have a little fun. We often see and hear claims in the media about how many resources recycling saves. On the next page is what we hope will be the ultimate list, provided by the industries themselves.

The Ultimate Table of "Recyclable" Equivalents

One Tree = 120 pounds of newsprint (4 to 6 months' worth of newspapers)
= 412 gallons of water (to make the paper pulp)

One Acre = 43,560 square foot
= 435 trees (figuring 100 square feet of space per tree (a square 10 feet on a side))

640 Acres = 1 square mile
= 278,400 trees

Recycling one ton (2,000 pounds) of paper saves these quantities of materials:
- 7,000 gallons of water
- 17 pulp trees
- 682.5 gallons of power plant oil or 10,401 kWh (enough to power an average home for six months)
- 3.3 cubic yards of landfill
- 60 pounds of air pollutants

To light one 75-watt light bulb for a year, 24 hours a day, takes 657,000 watts of energy (657 kW). To generate that 657 kW requires the following energy sources. Power plant generating efficiencies are listed in parentheses (%):

657 kW = 10,889 gallons of water through a dam's 30 megawatt (MW) hydroelectric generator (90%)
= 63 gallons of oil in an oil-fired power plant (30%)
= 516 pounds of coal in a coal-fired plant (35%)
= 59 cubic feet of gas in a natural gas-fired turbine plant (42%)

657 kW can be saved by manufacturers when they make new products from recycling:
- 404 pounds of steel
- 102 pounds of aluminum beverage cans (per recycled can batch, vs. virgin material batch)
- 371 pounds of glass

1 kWh = 3,413 Btu (British Thermal Units)

100,000 Btu = 1 Therm
= 1 cubic foot of natural gas
= 29.29 kWh

1 gallon oil = 1.3 Therm

Sources

American Paper Institute, New York, NY

Washington Natural Gas Co., Seattle, WA

Washington State Department of Ecology, Olympia, WA

Seattle City Light, Seattle, WA

Ball-Incon Glass Corp., Seattle, WA

Alcoa Aluminum Co., Pittsburgh, PA

The Steel Can Recycling Institute, Pittsburgh, PA

Rethink Questionnaire

Use a separate questionnaire for each group of related materials or each business activity.

1. Sketch the flow of materials from where they enter your business to where they exit.

Examples:

- "Paperwork Flow" includes purchase of papers, forms, notebooks, folders, etc., their storage, packaging disposal, delivery/distribution (inter-office memos to mailing), printing (on computers, in newsletters, etc.), photocopying, report assembly and distribution, filing, disposal.

- "Merchandise Flow" includes purchase, receiving, storage, delivery/distribution, packaging disposal, uses of merchandise, rotation, return or disposal.

2. Are these products necessary to our business activity? Can we use our in-place resources more effectively, and eliminate the need for one or more products in this flow? Explain:

_____

_____

_____

_____

3. How else might we (1) make this activity more efficient and (2) reduce our costs? Are all the steps in this flow necessary? Can we consolidate or eliminate steps? Explain:

_____

_____

_____

_____

4.a. Do we fully use the materials in this activity? Where do we under-utilize or over-utilize them? What can we do to improve that? Explain:

_____

_____

_____

_____

Rethink Questionnaire (continued)

4.b. Can we change from single-use or disposable units to reusable, more durable units? Explain:

_____

_____

_____

_____

5. Can we purchase products with (1) less packaging and (2) packaging that is recyclable or biodegradable? Explain:

_____

_____

_____

_____

6. How can our manufacturers and suppliers make less waste for our company? Can they eliminate packaging or consolidate loads in bulk? Can we return packaging to them for reuse? Explain:

_____

_____

_____

_____

7.a. How can our business make less waste for our customers? Can we eliminate packaging? Can we make the packaging recyclable or biodegradable? Explain:

_____

_____

_____

_____

7.b. Can we make the product recyclable or biodegradable? Explain:

_____

_____

_____

_____

8. Can we set up management and employee suggestion programs to reward people for helping the company reduce waste and improve efficiency? Explain:

_____

_____

_____

Sample Materials Efficiency Mission Statement

XYZ Company
March 12, 1994

The first paragraph should clearly state why you are doing this.

We at XYZ Company want our company to become a "world- class competitor." Toward that end, we can create a resource-efficient business that stands as one of the most forward-thinking and lowest-cost producers in our industry.

This is a team effort in which all members of this company are equal partners in making improvements and achieving successes.

Our goals are simple: reduce material and packaging waste, and make the most effective possible use of the materials that pass through our company. To do this, we must:

Here, the goals are clearly stated along with how they are to be accomplished.

- Follow the "Five Rs" — rethink, reduce, reuse, recycle, and results;
- Streamline materials flow through the company;
- Reduce the packaging and packing materials we use;
- Work with our manufacturers and suppliers to reduce or reuse their packaging materials; and
- Work to reduce the waste we pass on to our customers.

As of this date, Tony Andrews is designated as our company's conservation coordinator. As our key resource person, he will spearhead our efforts. Conservation team members include:

Team members are identified and employees are encouraged to voice their ideas.

Jessica Langford	Ext. 21
Tom Daily	Ext. 33
Sally Bradford	Ext. 44

Please approach them or our company officers with your ideas on improving our company's efficiency.

Basic Source Reduction Measures

Offices

☐ 1. Letterhead: experiment with a heavier grade and start writing business letters on both sides of it.

☐ 2. Make two-sided photocopies.

☐ 3. Use both sides of paper for inter-office communication.

☐ 4. For notepaper: use photocopy rejects, used envelopes, old memos, etc.

☐ 5. Reuse materials, such as file folders, inter-office envelopes, boxes, and paper.

☐ 6. Share reports and periodicals instead of duplicating or buying multiple copies.

☐ 7. Circulate and post memos rather than making a copy for every employee.

☐ 8. Make fewer individual direct mailings; bundle yours with direct mail packagers, and where you can, eliminate them or experiment with other methods of reaching mass audiences.

☐ 9. Use electronic mail where possible instead of paper.

☐ 10. Create a central filing system instead of maintaining duplicate personal files.

☐ 11. Recharge and reuse laser printer cartridges, and re-ink printer ribbons.

☐ 12. Remove your company name from unwanted mailing lists. Write to:

Mail Preference Service
Direct Market Association
5 East 43rd Street
New York, NY 10017-4610

☐ 13. Provide a ceramic or heavy (recycled) plastic mug for each employee, rather than paper or Styrofoam disposables.

☐ 14. Give away old magazines and newspapers to hospitals and clinics.

☐ 15. Use cloth towels rather than paper.

☐ 16. Use recycled paper or permanent metal mesh coffee filters rather than virgin white paper.

☐ 17. Contact a recycling company in your area to pick up office paper.

Food Services

☐ 1. Use linen towels, tablecloths, and napkins instead of disposable products.

☐ 2. Use soft drink dispensers, kegs, and bulk containers where appropriate rather than individual bottles or cans. Serve in reusable glasses.

☐ 3. Provide separate containers for recyclables (steel, aluminum, glass, plastic), composting (if appropriate), and garbage.

☐ 4. Invest, where appropriate, in a low-temp, water-miser dishwasher, switch to reusable dishware and flatware, and phase out disposables.

Basic Source Reduction Measures (continued)

☐ 5. Examine waste of portion control packs versus bulk food purchases in such items as condiments, cereals, drinks, and toppings. If portion control economies are better, ask your supplier or write to the manufacturer about getting the packs in materials that can be recycled, such as #1, #2, or #4 plastic.

☐ 6. Use pre-prepped foods wherever possible to reduce packaging and organic waste.

☐ 7. Send all oil and grease to a fat renderer.

Shipping and Receiving

☐ 1. Work out a system for reusing packing materials or returning them to the supplier.

☐ 2. Return cardboard boxes to distributors for credit.

☐ 3. Order products in bulk.

☐ 4. Return or repair pallets, and where possible, use pallets made of recyclable materials.

☐ 5. For internal shipping — to branch offices, stores, and warehouses — replace cardboard boxes with durable multi-use boxes.

☐ 6. Ask your suppliers to use recyclable and biodegradable packing materials for all shipments.

Reuse Checklist

☐ Contact your suppliers and customers to discuss materials and packaging you can agree to reuse, trade, or both.

☐ Use blank side of used paper for notes and rough drafts.

☐ Make two-sided photocopies.

☐ Reuse durable packaging from manufacturers and suppliers.

☐ Track equipment usage, and rent or borrow rather than buy items and equipment you rarely use.

☐ Start an in-house materials exchange program to advertise surplus items for your employees.

☐ Start a materials exchange network with businesses in your building, complex, or neighborhood, and participate with related industries and state agencies.

☐ Donate used office equipment to charitable organizations — contact each first to learn what they will accept.

☐ Buy durable goods you can repair and continue using.

Packing Materials Chart

Material	Weight*	Advantages	Disadvantages
"Eco-foam" — peanuts made from cornstarch	12 oz.	Biodegradable, water soluble; and works in assembly line packing machinery.	No anti-static version available for packaging electronics.
Popcorn	1 lb.	Offers same benefits as peanuts.	Can attract rodents and insects; no anti-static version.
Shredded corrugated cartons — usually 4"-long shreds	1 lb.	Biodegradable and recyclable cellulose fibers.	Fiber dust.
Shredded newspaper	1 lb.	Biodegradable and recyclable cellulose fibers.	Ink can rub off on packaged product, so product must be bagged.
Molded paperboard	1.5 lbs.	Biodegradable and recyclable cellulose fibers.	
Plastic foam sheets and bubble pack.	8 – 13 oz.	Reusable; anti-static version available.	Made from petroleum, sometimes with CFCs or HCFCs; not biodegradable or recyclable.
Polystyrene peanuts	4 oz.	Reusable; works in assembly line packing machinery; anti-static version available.	Made from petroleum, ethylene, benzene, and CFCs or HCFCs. Rarely recyclable. When they appear in litter and landfills, birds and small animals mistake them for food.

*Approximate weight per cubic foot

Chapter 4

Recycling

Most North American states and provinces now have commercial and residential recycling programs. Customers are either required to participate, or given incentives to sort out papers, metals, glass, and some plastics for recycling; and landscape trimmings for composting.

Because the programs are available, more and more businesses are participating and creating innovative and successful recycling programs. The list of potentially recyclable materials is long:

- Office and computer paper;
- Newsprint;
- Mixed papers;
- Scrap textiles;
- Glass and plastic containers;
- Wood and insulation;
- Cardboard and other packaging materials;
- Hard plastics;
- Plastic films and wraps;
- Car batteries;
- Aluminum, copper, steel, tin, and other scrap metals and foils;
- Oils, solvents, and antifreeze;
- Window glass; and
- Latex paints.

Of course, none of these items is recyclable unless the means are available to recycle them in volume. If there is no hauler to pick up your newspapers and no plant to de-ink and reprocess the pulp into fresh newsprint, then even if your newspapers are made of recyclable cellulose fibers, they cannot be recycled.

This is unfortunately true of most consumer plastics. Most North Americans have the misperception that plastic packaging is being recycled because plastics manufacturers mark "recyclable" on it. Although the National Association for Plastic Container Recovery (NAPCOR) asserts that all plastics can be recycled, the fact is that in North America, just over 29% of the 62 billion pounds the industry produces each year are recycled. Of that total, about half, 25 to 30 billion pounds, are disposable products.[1]

Recycling is a giant R & D project, bent on creating a forest, metal mine, and resin source in every North American business and household. To get this up and running costs money and takes time to shake out supplies and demands.

The true test of the program is to examine its successes. Here are some examples of gross savings from selected programs:

- As of 1991, the headquarters of Westin International Hotels in Seattle, Washington, has recycled 8.5 tons of scrap metal, paper, and glass; and 5.0 tons of cardboard each month. This has been accomplished using just one full-time employee as a recycling coordinator. Disposal savings and revenue equal about $9,000 a year.

- Washington State Department of Ecology reports that in more than 80% of its recycling case studies, businesses have reduced disposal costs, and in the other 20%, they have absorbed it as a cost of doing business — which means this cost has been passed along to their clients or resulted in the business becoming less competitive.

- Office blocks in Seattle, Washington, separate out cardboard, computer, high-grade white, and mixed paper and reduce garbage volume by 46 to 53% and costs by about half.

Notes on Consumer and Commercial Plastics

Before you try to set up a recycling program, you should know a little about plastics.

Lightweight, flexible, moldable, and durable, plastics have become indispensible in many applications. But most plastic waste ends up in landfills, where it accounts for about 7% of the total solid waste stream and about 20% of landfill bulk, according to EPA figures.

As of 1991, only 1,135 of 23,000 communities in the U.S. actually had plastics recycling programs. Some large-scale users, such as Anheuser-Busch of St. Louis, have developed their own industrial plastics recycling programs for strapping and shrink films. Specialty programs, such as the Aseptic

Packaging Council's juice box collection effort, were also underway in some public and private schools.

New plastics recycling technologies are being developed, but will not be commercially viable until the late 1990s or early 2000s. Also, plastic types will proliferate as new products appear. The seven basic plastic resins currently in use are explained in the chart below.

Basic Codes for Plastics

For consumers, the plastics industry identifies resins by seven basic codes:

 PET (polyethylene teraphthalate) — one- and two-liter soda bottles, some food, sauce, and sundries packages.

 HDPE (high density polyethylene) — gallon milk and juice jugs, some food packages.

 PVC (polyvynil chloride) — food and mineral water bottles.

 LDPE (low-density polyethylene) — some food product containers and lids, and plastic grocery and shopping bags.

 PP (polypropylene) — medical cases, cereal box liners.

 PS (polystyrene) — cookie, muffin and deli trays, fast food cutlery.

 OTHER — multiple plastic resins, from which layered products, such as potato and corn chip bags and some deli trays, are made.

Each resin is a category of subgroups. In the #4 area, for example, there is the opaque rigid yogurt cup, the transparent, lightweight film bag for supermarket vegetables, and the opaque, medium weight bag for checkout. A collection station for #4 bags will not accept #4 yogurt containers — they are a different resin and must be reprocessed separately.

Meanwhile, plastics disposal levels continue at a staggering pace:

- A typical North American cheese shop/delicatessen goes through 60 miles of 12 inch wide plastic film a year, wrapping and rewrapping meats, cheeses, and other perishable products to keep them fresh.
- At a typical gift trade show, participants discard enough cubic yards of Styrofoam peanuts to cover convention center floors several inches deep.
- At light industry trade shows, shrink-wrap machinery makers each day discard two to six cubic yards of film simply demonstrating their units.

Multiply these examples by hundreds of shops, shows, and machines across the continent, and you can see the quantity of plastic film and Styrofoam peanuts alone that is landfilled daily in America. And this does not even count the bubble packs, food service packs, pens, toys, electronics, and other plastics that are landfilled every day.

Until the late 1990s, any business using plastics will probably be throwing most of them out — films, piping, containers, packing materials, food service ware. If you wish to reduce your waste output and disposal costs, apply the five "R's" to plastics now.

As manufacturers of consumer plastics and multi-layer packaging face bans, restrictions, and recycling deadlines, they may pull certain ones from the market, reformulate others to fit established recycling streams or create their own nationwide recycling programs.

How to Create Your Recycling Program

The steps for creating your program are straightforward. The worksheets at the end of this chapter will walk you through the process as outlined by the Solid Waste Department of King County, Washington. The calculations in the worksheets will give you a clear picture of your business' waste and potential recyclables and of the recycling resources available to you. The Local Recycling Resource Options sheet on page 47 will tell you which worksheets to use, depending on your business size and location.

A key to your success is making space for the recycling operation. The recyclables collected from different indoor areas, buildings, and outdoor areas must be gathered at a central location for staging and hauling off-site. You'll need a staging area of about 60 to 100 square feet (using standard storage bins or dumpsters).

Cardboard will require the most space. If you are generating 1,000 pounds or more a week, it may be economical for you to invest in a compactor, or join other tenants in purchasing one. Most recyclers won't take unflattened cardboard, anyway. As whole boxes, 500 pounds of cardboard will fill a room 10 feet wide, 10 feet long, and 8 feet high. That same room will hold about eight times as much flattened cardboard.

Tin and aluminum can be stored in permanent containers or garbage cans; glass must be stored in hard-sided containers.

Set Up Your Inside Organization

After completing the recycling worksheets, you will know what you can recycle, and what the costs and savings are. Then you can set up your inside organization. First, select a recycling coordinator or recycling committee.

As you set up for recycling, have the coordinator or the committee:

1. Educate co-workers to promote the program at work. Start by collecting the most attractive recycling items, such as cardboard, computer paper, or aluminum cans. When you get that off the ground, start collecting other materials, such as newsprint, glass, or steel.

2. Work with the janitorial staff, building management, and recycler to equip and create logistics for collecting and moving the recyclables through your spaces out to the dock or parking lot for pickup. Inside, designate one or more specific places for collection.

3. Walk co-workers through the program before you start. You will have to re-set and re-label office trash bins, create new office habits, and secure new dumpsters from your recycling hauler to make this succeed. One possibility is to put out tiny garbage cans at each desk or work station, and big, centrally-placed recycling bins near each cubicle group. If you are collecting food containers, place collection bins (plastic, glass, aluminum, steel) in the employee lounge and lunchroom.

4. Create an employee suggestion system and give awards for waste reduction ideas that translate into company savings.

5. Publicize the success of your program to your employees and community. For example, The *Miami Herald* newspaper awards Eco-Hero T-shirts for kind-to-the-earth businesses that are making positive environmental changes in landscaping, recycling, and office products.

Be sure that the collection bins for each material are clearly marked. The best approach is to make each bin a different shape or color to avoid confusion over where to put each material.

Multi-tenant Recycling Programs

If you are the owner of or a tenant in a multi-tenant building, you may wish to start a building-wide recycling program. Take the same steps as those for starting a single business recycling program. Manager participation is essential to get participation in the program. It is necessary to get one person as a consistent point person to distribute information and motivate tenants. Posters are a helpful reminder.

Advantages to recycling in multi-tenant buildings, such as malls or high-rise office buildings include:

- It can be promoted as an amenity to draw tenants;
- It is a positive action for the regional environment; and
- It can improve the bottom line at the complex.

To start the recycling program, you may have to interview tenants about their waste. If waste output information is unavailable, you can use the chart on the following page to make rough estimates of the per-person weekly waste outputs for your building.

Material	Output in pounds
Wasted food	8–11
Cardboard	2–6
Paper	7–10
Steel	9
Aluminum	2
Plastic	2
Glass	2

Success revolves around making it convenient for everyone to recycle. This means creating space and making the bins available to all the tenants. It is also important to avoid confusion outdoors. A good approach is to provide different-colored dumpsters for each purpose. For example, red for recycling, green for garbage, and stickers that reinforce the message.

In areas where people recycle at home, they will come to work and want to recycle there. It's a sort of "trickle up theory." Also, it boosts everyone's morale to have consistent activities they can do both at work and home.

Purchase Recycled-Content Material

A final key is stimulating the recycling market by purchasing goods that contain reclaimed materials. More and more, recycled-material goods are becoming price competitive with virgin materials goods.

To find sources of recycled-content materials, inquire of your suppliers, look at the catalogs listed in Appendix D, and check with your IMEX and with your local solid waste utility and state environmental department.

Other Action

If you wish to take more action, write letters to suppliers and manufacturers of packages and products you feel should be made of recyclable materials. They are in business just as you are and will understand your concerns in dollars and cents terms.

You may think yours is but one letter, but rest assured, it carries weight. Most marketing and public relations departments estimate that for every one person who writes a letter, there are six to eleven more who feel the same way but don't pick up a pen. Make sure, too, that you write complimentary letters to companies you believe are doing a good job.

Finally, A Brief Look at Composting

If you produce a pound or more of food or landscaping scrap per day, explore the possibilities of composting. Resources include your local solid waste management or state environmental department, agricultural extension agent, regional EPA office, or the Solid Waste Composting Council — see Appendix D.

Composting, only an organic gardener's pursuit two decades ago, has now become big business nationwide. It promises to reduce landfill garbage dramatically, by removing landscape trimmings, food waste, paper products (non-coated, nor printed with heavy metal inks), disposable diapers, and even pet waste from the refuse stream.

Capturing this "biowaste" for reuse will affect up to half the items now thrown away, according to the EPA waste figures noted earlier.

Compost, the "complete health food meal for plants," is the end of the organic decomposition process. It is a dark, crumbly, earthy-smelling material, similar to potting soil. Its bulkiness improves texture and structure of soil and helps it retain moisture. Compost also locks nutrients and trace elements into the soil and contains beneficial bacteria that enable plants to resist disease and viruses.

Picking Out the Good Stuff

In more than 30 states, disposal customers are now required to separate landscape trimmings from other garbage for composting. The materials are processed at more than 2,000 large facilities nationwide, from commercial operators to park districts and zoos.

A growing number of summer camps compost both food and landscape wastes; many feed their food scraps to farm animals. About ten commercial facilities are also handling disposable diapers (the plastics are screened out after the process is completed).

Separation is the one problem that must be resolved before composting goes mainstream. Presently, most biodegradable materials are separated out at the composting facility. But sometimes, objects and hazardous materials get through. That causes contamination problems and reduces or kills the value of the compost batch. The solution is separation of materials at the source, or at some intermediate point, such as a transfer station. Change is coming.

Food Waste

Meanwhile, food waste is the next frontier. Already, several pilot and ongoing projects are proving its viability. These range from Seattle, Washington, commercial food waste pilot programs, to Staten Island, New York's Park Slope Intensive Zone project, which has been successfully composting residential and commercial food wastes for two years. McDonald's continues to experiment with it in the northeast and midwest; Burger King is currently doing pilot work with 34 restaurants around Minneapolis.

Your Compostable Output

How much material you make available for compost varies dramatically by business type. Where compostables may be 70% of waste from a food service or landscaping company, a sand and gravel or automotive business would have less than 1% in food and landscape waste combined.

You can handle moderate amounts of food scrap on your site with a "vermi-composting" or worm bin. For landscape materials, you can use cold or hot piles or bins to decompose them.

A number of researchers are exploring other options for on-site business composting, too, such as an automated system that businesses could lease from a composting service. The company would provide the equipment, training, maintenance, and disposal.

Contact the resources listed above and in Appendix D to keep abreast of developments. That way, as new garbage initiatives develop in your area, you won't be taken by surprise.

Local Recycling Resource Options

Small Businesses

If yours is a small business (less than ten people) working out of a residence or similar stand-alone structure, you may simply be able to sign up for your local curbside recycling program. Call your city or county solid waste department for answers, and use Worksheets II, V, and VII.

If yours is a small business operating in an office park, mall, or building, contact the management group about teaming with other tenants on a coordinated program, and rebating the savings back to participating tenants on a square-footage basis. Use Worksheets III, V, VI, VII, and VIII.

Medium-sized and Large Businesses

If yours is a medium-sized (10 to 100) or large business, follow these steps:

1. Call local recyclers; solid waste haulers; the department of solid waste, natural resources, ecology, or environment; or state recycling hotline to determine what materials can be recycled in your area. Use Worksheet I.

2. Calculate the quantities of recyclables you can expect to collect, the costs to collect them, and the money you can save by recycling. Use Worksheets II – VIII.

3. Work with your local solid waste department or recycler to organize and equip in-house education, collection, storage, and pick-up efforts.

All Businesses

Regardless of the size of your business, check your garbage cans, tour your office or facility, and talk with your janitorial staff about the feasibility of recycling.

Use this sheet to determine which recycling worksheets apply to your business.

Recycling Worksheet I — Preliminary Research

Begin the process of setting up your program here. With this first sheet, determine exactly what materials you can have recycled, exactly who does it, and how it is done. Fill out a separate worksheet for each recycler.

Name of recycler: _____

Phone: _____   **Contact:** _____

Address: _____

1. What materials do they recycle?   Minimum Required?   Quantity?

    ☐ Cardboard   ☐ Y   ☐ N   _____ lbs

    ☐ Newsprint   ☐ Y   ☐ N   _____ lbs

    ☐ Paper: ☐ mixed   ☐ separated   ☐ colored   ☐ Y   ☐ N   _____ lbs
             ☐ computer ☐ other _____

    ☐ Metal: ☐ delabeled ☐ cleaned   ☐ aluminum   ☐ Y   ☐ N   _____ lbs
             ☐ tin/steel ☐ foils

    ☐ Glass: ☐ delabeled ☐ cleaned   ☐ whole   ☐ Y   ☐ N   _____ lbs
             ☐ mixed   ☐ green   ☐ white
             ☐ brown

    ☐ Plastic: ☐ delabeled ☐ cleaned ☐ whole   ☐ Y   ☐ N   _____ lbs
               ☐ PET   ☐ HDPE   ☐ LDPE
               ☐ PE   ☐ PS   ☐ PP
               ☐ other _____

2. How often will they pick up from us? _____

3. What arrangement do they require? _____

4. Will they provide collection bins? ☐ Yes   ☐ No

5. Do they charge?   ☐ Yes   ☐ No
    If yes, how much? $_____ per_____

6. If we deliver, will they pay?   ☐ Yes   ☐ No
    If yes, how much? $_____ per_____

Recycling Worksheet II — Total Quantity of Garbage

a. Size of dumpster = _____ cubic yards

Your garbage bill usually shows the size. If not, call your garbage contractor.

b. Frequency of collection = _____ pickups/month

Your garbage bill also shows how many times the dumpster has been emptied during the billing period. Add up all collections for the year and divide by 12.

c. Average collected dumpster fullness = _____%

This may not be on the bill. You can estimate it from observation. If you are unsure, use 75% for this calculation.

d. Garbage density = _____ lbs. per cubic yard

For normal units, densities average:

- *Non-compacting dumpster = 240 lbs/cu. yd.*
- *Compacting dumpster = 700 lbs/cu. yd.*

For units with large percentages of heavy materials such as food waste, metals, glass, and construction debris, densities average:

- *Non-compacting dumpster = 360 lbs/cu. yd.*
- *Compacting dumpster = 1,050 lbs/cu. yd.*

e. Estimated garbage disposal = _____ lbs. per month

To get this figure, multiply a, b, c, and d together:

_____ X _____ X _____ X _____ = _____
   a   b   c   d   total lbs./mo.

Use this worksheet to determine how much total garbage per month your company produces in a stand-alone building or operation. If you share space and garbage collection with other tenants in a building, mall, or business park, skip to the next worksheet.

Recycling Worksheet III — Total Monthly Quantity Estimate by Business

If you share garbage service in a multi-tenant situation, and have no garbage/utility bills to which you can refer, use this chart to estimate your waste output.

Business Type	Generation Rate Lbs./Employee/Mo.
Wholesale	230
Retail	180
Food/Lodging	230
Office	50
Education (per student)	20
Other Services	170

a. Your number of employees = _____

b. Your garbage generation rate:

_____ x _____ = _____

employees x lbs./mo. (from chart) = total lbs./mo.

Recycle Worksheet IV — Self-Hauled Garbage Quantity Calculation

If you haul your own garbage directly to the transfer station or landfill, your driver will receive a receipt which shows the weight of garbage dumped and the charge for it.

a. Total weight = _____ lbs.

Enter the total of the weights from at least six months of receipts (if weights are shown in tons, multiply by 2,000 to convert to pounds).

b. Time period = _____ months

Enter the time period covered by the bills.

c. Self-haul disposal rate = _____ lbs. per month

Divide total weight (a) by time period (b).

Material Weights Checklist

Material	Quantity	Weight in Pounds
Glass		
8-ounce jar	24	9.40
32-ounce juice	12	12.00
64-ounce	6	8.90
105-ounce	4	10.20
134-ounce	4	10.75
long-neck soda/beer bottles	24	17.00
12-ounce soda/beer bottles	24	10.50
one-liter/quart bottles	12	13.50
750 ml wine bottles	6	11.60
750ml champagne	6	17.25
Aluminum cans, case	28	1.00
Steel #10 cans, food service case	6	3.50
Cardboard box, average food service		1.30
Cardboard box, heavy tomato/fruit		2.50

Now, you can estimate what quantities of recyclable materials you are generating. If you are a food service operator, you can calculate precise weights from your purchasing sheets or invoices. If you are in another business, skip to the next worksheet.

You can also plug in the weights of cartons and packaging to your ordering program, so you know the quantities of recyclable materials you will generate at the moment you order.

Recycling Worksheet V — Estimate of Recyclables by Business Type

Take the total pounds per month number from your completed Recycling Worksheet II, III, or IV and plug it into the column below labeled "Your Total Lbs/Mo" next to each material your company uses. Then, multiply that column by the number under the business category that best describes your type of business. The product will be the potentially recyclable amount of each material. * * *

Material*	Office	Retail	Whole-sale	Food/Lodging	Education	Other		Your Total Lbs/Mo		Potential Recyclable Lbs/Mo
Computer Paper	.06	.02	.02	.00	.03	.02	x	_____	=	_____
White Ledger	.09	.01	.01	.01	.03	.03	x	_____	=	_____
Newsprint	.04	.02	.02	.03	.03	.03	x	_____	=	_____
Cardboard	.11	.12	.21	.14	.12	.12	x	_____	=	_____
Mixed Paper	.24	.18	.09	.06	.21	.09	x	_____	=	_____
Glass	.03	.03	.02	.12	.03	.03	x	_____	=	_____
Plastic	.04	.09	.05	.13	.08	.08	x	_____	=	_____
Aluminum Cans	.01	.02	.01	.01	.01	.01	x	_____	=	_____
Tin Cans	.00	.01	.01	.04	.01	.01	x	_____	=	_____
Ferrous Metal	.01	.04	.05	.00	.02	.04	x	_____	=	_____
Non-Ferrous Metal	.00	.00	.02	.00	.01	.00	x	_____	=	_____
Yard Waste**	.02	.01	.04	.01	.02	.02	x	_____	=	_____
Food Waste**	.01	.11	.03	.29	.04	.05	x	_____	=	_____
Wood**	.05	.10	.18	.02	.06	.10	x	_____	=	_____

Total Potential Recyclables _____

* Include only the materials for which your area has recycling facilities.

** Yard, food, and wood waste are only now beginning to be recycled in many communities. Check to see if this option is available to you, or start your own program for these materials.

*** See next page for an example of how to complete this worksheet.

Recycling Worksheet V — Example

Take the total pounds per month number from your completed Recycling Worksheet II, III, or IV and plug it into the column below labeled "Your Total Lbs/Mo" next to each material your company uses. Then, multiply that column by the number under the business category that best describes your type of business. The product will be the potentially recyclable amount of each material.

Material*	Office	Retail	Whole-sale	Food/Lodging	Education	Other		Your Total Lbs/Mo		Potential Recyclable Lbs/Mo
Computer Paper	.06	.02	.02	.00	.03	.02	x	20	=	1.2
White Ledger	.09	.01	.01	.01	.03	.03	x	20	=	1.8
Newsprint	.04	.02	.02	.03	.03	.03	x	20	=	.8
Cardboard	.11	.12	.21	.14	.12	.12	x	___	=	___
Mixed Paper	.24	.18	.09	.06	.21	.09	x	20	=	4.8
Glass	.03	.03	.02	.12	.03	.03	x	20	=	.6
Plastic	.04	.09	.05	.13	.08	.08	x	___	=	___
Aluminum Cans	.01	.02	.01	.01	.01	.01	x	20	=	.2
Tin Cans	.00	.01	.01	.04	.01	.01	x	___	=	___
Ferrous Metal	.01	.04	.05	.00	.02	.04	x	___	=	___
Non-Ferrous Metal	.00	.00	.02	.00	.01	.00	x	___	=	___
Yard Waste**	.02	.01	.04	.01	.02	.02	x	20	=	.4
Food Waste**	.01	.11	.03	.29	.04	.05	x	20	=	.2
Wood**	.05	.10	.18	.02	.06	.10	x	___	=	___

Total Potential Recyclables   10.00

* Include only the materials for which your area has recycling facilities.

** Yard, food, and wood waste are only now beginning to be recycled in many communities. Check to see if this option is available to you, or start your own program for these materials.

This example is for an office which generates 20 pounds of waste each month.

Recycle Worksheet VI — Dollar Savings and Disposal Costs

At this point, calculate potential savings from implementing a recycling program at your business.

a. Current disposal cost = $_____ per month

You can get this figure from your garbage bill or your landfill or transfer station receipts.

b. Total quantity disposed = _____ lbs/month

Refer to your completed Recycling Worksheet II, III, or IV for this figure.

c. Recyclable potential = _____ lbs/month

Refer to your completed Recycling Worksheet V for this figure.

d. Recycling rate:

Assume you will succeed in recycling 70% of your total potentially-recyclable materials.

_____ x _____ / _____ = _____
  0.70   c   b   d (recycling rate)

e. Monthly savings:

_____ x _____ = _____ per month
  a   d   e (monthly savings))

Recycle Worksheet VII — Materials to be Recycled

1. What materials will we recycle?

   ☐ Cardboard

   ☐ Newsprint

   ☐ Paper: ☐ mixed ☐ separated ☐ colored

              ☐ computer ☐ other _____

   ☐ Metal: ☐ aluminum ☐ tin/steel ☐ foils

   ☐ Glass: ☐ mixed ☐ green ☐ white

             ☐ brown

   ☐ Plastic: ☐ PET ☐ HDPE ☐ LDPE

             ☐ PE ☐ PS ☐ PP

             ☐ other _____

2. Where will we collect them?

   ☐ Kitchen/Break Rooms

   ☐ Office

   ☐ Graphics

   ☐ Warehouse

   ☐ Shop _____

   ☐ Other _____

   ☐ Other _____

   ☐ Other _____

   ☐ Other _____

3. Where do we place the bins at each location?

   Kitchen/Break Rooms _____

   Office _____

   Graphics _____

   Warehouse _____

   Shop _____

   Other _____

   Other _____

   Other _____

   Other _____

Now that you know what your locality recycles and what types and quantities of materials you generate, you can decide what to collect at your business and where.

Recycle Worksheet VII — Materials to be Recycled (continued)

4. Who will flatten cardboard; rinse and clean foil, cans, and bottles; crush cans?

   ☐ Each individual at each location

   ☐ Staff member (whom?) _____

   ☐ Other (whom?) _____

5. How do we collect the materials? _____

   _____

   _____

   _____

   _____

   _____

   _____

   _____

   _____

6. Who in the organization handles collection? _____

   _____

   _____

7. Where do we store the recyclables for outside pickup or removal? _____

   _____

   _____

   _____

   _____

   _____

8. How will we collect the recyclables for storage?

   ☐ Vehicle collection run

   ☐ Participants bring items to collection area

9. How often? ☐ Daily ☐ Weekly

10. How often do we move the recyclables off-site? _____

    _____

    _____

Recycle Worksheet VIII — Dollar Cost and Revenue for Recycling Per Month

Dollar Cost

Materials You Will Recycle	Lbs./ Month	Cost of Space to Store Materials		Cost of Bin(s) or Dumpsters		Cost of Collection		Total Cost of Recycling per Month
Computer paper	___	$ ___	+	$ ___	+	$ ___	=	$ ___
White ledger	___	$ ___	+	$ ___	+	$ ___	=	$ ___
Mixed paper	___	$ ___	+	$ ___	+	$ ___	=	$ ___
Newsprint	___	$ ___	+	$ ___	+	$ ___	=	$ ___
Cardboard	___	$ ___	+	$ ___	+	$ ___	=	$ ___
Glass	___	$ ___	+	$ ___	+	$ ___	=	$ ___
Plastic	___	$ ___	+	$ ___	+	$ ___	=	$ ___
Aluminum	___	$ ___	+	$ ___	+	$ ___	=	$ ___
Steel	___	$ ___	+	$ ___	+	$ ___	=	$ ___
Tin	___	$ ___	+	$ ___	+	$ ___	=	$ ___
Frying fats/oils	___	$ ___	+	$ ___	+	$ ___	=	$ ___
Total Dollar Cost								$ ___

Revenue

Materials You Will Recycle	Lbs/ Month		Scrap Price per Pound		Total Revenue per Month
Computer paper	___	x	$ ___	=	$ ___
White ledger	___	x	$ ___	=	$ ___
Mixed paper	___	x	$ ___	=	$ ___
Newsprint	___	x	$ ___	=	$ ___
Cardboard	___	x	$ ___	=	$ ___
Glass	___	x	$ ___	=	$ ___
Plastic	___	x	$ ___	=	$ ___
Aluminum	___	x	$ ___	=	$ ___
Steel	___	x	$ ___	=	$ ___
Tin	___	x	$ ___	=	$ ___
Frying fats/oils	___	x	$ ___	=	$ ___
Total Revenue					$ ___

Recycle Worksheet VIII — Dollar Cost and Revenue for Recycling Per Month (continued)

Net Cost/Revenue

Materials You Will Recycle	Recycling Revenue		Recycling Cost		Net Profit or Loss per Material
Computer paper	$ _____	–	$ _____	=	$ _____
White ledger	$ _____	–	$ _____	=	$ _____
Mixed paper	$ _____	–	$ _____	=	$ _____
Newsprint	$ _____	–	$ _____	=	$ _____
Cardboard	$ _____	–	$ _____	=	$ _____
Glass	$ _____	–	$ _____	=	$ _____
Plastic	$ _____	–	$ _____	=	$ _____
Aluminum	$ _____	–	$ _____	=	$ _____
Steel	$ _____	–	$ _____	=	$ _____
Tin	$ _____	–	$ _____	=	$ _____
Frying fats/oils	$ _____	–	$ _____	=	$ _____
Net Profit or Loss					$ _____

Chapter 5

Successfully Handling Hazardous Materials

A University student feared the spiders in her apartment so much, she emptied a can of Raid on them one day. Then she discovered, to her dismay, that the airborne pesticide residue had settled on the surface water of her aquarium and killed her tropical fish.

This is the hazardous materials problem in a nutshell.

Hazardous materials can be potential liabilities for anyone that handles them, because they can cause harm far outside the areas where they are intended for use. For businesses, they can impact employee health, insurance costs, operations and disposal costs, and real estate transactions.

Once a hazardous materi-al enters your possession, you are responsible for it and any damage it may cause forever after.

Of course, hazardous materials have always had these impacts. Archeologists believe that ancient potters died of lead poisoning contracted from their glazes. The "Mad Hatter" from Alice in Wonderland was based on real hat makers who became brain-damaged from the mercury they used to cure felt. It is only in the last 20 years, however, that laws and regulations have begun laying responsibilities and liabilities for hazardous materials at the doorsteps of users and manufacturers and the government agencies that passed the laws.

The message is clear: Whomever acquires a hazardous substance is responsible for it from the moment it enters their possession. After you use a toxic material, it becomes hazardous waste. If you dispose of it unsafely, you and your company can be held liable indefinitely for that action, and for whatever damage that substance does. There is no statute of limitations on hazardous waste damage.

Definitions

The simplest definitions of a hazardous material, or toxic substance, is printed right on its package label. Look for words, such as:

- Caustic
- Flammable
- Corrosive
- Reactive

Or warnings, such as:

- Ventilate area during use.
- Irritates skin and eyes.
- Wear protective clothing.
- Harmful or fatal if swallowed.
- Keep out of reach of children.

All toxic chemicals are hazardous, but not all hazardous chemicals are toxic. Ethanol (grain alcohol), for example, is hazardous, since it is flammable and will burn readily at temperatures consistent with regulatory definitions. It can be ingested by humans, however, at 95% concentration (190 proof) in limited quantities without causing illness or death, so it is not considered toxic. On the other hand, dioxin, PCBs, creosote, asbestos and the pesticide 2,4,5-T are both toxic and hazardous.

The laws divide hazardous substances into categories according to the level of harm they can do to living things. There are extremely hazardous materials (EHM), from which come extremely hazardous wastes (EHW), and hazardous materials (HM), from which, generally, come hazardous wastes (HW). There are exceptions, however, such as ammonia, which is a hazardous material but not a hazardous waste.

Hazardous materials are usually judged on four characteristics:

- Toxicity — fatal or irreparably harmful to living things in tiny doses;
- Ignitability — having a low flash point;
- Reactivity — unstable in air or water; or
- Corrosivity — extremely corrosive (acidic, alkaline, or able to corrode steel).

Hazardous materials and HW present the same dangers as EHM and EHW, but to lesser degrees.

The laws also define the generators of hazardous wastes by the amounts they produce each month.[1] See the chart on the next page.

If you operate out of a household or are a conditionally exempt generator, your waste may be exempt from current laws because you generate less HW or EHW than they regulate. Your waste isn't any less dangerous, even though it is reclassified by some municipalities and states as moderate risk waste (MRW). Local and county solid waste departments across the United

States are now beginning to survey, quantify, and regulate this type of material and waste and to develop local collection and commercial minimization programs.

So, instead of mixing your HW with the regular garbage, contact your city or county solid waste management department to ask about available disposal options. These could include participating in hazardous materials collection events, dropping used oil and antifreeze with collectors, or connecting with a hazardous waste contractor.

Waste Generator	Waste Produced Per Month
"Household" and "Conditionally Exempt Small Quantity Generator" (SQG)	1 kg (2.2 lbs) or less of EHW, or spill cleanup debris containing EHW.
	100 kg (220 lbs) or less of HW, or spill cleanup debris containing HW.
	Accumulation of up to 2,200 pounds of HW on-site.
"Moderate or Medium Quantity Generator"	100.1 kg (221 lbs) to 1,000 kg (2,199.9 lbs) of HW, or spill cleanup debris containing HW.
	Accumulation of more than 2,200 pounds of HW on-site.
"Large Quantity Generator" (LQG)	More than 1 kg (2.2 lbs) of EHW, or more than 100 kg (220 lbs) of spill cleanup debris containing EHW.
	More than 1,000 kg (2,200 lbs) of HW, or more than 1,000 kg of spill cleanup debris containing HW.
	Accumulation of more than one kilogram (2.2 lb) of EHW on-site.

See Appendix A for more information on hazardous materials.

Materials Safety Data Sheets and Hazardous Materials Identification System

Basic information about toxic substances in the products you use is usually listed on their Materials Safety Data Sheets (MSDS). These are either furnished with the product, or available from the manufacturer on request. They include degrees of danger, hazardous effects, and types of protective clothing required for handling the products.

Caution: An MSDS is only as good as the person who wrote it for the company. No uniform MSDS guidelines or standards have been set yet, and trade secrets may protect the identities of some materials. Also, the company does not have to report any ingredient below one-tenth of one percent, although that is a dangerous level for many hazardous materials. So if you have questions, check the special precautions information and call the manufacturer, your supplier, and other product users.

More and more of these products now also carry the colorful Hazardous Materials Identification System (HMIS®) label. This shorthands the hazardous materials information in letters and numbers and includes a Personal Protection Index of protective equipment to use with the different levels of hazards — see illustration on page 68. The copyrighted system, created by the National Paint and Coatings Association, also provides training materials and wallet-sized reference cards. HMIS materials are available exclusively through the U.S. licensee, American Labelmark — listed in Appendix D. Use of HMIS is one way to satisfy OSHA's hazardous communication standard requirements. Call OSHA for details, or American Labelmark.

The Pro-Active Approach

There is an old Henny Youngman joke about a man who goes to a doctor. He says, "Doctor, it hurts when I do this." "OK," says the doctor, "Don't do that."

The most obvious way to avoid problems with hazardous and toxic materials is to not use them. If your company depends on them to create its products and services, however, shifting away will be a challenge. You may need customer cooperation, research, and perhaps exhaustive testing before commercializing the new product and process. You may also have to rewrite the specifications by which you manufactured the old products.

There are degrees of difficulty in the transition. A painter or flooring installer may be able to simply shift from solvent-based products to water-based. For aircraft manufacturers, however, new, low-volatile organic compound (VOC) paints come out of spray guns differently from other coatings. They also spread differently and need heating to speed drying time. The process change requires up to three years for research, testing, and specification changes, and costs nearly $200,000.

Companies facing this sort of situation may resist change. High out-front costs tend to obscure downstream benefits. A Southern California aircraft builder, for example, resisted employee calls to create an expensive, centralized chemical control program. The federal government finally fined it nearly $1 million for not having one. Taking the initiative early on would have been $1 million cheaper.

Local, state, and federal laws require you to take certain actions and make certain reports if you handle or use hazardous materials. To learn about the other laws and reporting requirements for your level of waste generation, contact your state environmental department and your regional office of the EPA — see Appendix E.

Beware of Pitfalls

Rushing to eliminate hazardous materials can create new problems, too. For example, to clear the air over Southern California, the South Coast Air Quality Management District has required industries there to phase out using products formulated with smog-forming chemicals such as petroleum distillates. Many of the replacement products, however, use ozone-depleting chemicals such as methyl chloroform.

The pressure of bans also prompts some businesses that depend upon hazardous materials to buy them up and hoard them, so their stocks can be "grandfathered in" before the deadlines. For example, in early 1992, the U.S. Government Services Administration (GSA) office in Lakewood, Colorado, bought a new air conditioning system and 1,200 pounds of CFC-11 to run it. It beat the 1995 CFC phaseout deadline, and the $1.00-a-pound CFC tax hike due in 1993. This bought GSA time for converting the unit to run on CFC-123, which is more costly, more corrosive on rubber and plastic, and 5% less energy efficient, but 98% less ozone destructive than CFC-11.

On the other hand, DuPont, the inventor of CFC, has now converted all 450 air conditioning units at its Delaware headquarters to CFC-123 and other, safer refrigerants and is scrambling to discover another wonder compound to replace CFCs.

Your best course of action to reduce your exposure to liability is to shift away from regulated substances and handle the ones you do use better. Follow the leads of companies, such as 3M Company of St. Paul, Minnesota, and Preservative Paints of Seattle, Washington. Both run company-wide waste prevention programs that invite all employees to create solutions and reward them for the ones the company uses. These efforts are cutting their hazardous material inputs, outputs, and costs and reducing their exposure to liability. Companies today cannot expect to operate profitably otherwise.

"Reducing our exposure to regulation by eliminating regulated substances from our processes and inventory is the only way to go if we want to be competitive."

**Robert P. Bringer, Phd.
Staff Vice President
Environmental Engineer
and Pollution Control
3M Company**

Priorities for Handling Hazardous Materials

Your business may have to comply with a variety of regulations in handling hazardous materials. Before referring to the step-by-step worksheets for analyzing your toxic and hazardous material usages, refer to the tables of materials substitutions developed by the Environmental Hazards Management Institute (EHMI) in Appendix A.

Jurisdictions in most North American states and provinces now prioritize handling hazardous materials in this order:

1. Source reduction — use less HM and EHM to get the jobs done.
2. Reuse — create in-house programs and participate in out-of-house programs, such as the local or regional IMEX for reuse of such HWs and EHWs as chemical compounds, solvents, lubricants, and coatings.
3. Recycle — create in-house programs wherever possible, such as lubricating your fleet vehicles with recycled oil. Utilize local recycling programs and resources.

4. Treatment — use in-house means, or licensed contractors, to detoxify or neutralize HWs and EHWs.

5. Disposal, incineration, or solidification (depending on material type and preferences of the local jurisdiction) — use contracted services to appropriately dispose of the waste. Use this option only if none of the first four options can be applied.

Getting Answers

To get specific information on technology assistance programs, advice, permits, exemptions, and laws, start with your state environmental office and your regional office of the EPA. The EPA produces several guides for specific industries on minimizing hazardous waste and preventing pollution — see Appendix H. You can also call your local agencies and refer to the *Guide to State Environmental Programs*.[2]

You may have to make more than one call to get your answers. Different authorities at the federal, state, and local levels may handle different areas of regulation.

For general questions — call the Environmental Hazards Management Institute and check your local Yellow Pages under "Consultants—Environmental," "Consultants—Engineering," "Engineers—Environmental," "Consultants—Environmental, Conservation & Ecological Organizations," or "Environmental & Ecological Services."

Whether you now operate a business, or you plan to start one, or start a new process, learn who your local authorities report to and deal with at the state and federal levels, and get a list of required permits and other environmental requirements from all local agencies.

If this feels like a multi-level maze to you, it is — for everybody. For example, to clean up the Chesapeake Bay and Puget Sound, two huge bodies of water on opposite sides of this continent, more than 100 different federal, state, local, and tribal agencies have to be coordinated in each place. The tally for these two bodies of water is nearly 250 agencies and nearly 1,000 people involved to get some decisions made. Each agency has jurisdiction over some part or parts of each area's shorelines and waters. Yes, the governments even frustrate themselves, but they are striving to streamline their processes, just as businesses are.

Several states have now moved on their own initiatives. New Jersey may have the toughest laws, including a community right-to-know, a right to sue for environmental redress, and an Environmental Cleanup Responsibility Act that prohibits sale of land until its hazardous wastes are cleaned up.

Oregon, however, was the first state to mandate pollution prevention planning for both the public and private sectors in 1989. Some of the material listed below is drawn from Oregon's excellent Department of Environmental Quality workbook, *Benefitting From Toxic Substance and Hazardous Waste Reduction*.

Step 1: Create Support From the Top

Start your hazardous materials management program with a clear statement of your commitment. Top management sets the tone for your company and the world to see; their support must be obvious and directed. To get the ball rolling:

1. Call a special meeting or meetings to review local, state, and federal requirements, and discuss how the company can meet them.
2. Create a written policy you can post, with specific objectives. Update the objectives as you meet them. That makes the written policy a dynamic document that people don't forget once it's posted.
3. Set up the objectives step-by-step, and start with projects that are easy to do, low-cost, and likely to succeed. People will soon begin achieving the initial goals and building their confidence. These successes will build pride and support at all levels, and encourage everyone to create new programs and tackle new objectives.

A sample policy statement is provided on page 69.

Step 2: Select Your Coordinator or Committee

Select the person or people who will inspect your process(es) and facilities, assess hazardous materials inputs and outputs (throughputs), and make recommendations for improvements.

You may hire a consultant for this or select from your own personnel. If you have already selected a coordinator or committee for other programs, such as recycling, they may be able to assume this responsibility also. Consultants are listed in your Yellow Pages under "Environmental" and "Hazardous Materials," and in environmental directories.

If you go in-house, pick employees from different activity areas of the company — accounting, purchasing, materials and inventory control, production, marketing, and environmental health and safety. This will provide the needed range of perspectives and expertise. Once your team is selected, let your personnel know by placing a notice on bulletin boards and in the company newsletter or video news. A sample notice is on page 70.

Step 3: Review Company Business Practices

Look to find and control hazardous materials throughout your operation — on the production line, in purchasing, inventory, recordkeeping, accounting, marketing, and training. You can achieve cost-savings with improvements in every area:

- Operating practices, such as:
  - Housekeeping;
  - Purchasing and inventory control;
  - Materials management;

- Process control;
- Leak and spill prevention;
  - Technologies, such as:
    - Process modifications;
    - Equipment additions and substitutions;
  - Raw materials, such as input substitutions; and
  - Products, such as reformulations.

Search records for hazardous waste reports and manifests and toxic chemical inventory reports. Look at procedures, and get toxic reduction suggestions from the people who buy your products or sell you raw materials and other products. Make this a team effort with your suppliers and customers. Use the Business Practices Worksheet on pages 71–74 to help you in the process.

Step 4: Assess Processes and Waste Streams

You can do the assessment in three phases:

1. An operations review.
2. A walk-through of your plant or facilities.
3. Documentation for setting reduction goals and exploring and implementing new options.

Phase 1: Operations Review

In Step 3, you reviewed items ranging from purchasing and inventory to flow diagrams and drawings.

Now, you'll note where you expect to find waste, and where you don't, in the flow of chemicals through your business. This is not a precise accounting, but it provides a starting point for assessing your processes. Start by trying to quantify each item, then assess its significance based on its relative contribution to emissions and waste streams. This process can also help you identify the initial low-cost, most-likely-to-succeed objectives for your policy statement. Use the Operations Review Checklist on page 75 for this phase.

Phase 2: Facility Walk-Through

To get the most from this phase:

- Notify employees of when, where, and how long you or the team will be touring.
- Schedule during times when all or most processes are operating. Be aware, if your company runs more than one shift, operating procedures can vary from shift-to-shift, operator-to-operator. You may want to repeat walk-throughs of particular processes on each shift.
- Plan the walk-through to cover all areas, including those that are generally ignored, such as storage rooms and maintenance sheds. Look for materials with a lot of dust on them. They are not being used.

- Follow each process from the point where the raw materials enter the facility at receiving, to the point where products and wastes are stored, shipped, or recycled. Look at everything as if you have never seen it before, and compare what you expected to find in Phase 1 to what you actually see.

Talk to everyone. Compare standard operating procedures for equipment to actual procedures as they are run in the plant. Are there any differences, and if so, do they affect the process for better or worse?

Ask why things are done the way they are. No one may have asked this question before, and it may start everyone looking at the process with a new perspective. Ask employees to start thinking of potential improvements.

Phase 3: Documentation

Take notes, make sketches, take photographs, or all three, to keep information fresh in your mind. Then use the worksheets on pages 76–79 to document your findings.

Step 5: Determine Chemical Use and Waste Generation

Once you have a picture of your toxic chemicals throughput, answer these questions:

- What quantities are you using for each process?
- Is each process as efficient as possible, and are you using each material as efficiently as possible?
- Are you generating the minimum amount of waste possible?

As you assess your operations, you may find cases where you can't do things any better, you are making the best possible use of materials, and no reduction in input or waste output is possible. In other cases, you may be able to improve processes and reduce or eliminate materials and wastes entirely.

If you own a small business, you may be able to complete the assessments in four or six hours. Larger factories or multiple-process firms may need a team of people with diverse skills to conduct the assessments over a period of weeks.

To arrive at an educated guess for the hazardous materials your facility manufactures, processes, or otherwise uses, you can use the formulas in the EPA *Toxics Release Inventory Report, Form R* (SARA Title III Sec. 313). Request a copy of *Form R* from your regional EPA office. For a precise inventory, however, you must do a complete mass balance of all materials, affected parts, filters, emissions, etc.

When you have completed all the worksheets in this chapter, you will be ready to begin the process of reducing the amount of hazardous materials you have on hand. This will be explained in the next chapter.

Hazardous Materials Identification System Illustration

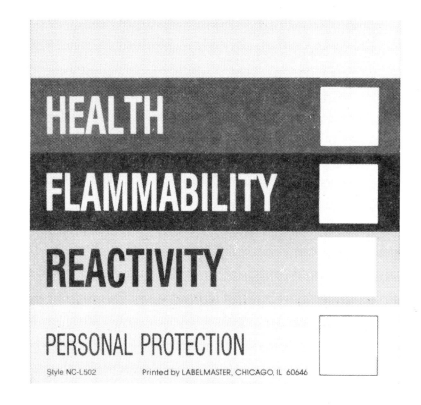

The top illustration shows the label used to identify hazardous materials. The chemical name is typed on the top of the label and a code is inserted in each of the boxes next to the four categories of identification. The label is very colorful to get your attention — the Health stripe is blue; the Flammability stripe is red; the Reactivity stripe is yellow; and the Personal Protection stripe is white.

The illustration on the bottom shows both sides of the pocket card employees carry. This card lists the codes for the labels and explains what precautions should be taken.

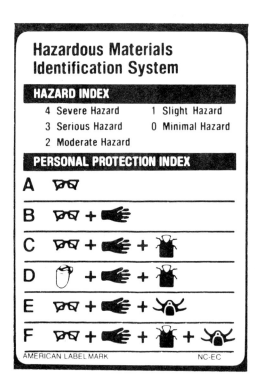

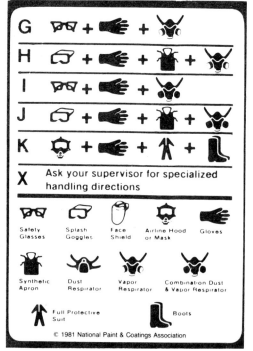

Sample Dynamic Environmental Policy Statement

XYZ Company
March 15, 1994

Protecting our employees and our environment is a high priority for XYZ Company, and we pledge to reduce and, where possible, eliminate our uses of toxic substances and production of toxic wastes. We plan to achieve these goals with a combination of methods, including:

- Source reduction (using less hazardous materials to get the jobs done);
- Reuse and recycling of materials wherever possible;
- Treatment and detoxification of wastes; and
- Disposal in ways that minimize harm to living things, air, water, and land.

Objectives

As of March 15, 1994, we will work during the next year to:

- Decrease the amount of chlorinated solvents we use by 50%;
- Convert 100% of our refrigeration and air conditioning systems to less harmful or non-CFC coolants;
- Convert 100% of our solvent-based coating inventory, where applicable, to water-based coatings;
- Explore use of recycled oil by August 1 for vehicles and machinery and phase in this product as a test in 50% of our fleet and machinery where applicable.

Achievements

Congratulations to the people in Personnel. As of March 5, you have reduced the amount of paper used for inter-office memos and documentation by 20% and cut our waste by 15%, helping all of us at XYZ Company achieve the objectives of our environmental mission. Thanks from all of us!

Update this statement regularly to keep it current and to keep employees current on their progress and achievements.
To spur creation of new ideas, offer financial and other rewards, such as comp and extra vacation time, bonuses, or incentive travel.

Sample Notice Introducing Hazardous Materials Reduction Team

Introducing the XYZ Company Hazardous Materials Reduction Team

March 20, 1993

At XYZ, we believe using less hazardous materials and producing less hazardous waste is everybody's business. As a first step, we have formed a team to start the environmental improvements process.

Team Members:	Phone
Joline Carlson (Team Leader)	Ext. 90
Bonnie Simons	Ext. 57
John Thomas	Ext. 69
Bob Sanders	Ext.45

Responsibilities of our Hazardous Materials Reduction Team:

1. Inspect our facilities to assess how toxic substances are used, how waste is generated, and where it goes.
2. Involve co-workers in identifying problems and suggesting possible solutions.
3. Help us set and meet reduction objectives.
4. Help spread the word of our efforts about our commitment to everyone's safety, the safety of our environment, the efficient uses of our materials, and the reduction of our waste.

Any time you have an idea you think can help, please contact anyone on the team.

Business Practices Worksheet

Question	Y, N	Comments

Purchase Practices

1. Is purchasing centralized through one person or one department?   ___

2. When purchasing, do you:

   • Avoid overpurchasing?   ___

   • Review MSDSs for hazardous components prior to purchase?   ___

   • Buy standard raw materials (like solvents) to minimize small leftover lots?   ___

   • Consider toxics use and waste reduction advantages when buying new equipment?   ___

Additional comments: _____

_____

_____

_____

_____

Vendor and In-House Practices

1. Have you discussed techniques and options for reducing hazardous materials use and minimizing waste with:

   • Chemical suppliers?   ___

   • Equipment vendors?   ___

   • Regulatory agencies?   ___

Business Practices Worksheet (continued)

Question	Y, N	Comments
2. Are your support services using these techniques and options in:		
• Laboratories?	___	_____
• Maintenance shops?	___	_____
• Garages?	___	_____
• Physical plants (for powerhouses, boilers, and cooling towers)?	___	_____

Additional comments: _____

_____

_____

_____

_____

Inventory Practices

	Y, N	Comments
1. Do you have a written inventory of all raw materials and products?	___	_____
Is it dated?	___	_____
Is it updated at regular intervals?	___	_____
Are materials, products, or their constituents identified as toxic or hazardous?	___	_____
Are listed toxic substances identified?	___	_____

Business Practices Worksheet (continued)

Question	Y, N	Comments

2. Do you have a hazardous chemical inventory list ?   ___

3. Do you have a completed State Fire Marshal survey form (SARA Title III Section 312 Report)?   ___

4. Do you have current MSDSs for all hazardous materials you store on-site?   ___

Additional comments: _____

Other Records

Do you have:

1. Informational literature on your company, including records of products, services, manufacturing processes, other areas of business?   ___

2. Diagrams, blueprints, and schematic drawings of your building, processing areas, and storage and shipping areas?   ___

3. Design information, including equipment lists, specifications and data sheets, process flow diagrams, and water use rates?   ___

4. Production information, including production schedules and records, operator data sheets or logs, product composition and batch sheets, and operating manuals?   ___

Business Practices Worksheet (continued)

Question	Y, N	Comments
5. Vendor information, including product literature, data sheets, and advertisements?	___	
6. Fire insurance inspection records?	___	
7. Employee training records?	___	
8. Plans and reports prepared by other committees (safety, quality assurance, etc.)?	___	
9. Environmental permits, including solid waste, hazardous waste, air, pretreatment and waste water discharge?	___	
10. Waste analysis results from laboratories & consultants?	___	
11. Standard operating procedures for your waste treatment facilities or units?	___	
12. Waste manifests, which are required for all hazardous waste transported and managed off-site?	___	
13. Biennial reports, if you are a large quantity generator (LQG)?	___	
14. EPA Toxic Chemical Release Inventory Reporting Form Rs, if you are a LQG?	___	

Additional comments: _____

_____

_____

Operations Review Checklist

Date: _____

	Significance at Plant		
Materials Handling Waste Sources	**Low**	**Medium**	**High**
Off-spec materials	____	____	____
Rejected products	____	____	____
Obsolete materials	____	____	____
Spills and leaks (liquids)	____	____	____
Spills (dry and powders)	____	____	____
Air emissions*	____	____	____
Overspray	____	____	____
Drag-out	____	____	____
Grits (floor sweepings)	____	____	____
Grits (drain cleanings)	____	____	____
Maintenance waste	____	____	____
Empty container cleaning	____	____	____
Container/packaging disposal:			
Metal	____	____	____
Paper	____	____	____
Glass	____	____	____
Plastic	____	____	____
Pipeline/tank drainage	____	____	____
Evaporative losses*	____	____	____
Other _____	____	____	____
_____	____	____	____

* These items may need to be tested or calculated. The best initial way to reduce emissions and evaporative losses is to keep container lids tightly closed.

Process Operations Waste Sources

Tank cleaning	____	____	____
Container cleaning	____	____	____
Process effluent	____	____	____
Spent rinse water	____	____	____
Equipment cleaning	____	____	____
Other_____	____	____	____
_____	____	____	____

Facility Assessment

Check items with observed problems or evidence of waste. In the right hand column, briefly note the reason for the check.

Company: _____   **Date:** _____

Person(s) making inspection: _____

General Site Conditions:

☐ Housekeeping (crowded walkways or work surfaces)   _____

☐ Discoloration on walls, surfaces, ceilings   _____

☐ Corrosion   _____

☐ Leaking containers   _____

☐ Other_____   _____

Evidence of Pollution:

☐ Odors   _____

☐ Fumes   _____

☐ Smoke   _____

☐ Steam   _____

☐ Dust   _____

☐ Evaporation   _____

☐ Eye, nose, throat irritation   _____

☐ Drag-out   _____

☐ Other_____   _____

Labeling of Materials:

☐ Contents   _____

☐ Strength   _____

☐ Hazards   _____

☐ Expiration dates   _____

☐ Accumulation dates   _____

Storage:

☐ Open containers   _____

☐ Stacked drums   _____

☐ Crowded shelves   _____

☐ Out-of-date stock   _____

☐ Materials no longer used   _____

Employee observations:

_____

_____

_____

Processes, Toxic Substances, and Hazardous Wastes

Use a separate worksheet for each process.

Company: _____ **Date:** _____

Process: _____

Draw a flow diagram of the process:

Toxic Substances

List those used as raw materials in this process.

Substance (trade or chemical name)	Amount used (lbs/month)	Where does toxic substance go? (product, waste, etc.)
_____	_____	_____
_____	_____	_____
_____	_____	_____
_____	_____	_____
_____	_____	_____
_____	_____	_____

Wastes

List each type of hazardous waste generated by this process.

Waste (identity, components)	Weight (lbs/month)
_____	_____
_____	_____
_____	_____
_____	_____
_____	_____
_____	_____

Cost of Process

Where costs are not available, use estimates.

Company: _____   **Date:** _____

Process: _____

Operating Costs

Toxic Substances   Cost per month

_____ $ _____

_____ $ _____

_____ $ _____

Subtotal, toxic substances $ _____

Labor and Equipment

_____ $ _____

_____ $ _____

_____ $ _____

Subtotal, labor, and equipment $_____

Utilities

_____ $ _____

_____ $ _____

_____ $ _____

Subtotal, utilities $ _____

Waste handling, storage

_____ $ _____

_____ $ _____

_____ $ _____

Subtotal, waste handling, storage $_____

Waste Treatment

_____ $ _____

_____ $ _____

_____ $ _____

Subtotal, waste treatment $ _____

Cost of Process (continued)

Waste Disposal

_____ $_____

_____ $_____

_____ $_____

Subtotal, waste disposal $_____

Other (supplies, QA, lab costs, etc.)

_____ $_____

_____ $_____

_____ $_____

Subtotal, other $_____

Total monthly operating costs

Total of all subtotals $_____

Total annual operating costs

(Total monthly cost x 12) $_____

Capital Costs

Summarize annual capital costs for each process. Your accountant can help you determine annual costs and perform a more detailed analysis of profitability and depreciation.

Equipment purchase $_____

Construction costs $_____

Construction/installation $_____

Connections to utilities $_____

Engineering $_____

Permitting $_____

Contracting $_____

Training $_____

Start-up $_____

Subtotal annual capital costs $_____

Total Costs

Annual operating costs $_____

Annual capital costs $_____

Grand total $_____

Chapter 6

The Reduction/Waste Minimization Process

This chapter shows you how to start your reduction process based on the information you gathered in the last chapter. Procedures for reducing hazardous materials vary widely, depending on the complexity of the production processes, the quantity and variety of materials used, and the wastes generated. There are some basic actions that nearly every company can take, however. These actions are discussed in this chapter, along with steps to help you create a reduction program tailored to your company's processes and procedures.

Step 1: Do the Basics

Before you address the complex issues, do the basic, easy-to-accomplish items. Use the Basic Hazardous Materials Reduction Measures on pages 91–92 as a checklist. Items 1–29 are low cost/no cost measures you can do immediately. Items 30–34 are moderate or high cost measures you can begin after completing the easy tasks. Keep a log of your efforts, and keep copies of your worksheets on file. An Action Log is provided on page 93 for your convenience.

Step 2: Rethink Your Processes

Rethinking processes may lead your company to change technologies, modify or replace equipment, and alter or automate processes. To help finance your improvements, check with your local utilities and with local, state, and federal environmental, financial, and business agencies. Besides having good advice, they may be able to offer you rebates, subsidies, loan packages, or tax credits.

Local utilities are becoming particularly good sources of flexible financing. From New England to the Pacific Northwest, they now know that manufacturing and process improvements can yield huge reductions in water and energy demands. These reductions enable them to avoid the political and public relations problems and costs of shortages, brownouts and blackouts, and the huge costs of finding and developing new water and energy sources.

In the past decade, electric utilities have become financing partners with businesses in everything from new windows and light bulbs to cogeneration systems and smelting equipment. Water utilities have become partners in everything from low-flow shower head give-aways and water-saver equipment rebates, to development of irrigation systems and drought-tolerant landscapes.

Here are some examples of process changes that can save you money:

- A metal finishing company changed to automated delivery of chromate conversion coating product, and its consumption of the product declined by 20%. The automated control reduced the frequency of scrapping the solution and improved the quality of the final product. Installing an automatic hoist on a degreasing operation will build in optimum drain/drip times by controlling the rate of withdrawal or "drag-out."

- We mentioned earlier the circuit board manufacturers that eliminated the need for CFC solvents and flux in some operations. Another electronics manufacturer changed from solvent cleaning to a water-based system, which cleaned six times more effectively, resulted in fewer rejects, and eliminated the hazardous waste.

- Decreasing the pressure of paint spraying equipment reduces overspray and lessens waste. Check with your supplier or manufacturer for specifications.

- In electroplating, placing drag-out stations and counter-flowing rinse stations after the electroplating tank reduces water consumption and make-up cost for the plating bath. The "dirtiest" rinse, used as make-up water for the plating bath, replenishes the components of the bath.

Beware of fix-all technologies that worked for other businesses. If you want them to work for your company and decrease waste and materials consumption, you may have to make your own design changes and modifications. These may involve changes in parts, layouts, or piping.

Raw Materials Changes

Work with your vendors and trade associations to find the right substitute for your needs. When exploring new options:

- Read the MSDS carefully before purchasing to evaluate potential hazards and health effects.

- Involve employees in the decision, and inform them that changes may be coming.
- Consider the substitute's effects on employee health and safety and its impacts on air, water, and solid waste.
- Consider the effects on the process involved and whether any process modifications will be required.
- Evaluate other regulations that may be affected.

Product Reformulation

A change in the recipe that reduces or replaces a hazardous component reduces toxicity and waste. Here is an example from the airline industry:

Manufacturers, such as Boeing, McDonnell Douglas, Lockheed, and others, are beginning to use water-based paints for coating low-stress, interior areas. Outside, however, where paints must withstand handling abuse and 700 mile-per-hour winds, no water-based coating yet resists abrasion and adheres to the metal as well as the solvent-based ones. The companies have helped reformulate these products with 30% less solvents and they use new electrostatic paint guns that lay twice as much paint on the surface as the old spray guns, cutting paint costs by as much as half. Waste vapor is collected as hazardous waste.

Recycling

Use and reuse of waste material can occur onsite or offsite. Officially, recycling is not considered reduction unless it becomes an integral part of a process, such as filtration. Many offsite recyclers take waste, recycle it, and sell the refined material back to the company at a price significantly lower than the cost of the original product. Check with your local authorities on what they consider "recycling" versus "reclamation" for hazardous materials.

Companies that recycle can realize savings in both the purchase of raw materials and in treatment and disposal costs. Here is an example :

A California printer purchased an ink recycling unit to blend colored waste inks with fresh black ink and black toner. After the recycled mixture is filtered to remove dried ink flakes, it is ready for use in place of fresh black ink. The recycling unit paid for itself in 18 months based only on the savings in black ink purchases, and in 9 months when the costs of disposing of ink as a hazardous waste were included.

Reclamation and Materials Exchange

Reclamation recovers valuable components from toxic or hazardous waste and reduces the toxicity and volume of hazardous waste. Examples include recovery of lead from spent wet cell batteries, mercury from button batteries, and silver from film processing rinse water. The reclaimed material is usually not used in the facility that generates it, but instead sold to another company.

Materials exchanges are agencies or businesses that can help match unused raw materials and potential wastes from one business with the need of other businesses. They are mutually beneficial, as buyers save on raw materials costs, and sellers avoid disposal costs. Small businesses can find excellent reduction opportunities through such organizations, although they need to be aware of their responsibility and potential liability for all materials and wastes exchanged. See Appendix F for a partial list of materials waste exchanges.

Step 3: Improve Your Processes

Old or inefficient processes often account for excess uses and outputs of hazardous substances and wastes. The following worksheets from Chapter 5 will help you determine which processes need to be improved:

- Business Practices Worksheet;
- Operations Review Checklist;
- Facility Assessment;
- Processes, Toxic Substances, and Hazardous Wastes Assessment; and
- Cost of Process Worksheet.

After you have determined which processes need improvement, you need to decide how to change them most effectively. Follow these steps:

1. Consult all the people who contribute to the process, from purchasing to packaging.
2. Identify potential options for meeting legal requirements.
3. Determine which options merit detailed analysis.
4. Evaluate the technical feasibility of each option.
5. Evaluate the economic feasibility of each option.
6. Evaluate the intangible benefits of each option.

Use the Process Improvement Options Worksheet on pages 95–98 to record your findings.

Keep the following points in mind when you are weighing costs and benefits:

- If benefits exceed costs, make the option a priority.
- If benefits nearly equal costs, look at intangible benefits and long-term payback to see if they tip the scales.
- If costs exceed benefits, it's not an option, unless it is required by law.

Any new reduction program must be flexible. It must enable you to respond to changes in raw materials, waste management costs, regulations, and technology.

As the name implies, the Process Improvement Options Summary sheet on page 99 should be filled out after completing the Process Improvement worksheet. The summary sheet can be used to present the idea to top management.

Some states require that you implement any process improvement options that are technically and economically feasible. Some states also want you to justify the items you choose, or don't choose. So be sure you record all your activities in the Action Log and keep all your completed worksheets on file.

Controlling Your Exposure to Liability

Besides local, state, and federal environmental requirements, the Securities and Exchange Commission (SEC) requires companies to disclose in their 10K Annual Reports any potential environmental cleanup liabilities they might face under the Superfund (CERCLA) law.

The laws on hazardous materials evolve constantly, so stay aware of current activity, so you will keep your company safe now, and keep ahead of regulatory and legal developments that are sure to come as testing methods improve and prosecutions get tougher.

Testing that measured "clean" last decade, with instruments that measured in the parts per million, would be considered "dirty" today with devices that measure in parts per billion and trillion.

There is no statute of limitations on damage caused by hazardous materials. Even if your corporation is dissolved, under CERCLA[1] and growing legal precedent, officers and shareholders continue to share liability for damage, and responsibility for cleanup and compensation. Exceptions are acts of God, of war, or an act or omission of a third party other than an employee or agent of the defendant.

Prosecutable environmental offenses now include:

- Patterns of illegal discharges coupled with false reporting — can be grounds for charges of mail fraud, conspiracy, filing false reports with the government, and accomplice liability for participants. Defendants can be prosecuted under the Racketeering Influenced and Corrupt Organizations Act (RICO).[2]
- Misuse or illegal sale of toxic materials.
- Illegal discharges to surface waters or sewage treatment plants in violation of permits or pretreatment standards.
- Dredging and filling wetlands or other navigable waters without permits.
- Improper transport or disposal of hazardous wastes.
- Failure to give timely or accurate notification of releases of hazardous substances.
- Air emissions in violation of permits.
- Submitting monitoring reports which contain false information.

The following items will help you reduce your liability:

1. Watch the neighbors:
   a. The property owner is responsible for keeping his or her land clean. Contamination can drift in from leaking drum barrels, seeping underground tanks, or other sources on neighboring properties. If you already own the piece of land, check your perimeter and, if possible,

neighboring properties at your earliest convenience. If you are planning to purchase the land, inspect it first. Hire a licensed expert for the inspection. Environmental studies are now required by lenders, purchasers, and insurers during the "due-diligence" process, so that parties to the purchase can use the "innocent landowner" defense if contamination is later discovered on the property. Due-diligence is proof that you have diligently inspected the property and found no problems.

    b. If you have a plant site or empty field next to your facility, negotiate with the owner(s) to create a means for controlling and accounting for all dumping there — see 3 below.

2. Be careful about your tenants:

    a. Update land contracts to include current environmental protection language.

    b. Take baseline readings of soil and groundwater at any property before leasing to a tenant that uses hazardous materials. Read again before tenant leaves to establish who is responsible if contamination is found.

    c. Don't combine incompatible tenants — odors and contaminants can drift. For example, a paint manufacturer next door to a food processor, or a metal or automotive shop next door to a florist.

    d. Spot-check existing tenants to make sure they are handling hazardous materials safely and disposing of waste appropriately. By keeping them aware of this critical area, you can prevent problems before they become serious.

3. Avoid any dumping on your land. You can perform disposal operations if you have obtained the necessary permits, but your accounting of this function must be air-tight. You must know where every load comes from and have every one monitored as it comes in and is discharged. If a non-permittable load is dumped, the carrier has first responsibility for cleaning it up. But if the carrier fails to do so, you must. You share the liability for whatever you accept.

Insurance

Liability brings up the question of insurance.

The Superfund provisions of CERCLA have had two main effects on current and would-be property owners. It has:

1. Virtually mandated due-diligence environmental testing of properties; and

2. Spurred owners to seek liability insurance to cover potential environmental cleanup costs.

As a result, the insurance industry has become a major, if unwilling "deep pockets" partner in this country's environmental cleanup projects. Property owners and purchasers who want insurance that will cover unexpected environmental cleanup costs must get a clean bill of health for their land. They must also make certain that the environmental testing or abatement firms they hire also have adequate liability insurance coverage.

Insuring against environmental liability has become a major source of contention between insurers and property owners because the insurers have already been stung for hundreds of billions of dollars in cleanup costs since the '70s.

In the early '80s, insurers began removing certain high-risk clients from their coverage pool. This has created two real estate imperatives for any company now: (1) check the property, and (2) make certain the expert or firm that checks your property is insured, too, and can share the cost of your liability if it makes a mistake. You may also request indemnification from the firm.

Informed Decision Making

There is no reason to panic if you do find evidence of a hazardous substance on your site. As with every environmental item here, take the process one step at a time. Before you do anything, be sure you have all the facts and have researched all your options. The following will help you.

- Get objective second opinions on the appropriateness of all technologies and actions to be used.
- Take a strong role in overseeing all parties and actions in remediation efforts.
- Trust your instincts: Does what you're hearing make sense? If not, keep asking questions until you are satisfied with the answers. If so, but you don't have knowledge in this area, get a second opinion anyway.

Other Considerations

Three other issues to consider are:

- Sick building syndrome;
- Asbestos; and
- Underground tanks.

If none of these apply to your business, skip to the next chapter.

Sick Building Syndrome

Sick building syndrome (SBS) is a growing concern in environmentally "tight" high-rise structures. Symptoms include occupants complaining of headaches, difficulty breathing, grogginess, nausea, burning eyes, sneezing or coughing, and finding relief at leaving the office.

The EPA estimates that 20 to 30% of offices in modern commercial and institutional buildings may experience air quality problems that could result in illnesses, absenteeism, low productivity, or discomfort. Sometimes, the cure can be as simple as adding humidity to overly dry, air-conditioned air.

After the 1970s "oil crises," the trend toward sealed buildings accelerated as a means of boosting energy and ventilation efficiencies. These techniques, however, reduced amounts of outside air drawn for ventilation, and instead re-circulated indoor air. This air contains pollutants from office machines, building materials, furnishings, tobacco smoke, human viruses and cosmetics, and can affect the health of employees in the buildings.

To guard against these problems:

1. Eliminate tobacco smoke. Establish a no-smoking policy, and set aside an outdoor smoking area distant from ventilation intakes. Likewise, locate the intakes far from loading docks and dumpster areas, and far from garage areas, equipment vents, and stacks that could contribute exhaust fumes to building ventilation systems.

2. Set mechanical systems to provide outdoor air quantities at rates equal to or above standards or codes. Where possible, filter outdoor and indoor air.

3. Regularly clean and disinfect the heating, ventilation, and air conditioning (HVAC) system with citrus-based or other safe cleaning agents as part of your company's preventive maintenance program.

4. Set up office equipment such as copy, fax and blueprint machines, laser printers, and photographic systems in a single area whenever possible with exhaust vented directly to the outdoors.

5. Eliminate or limit the use of carbonless copy paper (which can contain PCBs), adhesives, correction fluids, and air fresheners that can potentially emit strong odors and hazardous chemicals. Discourage employees from wearing heavy doses of perfumes or colognes.

6. Restrict remodeling activities to times of low building occupancy.

7. Obtain assurances from the seller or lessor that new building materials, furnishings, and equipment emit little or no irritating gases.

For more information on sick building syndrome, refer to the Heating, Ventilation, and Air Conditioning section of Chapter 7.

If employee health problems continue, contact environmental indoor air quality professionals.

Asbestos

Asbestos was used prior to 1977 for four main purposes:

1. To strengthen product material;
2. As a thermal (heat) insulator;
3. For acoustical insulation and interior decoration; and
4. For fire protection.

Unfortunately, before people discovered how dangerous it is, asbestos was used in a wide variety of products: hair dryers, stoves and slow cookers, ceiling and floor tiles, sprayed-on ceiling coatings, wall and pipe coverings, roofing and siding materials, brake and clutch linings, and more.

There is no safe level of asbestos for humans to ingest. However, it doesn't pose a health problem unless it is released as fibers into the air that people breathe.

So, unless it is "friable" (can crumble from hand pressure), needs repair or removal, leave it alone. It will carry on its assigned task without disturbing anyone or anything.

A corollary to that advice is, don't use small appliances manufactured before 1977, such as hair dryers and slow cookers, unless you are certain they do not contain asbestos.

Second, if you have structures with "popcorn" ceilings, or asbestos pipe sleeves, you can leave them in place if you do the following:

- Wrap asbestos insulation sleeves on water or heating pipes with wide duct tape, or spray-seal them with a heat-resistant epoxy or vinyl paint or other coating.
- Use a similar epoxy or other sealant on fraying asbestos siding, ceiling tiles, or "popcorn" coatings. Damaged roofing tiles, and badly damaged siding, may have to be removed and replaced by a licensed contractor.

Third, if you plan to remodel, or remove asbestos, get a licensed contractor to do it. If you do it yourself, you may be held liable for any damage to people's health that results from the release of asbestos into the air. Call your local air pollution control authority or department of public health for specific instructions before you take any action.

The health or air quality department can also point you toward contractors. If they don't, check the Yellow Pages under the specific problem, such as "Asbestos," or under the general category "Waste Disposal-Hazardous."

If you hire a contractor, make certain the company is certified by the state to perform this job. Check its references and record its name, license number, work dates, and disposal action. Asbestos is a hazardous waste that cannot be dumped in household garbage. It must be packed in sealed containers or double bags, and the contractor must notify the transfer station or landfill beforehand of his intention to carry it there for disposal.

If you must clean up a space where you've found asbestos debris, wear a head mask and protective clothing, put the debris into clearly-marked, double garbage bags or thick plastic bags, mop up the dust with wet rags, and drop them in the bags, too.

Underground Tanks

The owner of any property where an oil or gas tank is buried is liable for any damage to the ground, ground water, flora, and fauna that can be traced back to the tank or its contents.

If you have one or more underground storage tanks (UST) on the property, you are responsible for investigating which agency and which codes govern them in your locality. The buried tank permitting and enforcement authority will either be the local fire department, the local solid waste management or health department, or the state or provincial department of environment.

The viable lifetime of a tank can be as few as 5 years or as many as 30 years, depending on the nature of the stored liquid, the tank materials, soil acidity, and moisture. Eventually, most USTs will leak. For underground tank horror stories, look no further than our defense establishment and nuclear reservations such as Hanford, Washington, and Rocky Flats, Colorado.

If you need tanks for your business, and those on the property are underground, see about removing them and shifting to above-ground tanks.

If any of the USTs are unused, local codes may require you to (1) dig down and remove them, or if you leave them in the ground, (2) drain and fill them with a concrete slurry, or cured polyurethane. There are concerns about both these fillers, however. If the tank is filled with concrete, and it must ultimately be removed, it will be much heavier and harder to handle than if it was empty. If your area has a high water table, the polyurethane may provide all the buoyancy the tank needs to start floating up through the ground. Check with local experts before taking the fill action.

If you must remove a tank, call your old oil company for advice, or check the Yellow Pages under "Oils — Waste," "Tanks — Removal," "Waste Disposal," or "Environmental Services." Contractor tank removal costs can range into the thousands of dollars, so you may have to weigh the benefits of removal against the benefits of draining the tank and pumping it full of slurry or polyurethane.

In either case, document the action you take and keep the records accessible.

Instead of using a UST to handle your fuel needs, open a credit account with a nearby supplier or filling station. They will have their own up-to-code tanks and assume liability for tank leakage.

Basic Hazardous Materials Reduction Measures

Good Housekeeping

☐ 1. Routinely inspect and maintain equipment and conduct regular preventative maintenance repairs. Keep logs or a logbook of your actions.

☐ 2. Replace seals and gaskets regularly, and log the dates.

☐ 3. Repair leaks as they occur, and log the dates.

☐ 4. Use tight-fitting rings and bungs on containers to minimize evaporation and spillage

☐ 5. Use spigots or pumps to prevent spills.

Purchasing and Inventory Control

☐ 6. Purchase all materials only as needed, and consider just-in-time inventory management to minimize the amount of stock on hand. Set up an inventory tracking system to avoid over-purchase of materials by users in different parts of your facility.

☐ 7. Avoid overstock of raw materials, especially those with a short shelf life.

☐ 8. To reduce waste and leftovers, determine the quantities of materials you use, then purchase them in appropriately-sized containers. These may be a larger or smaller size than those you currently purchase.

☐ 9. Avoid transferring materials between containers, except for specific uses. Transfers invite spills, evaporation, and contamination; leftover material can pose a problem for storage and disposal.

☐ 10. Maintain records of hazardous substance purchases and for purchases of all production materials. This satisfies reporting requirements and helps you to understand when and where these substances are used and in what amounts. Look for trends that may occur on a daily, monthly, or seasonal basis.

☐ 11. Maintain current MSDSs for all raw materials and products. Prior to purchase, review MSDSs thoroughly to ensure that the product is compatible with your process and equipment and safe for your employees to use.

   Note: Some materials have separate MSDSs, such as resin and catalyst, for each component and for the mixture.

☐ 12. Don't accept free samples unless you are absolutely sure you will use them. Disposal costs may surprise you later.

Materials Management

☐ 13. Know the storage requirements for your materials. The requirements are listed on the container labels, in hazardous materials laws, and in local codes. As an additional precaution, call your local fire department for guidance, and invite them to your facility to give their stamp of approval.

☐ 14. Space rows of drums to allow for easy transfer and inspection for damage or leaks.

Basic Hazardous Materials Reduction Measures (continued)

☐ 15. Stack containers according to manufacturers' instructions to reduce tipping, puncturing, or other damage.

☐ 16. Segregate each type of hazardous substance and hazardous waste to avoid cross-contamination, mixing of incompatible materials, unwanted reactions, and to facilitate materials exchange, recycling, or reclamation.

☐ 17. Separate hazardous and non-hazardous wastes. Waste mixtures must be managed and disposed of as hazardous wastes.

☐ 18. Store containers on pallets to prevent corrosion which can result from containers contacting concrete floors — this is usually required by labels or regulations, anyway. Add containment berms to capture and contain leaks and spills.

☐ 19. Keep aisles free of obstructions.

☐ 20. Clearly label containers with information on contents, handling, storage, expiration dates, and health and safety hazards. This information reduces improper use of materials and aids in inventory control, material tracking, and storage.

☐ 21. Train employees to manage all materials and wastes with care. Keep a training log.

☐ 22. Wipe up spills whenever possible rather than hosing down an area.

☐ 23. Control the loading, unloading, and transfer of hazardous substances.

☐ 24. Handle materials properly.

☐ 25. Use storage tanks and vessels only for their intended purposes.

☐ 26. Install leak detection equipment for storage tanks.

☐ 27. Install spill containment equipment and train employees to use it.

☐ 28. Maintain the integrity of tanks and containers.

☐ 29. Install secondary containment around tanks or storage areas to limit spills.

Moderate/High-cost Reduction Measures

☐ 30. Design new, or redesign, current systems, and automate where possible to control additions of chemicals to batches and control drip time and drag-out.

☐ 31. Examine counter-current rinsing as a way to save water and chemicals in batch processes.

☐ 32. Examine changes in flow rates, temperatures, pressures, and residence times.

☐ 33. Improve scheduling or processes, or dedicate equipment to certain processes to minimize the amount of cleaning needed, especially in painting operations.

☐ 34. Test solvent baths to determine whether they need changing, rather than changing them according to a schedule.

Action Log

Action	Date	Results/Follow-up

Sample Action Log

Action	Date	Results/Follow-up
Attended hazmat workshop	5/15	
Checked expiration dates on toxic materials. Made note to decrease next purchase of material by 25%	5/17	
Put up sign reminding employees to measure, not estimate all additions of chemicals to processing tanks.	5/17	
Briefed all employees on state's hazmat use/waste requirements. Asked for ideas.	5/26	Idea meeting 6/12
Started spill and leak prevention system and trained all employees	5/27	
Met with accountant to set up cost accounting system for hazmats and haz-wastes.	6/2	
Installed a flow-control on rinse-water tank after the planting tank	6/8	Reduced water consumption — will know % next billing period.
Consultant on-site for technical assistance	6/8	

Process Improvement Options Worksheet

Make copies of this worksheet and fill out a separate one for each process improvement option you are considering.

Company: _____ **Date:** _____

Process: _____

1. Indicate the type of option:

   ☐ Toxics use reduction

   ☐ Good operating practice

   ☐ Technology change:

      ☐ Process

      ☐ Equipment

   ☐ Raw material change

   ☐ Product reformulation

   ☐ Waste reduction

   ☐ Recycling/ reuse

   ☐ Material reused for original purpose

   ☐ Material reused for a different purpose

   ☐ Materials exchange

   ☐ Personnel related

2. Briefly describe the option: _____

   _____

   _____

   _____

3. Toxic substance(s) affected: _____

   _____

   _____

4. Waste stream(s) affected: _____

   _____

   _____

5. Product(s) affected: _____

   _____

   _____

Process Improvement Options Worksheet (continued)

6. Personnel affected: _____

_____

_____

Technical Feasibility

7. Describe why you think this option is feasible: _____

_____

_____

_____

8. Describe affected areas and personnel: _____

_____

_____

_____

9. Are required space and utilities available? ☐ Yes ☐ No   Explain: ____

_____

_____

_____

10. Will production quality or services be affected? ☐ Yes ☐ No   If yes, explain: _____

_____

_____

11. Will production or services be stopped to modify or install a new system? ☐ Yes ☐ No   If yes, for what period of time? _____

_____

_____

12. Describe any new training procedures or special expertise required to operate or maintain the new system: _____

_____

_____

_____

13. Are new material handling, storage, or disposal techniques required? ☐ Yes ☐ No   If yes, explain: _____

_____

_____

_____

Process Improvement Options Worksheet (continued)

14. Other considerations or limitations: _____

_____

_____

Economic Feasibility

15. Estimate increases or decreases in operating costs attributable to the option:

	Cost Changes Per Month	
	(+)Increase	(-)Decrease
Health & safety	$ _____	$ _____
Insurance & benefits	$ _____	$ _____
Labor & equipment	$ _____	$ _____
Quality assurance	$ _____	$ _____
Raw materials	$ _____	$ _____
Supplies	$ _____	$ _____
Training	$ _____	$ _____
Toxic substances	$ _____	$ _____
Utilities	$ _____	$ _____
Waste disposal	$ _____	$ _____
Waste handling & storage	$ _____	$ _____
Waste treatment	$ _____	$ _____
Other _____	$ _____	$ _____
Total Operating Costs	$ _____	$ _____

16. Estimate capital costs of implementing the option

	Direct Cost
Equipment purchase	$ _____
Construction/installation	$ _____
Connections to utilities	$ _____
Materials purchase	$ _____
Contracting	$ _____
Training	$ _____
Start-up	$ _____
Total Direct Capital Costs	$ _____

Process Improvement Options Worksheet (continued)

	Indirect Cost
Engineering/planning	$ _____
Permitting	$ _____
Contracting	$ _____
Training	$ _____
Start-up	$ _____
Total Indirect Capital Costs	$ _____

Tangible and Intangible Benefits

17. Estimate all new revenues and reduced costs that would result from implementing the option.

Source of Revenue or Reduced Cost	Revenue or Avoided Cost per Month
_____	$ _____
_____	$ _____
_____	$ _____
_____	$ _____
_____	$ _____

18. Will implementing the option:

    ☐ Reduce regulatory burden? Explain: _____
    _____
    _____

    ☐ Reduce liability? Explain: _____
    _____
    _____

    ☐ Improve health and safety? Explain: _____
    _____
    _____

    ☐ Improve employee relations? Explain: _____
    _____
    _____

    ☐ Improve community relations? Explain: _____
    _____

Process Improvement Options Summary

Company: _____ **Date:** _____

Process: _____

1. Option proposed: _____ **Date:** _____

2. Description of option: _____

   _____

   _____

   _____

   _____

   _____

   _____

   _____

   _____

   _____

   _____

   _____

   _____

   _____

3. Option approved for further evaluation? ☐ Yes ☐ No   Date: _____

4. Reason for acceptance or rejection: _____

   _____

   _____

   _____

   _____

   _____

   _____

   _____

   _____

   _____

   _____

   _____

   _____

   _____

   _____

5. If option is approved:

   When will the option be implemented? _____

   Who will oversee the implementation? _____

Chapter 7

Increase Your Energy Efficiency

Suddenly, the energy arena is exploding with possibilities. Energy supply planners in the late '70s wrote off conservation as an eccentric pursuit and projected huge demand growth that could only be supplied by more nuclear, hydroelectric, oil- and coal-fired plants.

Instead, "since 1979, millions of individual decisions to save energy have given this country more than ten times as much new energy as all net expansions of energy supply put together," states Robert Sardinsky in the introduction to *The Efficient House Sourcebook* (Rocky Mountain Institute Press). The U.S. Department of Energy (DOE) estimates that conscientious Americans have saved 47 billion barrels of oil since the 1970s. However, DOE asserts the oil industry can still cost-effectively improve its energy use by another 30 to 50%.

Your company can "create" energy by cutting your waste and investing in efficiency. You gain bonuses, too, such as reduced costs for labor, equipment, operations, and maintenance and a competitive edge in the global marketplace.

Every change you make has a ripple effect to other areas, just like dropping a pebble in a pond. On a small scale, for example, your investment in low-flow faucets and shower heads can pay for itself in three months in water heater energy savings. On a large scale, recall the LaSalle Partners example in Chapter 1. It changed only the reflective power of lighting fixtures in its Chicago headquarters building. That halved the number of fluorescent lamps it needed, reduced purchase, labor, maintenance and energy costs, and yielded $70,000 in savings per year. The change also cut energy demand by so much, LaSalle avoided having to spend $500,000 on new electrical switch gear.

Out west, the Las Vegas Strip sports more lights today than it did ten years ago, yet it uses less wattage now. Highly-reflective surfaces enable sign designers to create powerful marquees with 10- and 25-watt bulbs.

Your energy utilities today don't want to invest billions of dollars in new generating plants. They want to make the best use of the generating capacity they already have. In simple terms, it's cheaper for them to send you cases of $10.00 compact fluorescent bulbs, than to build a new plant.

Basic Concepts

To achieve the best results, keep the following energy concepts in mind as you create your program.

Demand Side Management and Peak Load Management

Utilities promote "demand side management" (DSM) and "peak load management" (PLM) to help customers cut energy waste and build utility surplus. As incentives, they offer rate adjustments, efficiency consultations, and technical and financial assistance. This helps them avoid having to create new generating capacity.

The utility company sizes its plants to meet the peak demands, or loads, of their customers. You pay the utility to keep enough capacity in reserve to meet your maximum energy demand, or "peak load," even if you only reach that level once a year.

As you cut your energy demands and waste and spread your load out through the day, you cut your costs, and you help your utility gain generating capacity. You pay some retrofit costs, gain efficiency, and lower energy rates. They gain capacity, avoid investment costs, and sell your formerly wasted energy to other customers.

The Long-term View

Consider each conservation improvement an investment in your company's future. You reduce energy loads now, cut long-term overhead, and improve margins, because you also spend less on purchasing, labor, and inventory and become less vulnerable to future price increases for the resources you need.

Your investment in conservation also keeps you ahead of upcoming regulations. For example, if you upgrade your lighting now, you can stay ahead of Congress. In 1993, it is wrestling with new lighting standards that could make many inefficient incandescent lamps obsolete. Congress did the same thing to fluorescent lamps in its National Appliance Energy Conservation Amendments of 1988 (PL 100-357), which banned manufacture of inefficient, aluminum-wound ballasts after April 1, 1991. Today, only the more efficient, copper-wound ballast models are available.

Why let developments catch your company off-guard? Stay informed, and keep yourself ahead of the game.

Life Cycle Costing

The operating costs of a "great buy" item can quickly wipe out any savings you achieved from the low purchase price. For example, in its first year of operation, a commercial motor that is the wrong size for its function can use energy amounting to ten times its original cost. It's as if you got a $10,000 deal on a new Jaguar and spent $100,000 for gas the first year.

Always assure yourself that what you are buying fits your needs. Calculate all the costs associated with the purchase, such as operation, maintenance, repair, and future costs of energy. Solicit advice from your utility company, and from energy management specialists as needed. Often, the more expensive equipment will deliver lower life cycle costs because it is built to last and run efficiently for the long term.

Beware of trapping yourself with the following concepts:

- Short-term return-on-investment (ROI) requirements. Most energy efficiency measures cost money out front. While some can provide 100% and 200% annual paybacks, many yield less, according to the Rocky Mountain Institute (RMI).

  Unreasonable payback timelines can backfire, as one resort-hotel discovered. Its engineers couldn't get the parent company's management to invest in variable speed drive motors, heat recovery units, and other efficiency equipment because they calculated the paybacks at 2.5 to 2.7 years, and the chain's standard was 2.0 years. What management failed to understand was that the investments would enable them to avoid costs for the lifetime of the property, decades beyond their two-year ROI limit.

- Iron-clad equipment specifications. Technologies are changing so fast, you must allow yourself flexibility to improve with the times. Ironclad standards lock you into equipment that can double or triple your operating costs when compared to newer, more efficient units. Review your specifications biannually, and plan to make changes even more often if laws and codes change and as new, cost-effective technologies come to market.

Map Out the Treasure Hunt

Think of energy efficiency work as a treasure hunt. Every function you improve and every waste you eliminate is money in your pocket.

Here is a suggested priority list, or map, for improving your energy efficiency. Each item is explained in greater detail throughout the remainder of the chapter.

1. Create a commitment from the top. Support your energy efficiency coordinator, invite employees to participate in the program, and reward them for suggestions your company implements.

2. Immediately implement low cost no cost efficiency measures to eliminate waste. These are easy to do, give you an immediate sense of accomplishment, and help you realize big dividends.

3. Do an energy audit. This shows specifically where your business uses and wastes energy resources, the costs, and where you can make improvements. Explore what the most appropriate form of energy is for each job — electric, gas, oil, solar, wind, cogeneration. Start with the worksheets in this book, then contact your energy utilities or a qualified energy management consultant for more detailed surveys.

4. Create an energy management plan based on the audit. Analyze costs and benefits of short-term and long-term actions, then prioritize and schedule them for implementation. Include ways to measure progress, such as reductions in your energy utilization index. Regularly review and update your ROI requirements and equipment specifications.

5. Market your "green image" to suppliers, customers, and the public — see Appendix B for tips.

Step 1: Create a Company-wide Commitment from the Top

Make a public statement of your commitment to energy efficiency. Do this with management and employee meetings or presentations and a posted, written statement that answers the questions, "Why are we doing this?" and "What do we expect to accomplish?"

People in your company will participate in efficiency programs if they understand the answers to these questions, and if you keep them informed of, and celebrate their achievements.

Reassure employees that:

- You will maintain comfort levels as you develop the program;
- Their efforts are needed, appreciated, and recognized; and
- The program is not a means of singling out people who waste energy.

A sample energy efficiency statement is on page 129.

Step 1A: Select an Energy Efficiency Coordinator or Advisory Committee

Choose a coordinator, or coordinating committee, and announce your choice with a posted statement, or in the company newsletter, by E-mail, FAX, or other written form. A sample announcement is on page 130. If you already have a coordinator or committee for recycling or hazardous materials management, they may be able to coordinate your energy efficiency program, too.

The coordinator or committee will lead your conservation efforts. Their tasks and functions can include these options:

- Find advice and loan and grant money;
- Promote the program;
- Direct the conservation plan, and monitor and document its implementation; and

- Review administrative and purchasing practices; the physical plant; and usage practices for lighting; plumbing; envelope; heating, ventilation, and air conditioning (HVAC); and landscaping.

This process could take hours or months, depending on how simple or complex your business operations are.

Step 1B: Assign Responsibilities

Your conservation coordinator or committee will now be responsible for implementing low cost/no cost options and for surveying the energy use at your company.

If you have departments, you may want to set specific goals for each one, just as individuals, or individual departments are held responsible for their portions of the budget. Your coordinator will regularly mark their progress and document their achievements.

If your company operates as a single unit, you can make the objectives company-wide and have the coordinator handle the program.

Step 2: Implement Basic Efficiency Measures

Energy is not a fixed cost. You can control how you use it, and what you pay for it. Cut the quantity and cost of energy your business uses, and you free up resources to use somewhere else.

Controlling your energy use is one of your best tools for staying competitive. Start saving energy immediately by implementing Group 1 of the Basic Energy Efficiency Measures on pages 131–134.

As stressed in previous chapters, do not try to implement all these measures at once. It will only frustrate you and your employees and prompt you to quit this enterprise prematurely. Start with one item, then add on, step-by-step, as you gain confidence in each achievement. When you need advice, take advantage of the resources available to you locally, in the trade, and further afield — see the Appendices.

Cautions

As you proceed, beware of energy-efficiency claims that manufacturers may make about their products but cannot prove. Get an expert opinion, testimonials from actual users of the product, and review test and customer satisfaction data.

Some specific items to be aware of are:

- Standby-equipped machines — the American Council for an Energy Efficient Economy (ACE[3]) has found that many offer little energy savings. The standby feature may do no more than shut off a machine's panel lights between uses. So, research what each machine's standby feature actually saves before you buy one.
- Printers — shut them off between uses, particularly laser printers, which are always "hot" while running. Also, laser printers generate ozone, so

keeping them off when not in use improves indoor air quality. If you must keep it on, get an ozone filter for it. If you need the laser for its document print quality, use it just for outgoing materials. For internal drafts, use a more energy-efficient ink- or bubble-jet printer.

- Transient voltage surge suppressors — they have many advantages, but energy savings isn't one of them. They don't maintain uniform voltage, enable your equipment to operate more efficiently, or stop spikes or transient-caused over-registration.

- Shutting down a computer daily will not significantly shorten its useful life. According to the Washington State Energy Extension Service, computer lifespans run about 20 years, but they become obsolete in less than ten years, and in the worst case, daily shutdowns may take five years off the processor's life. If you use a hard drive machine, it can handle about 100,000 on-off cycles before failure.

Step 3: Conduct an Energy Audit

This step assumes your company is already implementing Group 1 of the Basic Energy Efficiency Measures, and you are ready to conduct an energy audit to determine what further improvements are necessary.

Start by surveying where, how, and how much energy you use, and what it all costs you. Assemble your previous year's energy bills. From the information on your bills, convert energy used to British Thermal Units (Btus) using the Btu Conversion worksheet on page 135. Now, in the appropriate ledger boxes of the Energy Ledger on page 136, plug in the Btu numbers from your previous year's energy bills. Electricity billing periods vary from 25 to 40 days. Adjust your ledger accounting to make things consistent. You may want a qualified energy auditor to do this step for you.

This ledger figure is your baseline energy utilization index (EUI). The EUI will help you:

- Decide where to concentrate conservation efforts, and see what effects they have;
- Spot and assess utility billing changes; and
- Estimate your future energy costs.

If your EUI suddenly changes, and the change isn't due to unusual weather conditions, you will know it's a problem with one of your systems.

For example, a sudden rise in your EUI may indicate an HVAC, refrigeration, or process energy problem that is costing you money. The solution will probably show up as an item spotted by your repair people in their preventive maintenance logs.

Step 3A: Determine the Most Cost Effective Source of Energy

According to the U.S. Department of Energy's Energy Information Administration, about 24% of America's electricity is generated by oil-fired plants, 28% by natural gas, 31% by coal, 8% by hydro-electric dams, 7% by nuclear plants, and nearly 2% by "alternative" renewable generating sources, such as solar, wind, refuse-burning (waste-to-energy, or WTE) power plants, landfill-generated methane, and industrial cogeneration.

Nationally, the Energy Information Agency says average costs of generating energy sources in the early 1990s compare as shown in the chart below. Each utility adds its own charges to those listed. All costs are baseload unless otherwise noted.

Source	Cost
Coal, natural gas, hydroelectric, geothermal, cogeneration (biomass, natural gas, etc.)	3.0 – 5.5 cents per kWh
Oil	5.0 – 6.0 cents per kWh
Biomass, WTE	6.0 – 9.0 cents per kWh
Wind, intermittent – as available (IAA)	8.0 – 9.0 cents per kWh
Gas or oil electric	9.0 – 10.0 cents per kWh (peak-load)
Nuclear electric	9.0 – 11.0 cents per kWh
Solar thermal (IAA)	8.0 – 11.0 cents per kWh
Solar electric (IAA)	25.0 – 35.0 cents per kWh

These figures are national averages. Actual prices will vary by location. Begin your research by comparing rates from different sources in your area and their costs for your applications. Rates vary by your demand and the supplier's rate schedule.

If you have a choice between natural gas and nuclear-supplied electricity for cooking and water and space heating, you will most likely be better off in the long-run switching to gas. If you operate in a sunny climate, you may find that it pays you to install your own solar thermal panels for water and space heating, and use conventional energy to run equipment and cook.

Your utility companies can help you run cost comparisons on net energy implications of different power sources in your area. You may find that using a combination, such as gas, solar, and cogeneration will be more economical in the long-run than using only one source. On the other hand, you may find that one source is cheaper now and will continue to be so.

Generally, energy charges vary by utility or supplier and by class of customer. Your utility will have different rate schedules for residential, small commercial, large commercial, industrial, farm, irrigation, and outdoor lighting customers.

Electricity Billing. Check your electric bill. If you are a commercial customer using less than 30 to 50 kW a month, your utility will probably charge you residential rates. If you use more, it may bill you at another rate. The most common commercial rate charges are for:

- Service — the basic fee, which pays for the utility's fixed costs. It is generally based on your transformer size and whether you have single or three-phase power. It is also independent of demand. Some utilities, however, do include initial usage of power and energy in this charge and vary fees based on what it costs them to provide your company with service.
- Energy — measured in kilowatt hours. Depending on the utility fee structure, this charge may increase or decrease as you use more or less kWh.
- Demand or peak load — based on the maximum electric power demand, in kW, that your business registers on the meter during a given period — 15 to 30 minutes during the month. The utility must keep that generating capacity available to meet your peak requirements. If you don't review your energy consumption patterns regularly, your utility will charge you for that demand level, even if your business never registers that high a load again.
- Power factor — this is charged for the power you use that does not register on your demand or energy meters, such as for induction motors, transformers, and some lighting ballasts.

Fossil Fuel Billing. Fossil fuel billing is more basic. Suppliers generally levy a "Customer Charge" for basic service, to cover their fixed costs, and "Commodity Charges" for the quantity of fuel consumed. Usually, rates decline as consumed quantities increase. Some suppliers adjust the commodity rates based on seasonal and other factors.

Natural gas suppliers' Customer Charge includes your connection to the gas line. Propane charges may include tank installation fees. Oil and coal bills may include an account setup fee.

Natural gas is charged by the "therm," or heat content of the gas. Oil and propane are charged by the gallon, coal by the short ton, steam by the pound.

To reduce your company's peak load and energy costs:

1. Get the rate schedules that apply to your type and size of business from your utility or supplier. Make sure you are being billed on that schedule, and not on a higher one. Remember that applicable state and local taxes are added to each bill.
2. Reduce your consumption, using the Basic Energy Efficiency Measures and more specific measures listed in this book.
3. Reduce your demand periods by spreading it over the day. This can be as simple as staggering times you turn on equipment when you arrive for the shift, or as complex as investing in equipment timers and shifting operations away from peak demand periods to low demand periods.
4. Correct your power factor so you are not penalized for consuming power that does not show up on your meters. This involves installing capacitors on particular equipment and requires the help of your electric utility, electric equipment supplier, or electrician.

5. Investigate time-of-day metering. If you are a large power consumer, splitting your metering into on- and off-peak hours may spread your demand and reduce your rates.

As you do your audits, you may find that one item, such as lighting, alone accounts for half your energy demand. If so, stop there and improve the energy-efficiency of your lighting. The elements that make up the other half of your electrical demand (office equipment, refrigeration, water heating), will not pay you enough dividends to track down and improve until they account for a proportionately larger percentage of your improved system.

Create Your Energy Management Plan

Now that you know which areas need further improvement, you can begin your energy management plan. The rest of this chapter is devoted to instructing you on how to improve specific areas. If a section does not apply to you, skip to the next one that does apply.

Lighting

From the Energy Ledger, you now know your business' total kilowatt hour consumption per year. Questions:

1. Can you spread out your demand for lighting energy? For example, can you turn them on in the morning over an hour period rather than all at once?

2. What percentage of your total kWh do your lights consume?

Lighting improvements cut energy demands and consumption, reduce heat output indoors, and cut demand for cooling.

Count your lights. As you do, you may find you have one or several different types in each area. Count them all: entrance, reception, sales, administrative, accounting/bookkeeping, conference room(s), bathrooms, storage, shop(s), receiving, warehouse, loading dock, etc. And cover all types: signage, spotlights, indoor, and outdoor. Use the Lighting Assessment Worksheet on page 137 to record your findings.

Take a moment and calculate possible savings from improving your lighting. Assume that you leave one kilowatt of outside lighting on for twelve hours per day. The current annual energy use is:

   12 hours x 1 kW x 365 days = 4,380 kilowatt hours

Now, assume that photo cells are installed to reduce the outside lighting use to eight hours per day. The new energy use is:

   8 hours x 1 kW x 365 days = 2,920 kWh.

The annual energy saving with this measure is:

   4,380 kWh - 2,920 kWh = 1,460 kWh.

The type and complexity of the savings calculations varies with the item or system you analyze.

Recall this calculation as you fill out the worksheets for your lighting and equipment usage patterns. Before proceeding to the worksheets, however, make sure you have implemented, or are in the process of implementing, the Basic Lighting Efficiency Measures on pages 138–139.

Your business requires different types and intensities of lighting for different seasons, buildings and tasks. For example, you may have outdoor signage out front for your showroom or retail space, but no signage in back for your warehouse or shop. In summer, you may not switch on exterior lights until 9:30 P.M., but in winter, it gets dark by 5:00 P.M., so the lights may come on earlier. During the holiday season, you may add decorative lights, and keep them on constantly. Use the Illumination by the Hour worksheet on pages 140—141 to help you determine which lights are required during which time periods.

One note from school districts around the U.S. (quoted by the Georgia Governor's Office of Energy Resources): Districts discovered they can save energy and reduce vandalism by blacking out all lights at school facilities at night. This runs against conventional law enforcement recommendations to maintain well-lit areas. Their experiences show, however, that blackouts discourage youths from hanging around school buildings, and that any lights which are on cause suspicion for neighbors and police.

This discovery offers a benefit to your business. Check with your insurance and law enforcement agencies. Meanwhile, use one of the illumination worksheets for each building, facility, and season.

Green Lights

In January of 1991, the Environmental Protection Agency's Global Change Division introduced the Green Lights Program. The program helps businesses discover how to profit from converting to better quality, more energy-efficient lighting. Each business that agrees to join the program audits the lighting in its commercial space. If the numbers support a retrofit, the business must voluntarily upgrade 90% of its lighting within a five-year period, and document the savings.

Every business that signs with Green Lights gains access to a powerful package of resources: EPA guidance and forms, a Decision Support Software package for lighting auditing and accounting, and a growing network of "trade allies" — utilities, producers and suppliers of energy-efficient equipment, and in some cases, financial institutions, which can supply products and services. If you would like to join the Green Lights program, contact your regional office of the EPA.

Lighting and Fixture Replacements

Three things to remember:

1. Anywhere you need light, you can use low wattage lamps.
2. Specific tasks, such as merchandise inspection and detail and craft work need brighter lighting than open, non-work areas.

3. The final judges of lighting intensity are the people who actually work with them — your colleagues and employees. They may want more or less light than the U.S. Department of Energy and Illumination Engineering Society recommends in its listing on page 142.

Lighting and fixture upgrades are a good long-term investment, and more than a thousand energy-efficient lamps and fixtures are available now, enough to satisfy any lighting and interior design need you have.

In its *Alternative Energy Sourcebook* (7th Edition — see Appendix D), Real Goods Co. published comparative research between buying and using a compact fluorescent bulb (Panasonic 27 watt) versus incandescent 100-watt bulbs (which burned out every half year). Here are the calculations:

	Panasonic 7 Watt Bulb	Incandescent 100 Watt Bulb
Comparison period: 4.5 years		
Energy cost: $0 .10 per kWh (U.S. average)		
"On" time: Six hours per day		
Bulb cost	$29.00	$0.50
Product life	4.5 years	.45 years
Annual energy cost	$5.91	$21.90
Bulbs replaced in 4.5 year period	0	10
Total cost	$55.60	$103.55

If we add the costs of labor to purchase and change the incandescent bulbs, their total comes out even higher.

For a comparison guide to available lamps, their life expectancies, heat to light ratios and color rendering abilities, contact your electric utility, lighting supplier or lighting consultant, or the references listed in Appendix D

Every lamp fits into a fixture, which can enhance or kill its lighting ability. You want fixtures that give you good aesthetic design and reflect the best possible light from your lamps. Basically, this means finding fixtures with reflecting surfaces that are parabolic (curved) rather than square, and designs that are more open than closed.

At the same time, you may want to factor in how daylight entering your workspaces changes throughout the day and the seasons and affects overall light color and quality. Whether you are doing a small changeover, or a major retrofit, the tasks of balancing design requirements with lighting quality can be complex.

You may want to work with an adviser from your electric utility, or with your lighting supplier, designer, or consultant. Get referrals from your lighting supplier, electric utility, or state energy agency, or find them in the Yellow Pages under "Architects," "Consultants," "Designers," or "Lighting."

If you are only changing lights around your task areas or home office, you can simply go by the new lamp's fit in your socket, and the lumen, color, and electric cycle information noted on the lamp or package.

Americans are accustomed to a soft yellow glow from incandescent lamps, and to a harsh, white glow from fluorescents. The new, lower-wattage compact fluorescent lamps now have coatings that produce a softer light and come closer to the warm, sunlight yellows we expect out of our artificial illumination. Ask for them from your lighting supplier.

Caution: If you are offered cheap lights, or cheap fluorescent ballasts from a company you don't know, refuse them. Quality of the units, their light outputs, and longevity are all suspect.

Fluorescent Lights

Designed for diffuse lighting of uniform brightness, fluorescent lights create light using an electric ballast that ignites rare earth vapor (usually mercury) to make interior coatings (usually phosphors) glow. Available in white and in colors, shaped in globes, straight tubes (four-foot or specialty lengths), curves, circles, and angles.

Dimming. Nearly all bi-pin (two pins at each end) lamps can be dimmed with fluorescent rheostats (dimming switches); most single-pin, compact fluorescents can't be dimmed.

Hum, Light Quality Changes, and Flicker. Any or all of these annoying problems indicate that the ballast or lamp is wearing out, or a socket or ground problem. If you have a problem, check the lamp's age — if it is darkening at one or both ends, it must be replaced. If the lamp is fresh, get the product information from its label and from the ballast, and contact your lighting supplier for an answer.

Fluorescent lamp environmental advantages:

- They last up to ten times longer than incandescents, so they cut solid waste output (and purchase, storage, and replacement labor costs) up to 90%.
- Over their lives, they use 35 to 90% less energy than incandescent lamps, which means up to a ton less CO_2 per lamp is generated to keep them lit by coal- and oil- fired power plants.
- Within the category, units with solid state (electronic) ballasts are 20% more energy efficient than standard magnetic (wire-wound) ballasts.

Environmental disadvantages:

- The lamps contain mercury, and old ones can contain cadmium, so some states classify them as hazardous material. If you dispose of them in large quantities, you may have to treat them as hazardous waste. Contact your local environmental agency, solid waste department, or garbage hauler.
- Manufacturers of the lamps are working to eliminate the mercury, and a small fluorescent lamp recycling industry is emerging — see Appendix D. Recycling cost, as of 1993, runs about $0.40 per lamp.

- In coming years, you may anticipate a trade-in and recycling fee program for these lamps similar to those now run in most states for wet cell batteries and used tires. Buyers of new units trade in their old ones and pay a "battery core charge" or "tire disposal fee" to cover costs of reclaiming the products. Anticipate paying a "lamp disposal fee" at the time of purchase or trade-in.

Tube Fluorescents

Upgrading your fluorescent tube lights can pay you big dividends. For example, if you have standard sized T-12 (12/8" or 1 1/2" diameter) fluorescent lamps and ballasts, retrofitting with T-8s (8/8" or 1" diameter) gives you 20,000-hour average life lamps that will cut your lighting energy cost by 35 to 40% below T-12s. Your ROI in avoided costs, 15 to 20% a year, with payback in half the lifetime of the lamp.

Your investment: new ballasts and new tube lamps, whose costs, if you buy them in quantity, are similar to T-12s. If you buy them singly, T-8s may cost you $1.50 more per lamp.

Energy-efficient tube lamps are available in various diameters, in straight, standard, and specialty lengths; rings and curves. Again, to choose the best for your space, contact your private or electric utility lighting consultant for advice.

Compact Fluorescents

The compact fluorescent (CF) lamps provide diffuse lighting. If you want to be able to dim them, you need specific lamps and equipment. Talk with a lighting specialist. For energy and cost efficiency, and for the environment, the CFs have the same advantages as tube fluorescent lamps.

Businesses of any size will benefit from replacing incandescent lamps indoors or out with compact fluorescents (CF). For the more yellow sunlight-style light quality, ask for "tri-phosphor" CF lamps.

There are several compact fluorescent variations:

- Two designs: (1) a ballast with a replacable lamp, and (2) a bulb unit fused to the ballast. The ballast is good for the lifetimes of four or five lamps, so whenever possible, buy the ballast with replacable lamps.
- Two ballasts: (1) electromagnetic, which uses a copper-wound iron core and can hum and flicker in standard fixtures, and (2) electronic, which is solid state, more efficient, produces less heat, and generally is silent and does not flicker in standard fixtures.
- Warm or cold colors: Get the color that appeals to you. The yellow spectrum is usually a "tri-phosphor" coated bulb.
- Hum: could be the ballast, the fixture, or both. The best way to guard against hum is to use CF lamps with a built-in 60 cycle, or "Hertz" (Hz) filter and operate at or above 20,000 Hz. If that kind of lamp hums, ask your lighting supplier about retrofitting or changing your fixture.

Replacement Indoors. The media makes it sound as if you can simply buy a CF and replace any old incandescent bulb with it. Not so. The CF bulb sizes, shapes, and bases differ from incandescents, so they won't fit in most standard lamps or enclosed wall and ceiling fixtures.

Before you buy a CF, bring back samples to the office and test which size fits inside your fixture designs and which base fits into your fixture sockets. For some fixtures, you can get retrofit kits that accommodate sockets to CF bases. Also, see which CFs provide the least noise and the best light quality.

In recessed ceiling fixtures, such as down lights or "cans," you can generally make a straight-across CF-for-incandescent trade. If not, call your lighting or electrical supplier about a socket retrofit kit.

Replacement Outdoors. As temperatures drop toward freezing, most compact fluorescents become harder to ignite, and once on, produce dim light. For cold weather climates, use the lamps that can operate in weather as low as -20°F.

Ordering and Specification. Whenever you order compact fluorescents, specify "No PCBs." Also, you can specify the percent flicker you want, and if you use electromagnetic ballast lights, get the "A" level or lowest noise rating. You can find the full list of CF specifications in the California Energy Commission's publication, *Energy Efficient and Electronic Ballasts*. See Appendix D for more information.

Halogens

Halogens can be used for any indoor spot-lighting application where you now use incandescents, such as work, accent, and examination areas.

A halogen lamp is an efficient incandescent lamp, designed for spot lighting. This bulb's tungsten filament is surrounded with halogen gas (usually iodine or bromine), which redeposits evaporating tungsten molecules on the white hot filament and slows its decay. Halogens light at a higher temperature than standard incandescents and must be contained in a quartz glass housing. That's why they are also called Quartz Halogen and Tungsten Halogen (T-H) lamps.

A standard 60 to 90-watt halogen supplies the same lumens and less heat than a 150-watt incandescent. Halogen light color is whiter, too, so it can be dimmed without giving off the dingy yellow color that dimmed incandescents do.

Halogens have several lamp designs. Most fit standard fixtures. For example, you can replace standard floods with halogens in track lighting, and those with screw-type bases can generally replace incandescents in any ceramic socket fixture. Beware, however, of sockets that carry the warning, "Use no more than 60W (or 75W) bulb in this fixture." The 60 to 75-watt units are paper sockets and can catch fire in the high heat contact of halogen bulbs.

To get the right mix of bulbs and learn tricks to extend halogen life beyond their rated 2,000 to 6,000 hours, contact your lighting supplier or designer.

Metal Halide, Sodium Vapor, and Induction

Use these lamps for large area illumination—in warehouse and factory spaces, and outdoors (as lighting for storage and parking areas, roads, and walkways).

These brilliant lamps are used for diffuse lighting in large areas such as plants, wholesale and retail warehouses, outdoor properties, highways, and billboards. They work on the same principle as fluorescents, that is, a ballast ignites a metal vapor that glows brightly in the sealed lamp envelope.

Energy savings: Replace 300-watt incandescent street lamps with 35-watt sodium vapor lamps, and you maintain your lumen value and cut your exterior lighting energy costs by 85%.

The halide and induction lamps tend toward a whitish light color, low- and high-pressure sodium toward amber. For advice, contact your lighting supplier or lighting design consultant.

Dimmers, Occupancy Sensors, and Trip Switches

Occupancy sensors alone can save up to 15% of the energy normally consumed in a large room, and up to 30% in a small room, compared to manual switching. For example, REI now uses some of the most advanced and efficient lighting technologies available. In their warehouses, lights stay on at 30% of capacity until a worker enters the area. Then, lights come up to full power. After the worker leaves, light levels automatically drop again. This lighting technology is expected to save over $32,000 and 804,000 kilowatt hours annually. This is approximately enough energy saved to heat 58 homes for a year.

Using dimmers, occupancy sensors, timers, and trip switches can cut your operating expenses and save valuable energy.

Most dimmers for incandescent and halogen lamps are off-the-shelf items. Fluorescents, however, need lamp-specific equipment:

- Circuit based dimmers; or
- Current limiters, available hard wired, as inserts and dummy lamp tubes.

You can buy occupancy sensors, timers, and trip switches at most electronics and hardware stores and install them at your offices. Millions of people use them at home to switch lights and appliances on and off automatically, at preset times. Computer programs now available also enable you to centralize complete control of your electric devices from your home or office PC.

Consult an expert to make certain you get the most cost-effective equipment and design possible for larger control jobs.

Daylighting

Daylighting is basically letting the sun into your work areas with skylights and window areas and coupling your interior lights to controls that automatically dim or shut them off when bright daylight is available.

The technique can reduce heat from artificial lights by up to 66%; cut lighting energy requirements by 25 to 50%, and total energy costs by up to 7% under standard lighting systems. [1]

Daylighting can be used as interior lighting for any space. It is most cost-effective, however, when it is designed and built into new construction or a remodel.

Daylighting can be cost effective whether it is done in a remodel, or designed and built into new construction. There is more to this than meets the eye, however. Daylighting changes structural heat gains and losses. It can also create glare and uneven illumination patterns, which prompt occupants to close drapes or blinds, cut daylight, and boost demands for artificial light and cooling.

In your design, you want to minimize direct sunlight, and design glazing and thermal barriers to minimize glare and veiling reflections, solar heat gain, and heat loss. You'll also want to install automatic controls that minimize your use of artificial lights.

If you plan on using daylighting to cut your energy costs, get professional advice from your utility, state energy extension office, lighting supplier, or interior or architectural designer.

Electrical Appliances and Equipment

Keep these basics in mind when you use or choose appliances and equipment:

- Use life-cycle costs to make your purchasing decisions;
- Size each unit to its given task; and
- Maintain and service each unit.

You don't judge a book by its cover, so don't judge your appliance or equipment by its initial cost. The more expensive first cost can often be the least expensive long-term cost.

An example created by the Bonneville Power Administration (BPA) for two copy machines illustrates life-cycle costing. The example assumes constant dollars:

	Initial Cost Basis		Life Cycle 5-Year Cost	
	Machine A	Machine B	Machine A	Machine B
Purchase price	$ 800	$ 500	$ 800	$ 500
Energy cost	$200/year	$300/year	$1000	$1500
Maintenance cost	$40/year	$50/year	$200	$250
Total			$2,000	$ 2,250

Over the depreciation period, the more expensive machine costs less to operate than the less expensive one. For copy machines, the driver is energy cost.

Copy machines use a step-up transformer that boosts incoming voltage so the printing drum can take a static electric charge and hold the toner for printing on paper. The printed paper is then heat- and pressure-treated to bond the toner particles to it, at about 400°F — using a 550 to 700-watt lamp, depending on copier model. Thus, using a copy machine is akin to running a toaster or hair dryer all day long.

Just as you don't judge a book by its cover, don't judge a product by its initial cost. Do a life cycle analysis for each purchase. The more expensive first cost can often be the least expensive long-term cost.

Use the Electrical Equipment Inventory worksheet on pages 143–144 to compile a basic inventory of your electrical equipment, their wattage loads, and their maintenance records.

Production and Process Machinery Motors

Every system and process in every plant is different, but most have one thing in common — motors.

Electric drive motors in the United States account for more than half of this nation's electricity use. On a Btu basis, they also use far more energy than all U.S. vehicles combined, according to the U.S. Department of Energy. In audits of typical industrial and commercial facilities, the Washington State

Energy Extension Office found that half of all motors surveyed ran at less than 60% of full load, and about a third operate at less than 50%.

Recall the "new Jaguar" example in the "Life Cycle Costing" section above. If you have the right motor, drive, and control system for the job, you can achieve dramatic energy and operating savings. For a centrifugal pump or fan, for example, which has a variable load, using a variable speed drive motor system can dramatically cut the power and energy you use to run it (provided there is no excitation current). Such a motor running at 50% power, for example, uses 87% less electrical energy than at full power.

Also, during the long lifetimes of motors and drive systems, energy and maintenance costs rise. So, re-evaluating reliability and paybacks regularly will serve your interests and give you the reasons to justify improving these systems.

Check Appendix D for resources on evaluating, purchasing, and using motors. For the motors you now use, take your conservation and efficiency steps with the Basic Motor Efficiency Measures on page 145 and with the Motor Inventory Questionnaire on pages 145–146.

Many efficiency improvements will pay for themselves in less than two years, according to figures compiled by the Washington State Energy Extension Service. For example, even with a low energy cost of $.04 per kWh, a single point of efficiency improvement for a fully loaded, continuously operating (8,000 hours of use) 50 horse power motor can save as much as 3,564 kWh, valued at $142 annually. Thus, a motor with three points of improved performance could cost up to $852 more than a standard motor and still be cost effective using a two year payback period.

In most applications, future energy savings justify the purchase of an energy-efficient motor. A simple calculation or computer analysis can readily predict the expected payback, taking into account motor prices, energy costs, and efficiency ratings of the motor models.

Once you have inventoried the motors, catalog them by which you can replace or upgrade to get these potential energy savings paybacks: (1) rapid, (2) intermediate, and (3) long term. This will make clear each one's advantages and disadvantages to you:

1. Rapid payback: In each case here you are now using an inefficient motor. These are your first candidates for replacement. They run long hours, have high reliability demands, have inadequate controls, are oversized, or are functioning where variable speed drives will do better. Replace these motors with more efficient ones soon, for example, during the next regular plant downtime or scheduled changeout.

2. Intermediate payback: these motors are adequate in their current application, but can be replaced with a better model when they wear out. Begin shopping now for the replacement.

3. Long term payback: these motors are reasonably efficient or are used less than 2,000 hours each year. They require no special treatment, and can be replaced with a similar motor in the future.

Electric drive motors, a common denominator in all mechanical processes, is one of your keys to energy efficiency and long-term dollar savings.

Shopping Tips

When you shop for the most efficient motor at the lowest cost, keep these points in mind:

1. Use a consistent efficiency standard for comparing motors. Efficiency ratings may vary widely within a price range. The most common motor efficiency standard in the United States is IEEE 12-Method B, which uses a dynamometer to determine mechanical output.
2. Comparison shop for motors by efficiency rating, not by labels that say "energy efficient."
3. Negotiate price. Industrial size motors are rarely sold at manufacturer's list. Every supplier has individual unit and quantity discounting policies. Ask about them, or if you don't enjoy bargaining, bring someone with you who does.

Compressor Systems

Compressor systems are important if you are a building manager or owner or your business is in construction, manufacturing, or automotive.

Compressed air is used in commercial applications from HVAC equipment controls to driving pneumatic systems and shop tools. Motors are used in all compressors, so refer to the motor section above for energy conservation guidelines. When the compressor motor burns out, replace it with an energy-efficient motor instead of a new standard or rewound motor. It will cut your energy use by 2 to 5%.

A qualified person on your staff, or a qualified contractor, should handle maintenance and repair on your compressor systems. To keep things running at maximum efficiency, use the Basic Compressor Efficiency Measures on page 147.

Refrigeration

Refrigeration is your largest energy consumer after boilers and domestic water heating.

This area includes computer room air conditioning systems, building chillers, refrigerated cases, walk-in coolers, blast freezers, and controlled atmosphere refrigerated warehouses.

All use motors and compressors, and for each degree F that you can reduce their condensing temperature, you cut your compressor power requirements by about 1%. The primary energy-efficiency measures for refrigeration systems are listed in Group 3B of the Basic Energy Efficiency Measures on page 133. Again, other than the basic refrigeration efficiency items — adjusting thermostats, checking for condensation and air leaks, turning off door heaters during low-use hours — most maintenance and repair work here should be done by a qualified person on your staff or by a qualified contractor.

To keep things running at peak efficiency, check the Basic Refrigeration Energy Efficiency Measures on page 147–148.

A reminder about the hazardous materials risks of your refrigerants: Check for leaks of CFCs, and get all maintenance performed by licensed and bonded refrigeration contractors. Ammonia refrigeration is not as energy efficient, but using it does not expose you to hazardous materials liability.

Cooking Equipment

Kitchens generate great quantities of heat from stoves, ovens, warmers, refrigeration equipment, and other sources. As any kitchen is created or redesigned, consider the best uses of energy generated in this space. These include, but are not limited to the following:

- Recapturing heat to supplement hot water heating;
- Heat exchangers to supplement cooling; and
- Reversible fans between kitchen and dining areas that use heated kitchen air to warm dining areas during cold months, and cool dining area air to chill kitchens during hot months.

If your business is a restaurant, hospitality, or food service organization, find ways to recapture and use waste heat.

Industrial kitchen designers may not have the HVAC knowledge required for integrating the kitchen's heating, cooling, and ventilation outputs with the dining areas, nor with the rest of the building. For these, contact an HVAC specialist, and review ideas from such sources as ACE[3], the Electric Ideas Clearinghouse, and others listed in Appendix D.

To use your energy more efficiently in existing kitchens and food services, follow the guidelines in the Basic Cooking Energy Efficiency Measures on page 148–149.

Water Systems

The variable in water systems is your local water. Water carries minerals. Minerals precipitate out on piping and interior tank surfaces — the arteries, veins, and heart of your water heaters, dishwashers, boilers, and fountains. To keep your water equipment alive as long as possible, you must:

No matter what industry you are in, it is important to maintain your pipes and water systems.

- Regularly clean or flush tanks to remove sediments and precipitates; and
- Maintain proper water treatment to keep interior pipe and tank surfaces clear of scale. You can treat the water with ozone or chemicals to accomplish this.

Both these functions will have to be done by a qualified person on your staff, or by a qualified contractor.

Domestic Hot Water (DHW)

Your type of business determines how much heated water you consume. Commercial and residential office buildings tend to be low quantity users; health care, food service, and laundry industries tend to use large quantities — for boilers, primary water heating, and remotely located or special purpose DHW.

The Basic Water Heater Energy Efficiency Measures on pages 150–151 will help you save energy and prolong the life of your water heater(s). For greater detail on DHW, refer to *The Water Heater Workbook* — see Appendix D.

Other Water Heating Options

On Demand. This system is convenient, but very expensive compared to standard gas and electric tank units. They only operate with sufficient water pressure and at present do not have wide support networks in North

America. Those which are natural gas powered also generate carbon monoxide as a combustion by-product and must be used in well-ventilated spaces.

Heat Pumps. They work on the refrigeration principle, removing heat from the air and putting it into the water. The units can be up to 3 1/2 times more efficient than normal electric water heaters, but are more costly to buy and maintain than standard water heaters. Investigate the life cycle costs of this technology for your climate area before buying into it.

Combined Space and Water Heating. This option is possible in new construction and remodels. It offers the most advantage in winter and cool or cold climates because the space heater heats water for relatively little added cost. In summer, however, the space heater comes on only to heat water. Technology is improving in this area, so investigate the latest advances before committing to this option.

Dishwashers

There are two types of institutional dishwashers, low-temperature and high-temperature.

Make sure the dishwashers you use in your restaurant, food service, or hospitality organization are energy efficient.

High-temp units wash with 180 to 185° F water, which sterilizes dishware and leaves it so hot, it air dries quickly. The units are designed with electric water heat boosters — either built-in or as a companion item. Feed water from the domestic hot water (DHW) tank can be as low as 130°F and as high as 160°. Energy-wise, there are two questions to answer:

- What does the manufacturer recommend?
- What are your energy sources for the DHW and the booster? If your DHW is heated by natural gas (relatively inexpensive), and the booster is electric (relatively expensive), you may find that in the long-run you save money heating the DHW feed water to 160° (or the manufacturer's recommended temperature) with gas, rather than having the booster do all the work (50 to 55° up from 130°) with electricity.

Low-temp units wash at 130 to 140° F and use a chlorinated sanitizing agent in the rinse.

Environmentally, both use the same type of soap, the same amount of water for wash and rinse cycles — 1 to 2 gallons, and both run on either 220V or 115V, depending on the model. Both high- and low-temp systems recycle clean rinse water as wash water for the next load.

Here are the differences:

- Hard water — high-temp units can precipitate out minerals or ore on the dishware, leaving a powdery residue (whitish or greyish if mineral, reddish if ore) that requires extra cleaning. Low-temp units don't.
- Septic systems — both types can be used with septic systems. Their effects are a tossup. The high-temp unit water is about 150° F by the time it hits the drain, and there is no proof this adversely affects septic system bacteria. The low-temp chemical rinse contains 50 parts per million

(ppm) of chlorine (drinking water contains 1 ppm), but this dissipates within five minutes of exposure to air, heat, and solids.

- Effectiveness — as long as the high-temp unit's wash water consistently runs at 180 to 185° F, it is as effective as the low-temp.

To get more specific answers, call your restaurant supplier or dishwasher manufacturer.

For pots and pans, you can reduce wash water demand by using one deep sink filled with detergent water for washing, one filled with clean water and a cup of bleach for rinsing and sanitizing, and only then, using the tap for a final rinse. Change deep sink water as needed. Before using this technique, however, check with your health department to see if it is an approved method.

If you rinse bottles and cans for recycling, use a single tub of water for this purpose, and change it when it gets dirty.

Boilers

Boilers heat water to make steam for industrial processes and to make hot water for space heating and DHW. Since they burn fuel, the keys to their energy savings are combustion efficiency and minimum run times. Boiler care and maintenance should be handled by a specialist who is licensed, well-recommended, and well-versed in energy conservation.

This section won't make you a boiler expert. Instead, it will provide you with enough information to understand the process, so that you can ask informed questions of your specialist and get understandable answers.

The first step in saving energy is getting the right-sized boiler for the job. Until recently, most boilers were oversized to accommodate peak building loads that might come up only once a year. But, the '70s energy crises have pushed engineers to take new tactics. Engineers now:

Building owners and managers and manufacturers can dramatically cut energy costs by boosting the efficiency of their boilers.

- Add new controls to old, oversized boilers, which enable them to vary their firing rates to meet actual demands; and
- Install new, correctly-sized boilers with modern controls where old ones have worn out, or in new construction.

In fact, new installations often involve two boilers. The first, or "base boiler," fires under normal heating requirements; the second, or "backup," fires for high demand. Generally, one provides space heat while the other, which is usually smaller and less energy-demanding, heats domestic hot water.

Boiler Efficiency

Most boilers are fired by oil or gas (and in rare cases, coal or electricity). Combustion efficiency (CE) ranges from 75 to 95%. The CE is the portion of the fuel's energy that is not lost as exhaust up the stack. Engineers determine CE by taking two measurements from the stack gases — exhaust temperature and content of oxygen (O_2) or carbon dioxide (CO_2) — then they match their readings against CEs on a fuel-specific chart.

Stack temperatures for hot water or steam boilers generally range from 250 to 600° F. The lower the temperature, the higher the CE. Generally, stack temperature should be no more than 150° F above the boiler's steam or hot water temperature.

The oxygen carbon dioxide measurement indicates how much excess air is coming up the stack. To burn, fuel must be mixed with air, and no fuel-burning equipment makes that mix perfectly. Excess air is the air present beyond what is needed to burn the oil or gas. Too much carries heat up the stack; too little or none carries unburned fuel up the stack and offers a potential explosive condition. Both indicate low efficiency.

At the same time the engineer or specialist takes the stack measurements, he or she should also check carbon monoxide (CO) levels, and check for cracks or leaks in the stack itself, which should be promptly repaired.

For your own records, know your boilers. Use the Basic Boiler Inventory worksheet on page 153 to keep track.

Armed with this background information, make sure your boiler specialist also covers the basic steps listed in the Basic Boiler Energy Efficiency Measures on page 154.

Heating, Ventilation, and Air Conditioning

Businesses traditionally consume more energy pulling heat out of their spaces than putting heat in. This is because buildings accumulate heat produced from interior lights and machinery as well as absorbed from the sun. Consequently, air conditioning and ventilation must be used more than heat.

Avoid medical liabilities by quickly correcting any problems with your HVAC system; if you are constructing a new building, work closely with your architects and mechanical engineers to avoid costly long-term problems.

You will want a heating, ventilation, and air conditioning (HVAC) specialist to handle the bulk of the system's details. This includes keeping log books, adjusting dampers, outside air intake, air flows and pressurization, and conducting system-wide preventative maintenance.

There are actions you can take before you call in the specialist, however. Use the Heating, Ventilation, and Cooling Systems Worksheet on pages 155–156 to familiarize yourself with your system and determine where improvements can be made. Specific efficiency measures for HVAC systems are listed in the Basic HVAC Energy Efficiency Measures on pages 157–158.

Indoor Air Quality and Sick Building Syndrome

The HVAC system you install must provide healthy air for occupants in all building spaces.

HVAC in an environmentally tight structure can cut energy costs, but it can also have a bad effect on building occupants. The HVAC system can recirculate virus germs, pollutants (such as gasses from building and furnishing materials, smoke, perfume, and chemicals from office machines), bacteria, and other disease factors.

Sicknesses can mount, and absenteeism can jump when this happens in sealed buildings where occupants cannot open windows and doors and gain access to fresh, outdoor air. This condition is called "sick building syndrome" (SBS).

Indoor air quality (IAQ) depends on several items:

- Type of space, building materials, furnishings;
- Location of building;
- Indoor business activities and air pollutant levels;
- The condition of the supplied air;
- The air circulation patterns in the space; and
- Occupancy level.

There are several immediate actions you can take to clear the air. Please refer to Chapter 6 for more information.

Heaters

By keeping heating and air conditioning units "tuned" and their filters cleaned, you achieve energy efficiency, save up to 5% of operating expenses, and reduce emissions from heaters that run on oil or gas.

- Oil furnaces burn diesel fuel, operate at 62 to 75% efficiency, and produce combustion exhaust which contains pollutants, water vapor, and between 500 to 800° F of heat, just as vehicle and boat engines do. As with any internal combustion device, furnace fuel and air filters should be cleaned regularly, about once a month when in normal service.
- Gas furnaces burn at up to 95% efficiency, and more cleanly than oil, exhausting water vapor and about 110° F heat.
- Electric baseboard heat output is nearly 100% efficient, but has the drawback of high electricity cost in many parts of the United States.
- High efficiency wood burning units are also available for space and water heating. They exhaust 400 to 800° F up the chimney and may pose a pollution problem, however.

This is the time to refer back to your cost checklist for heating energy or fuel. If it looks high, contact your fuel oil or natural gas company for a review of your furnace efficiency.

Whatever heating or cooling source you use, make sure you use it in a well-insulated space, where you have fine-tuned the energy efficiencies of all the electric and fuel-consuming items in the space.

Heat Pumps

There are two types of heat pumps: air and ground-based. The ground-based units are more efficient because ground temperatures are stable compared to air temperatures, which vary widely on any given day. Ground-based pumps are also much more expensive than air units.

Because both models work on the refrigeration principle, they must have enough temperature differential to create an efficient heat exchange. If they

Heat pumps can be used in both residential and office structures, but their efficiency varies by climate and type.

don't, they use their built-in electric strip heaters, or draw on your existing heater or air conditioner to supplement their work. This is inefficient, because to get the benefit of the heat pump, you must now run a second piece of equipment, your heater or chiller.

Heat pump promoters point to their relatively low costs for delivering high energy efficiencies (which can be double the efficiency of your heater or cooler). Before buying into this technology, research it thoroughly for your climate area, and get opinions from neutral third parties, such as testimonials and cost/benefit numbers from people in your area who use them.

If you are already using heat pumps, be aware of the efficiency measures on page 159.

Water Heat Recovery Systems

Waste heat presents cost-cutting opportunities for any business that uses large volumes of water, such as restaurants, hotels, factories, hospitals, laundries, breweries, dairies, or spas.

A water heat recovery systems is a good option for businesses from medium-sized restaurants to large manufacturers.

You can recapture that heat to prewarm cold water. Sources can be commercial refrigeration, air conditioning, and any equipment that dumps waste hot water. The Washington State Energy Extension Office estimates that you can reclaim 60 to 70% of the heat and use it to add 45 to 70° F to your cold water, cutting your energy and costs for water heating, reducing work loads, and extending the lives of the very equipment that waste the heat. The higher your utility costs, the faster your payback will be.

The key is using a heat exchanger between the piece of equipment exhausting heat and the source of your cold water. Most state energy offices have diagrams and worksheets you can use to pencil out the economics for your business. See Appendix D for more information.

For example, you can enjoy paybacks in dishwashing of one to five years on a $2,500 to $4,000 investment. The system is arranged so the heat exchanger transfers heat from waste hot water back to the incoming cold water line. The newly warmed water then moves to the gas or electric heater, where it is boosted to the required wash temperature. You save the cost of energy for warming the water and extend the life of your water heater by reducing its heating load.

Consider this system where you operate refrigeration and air conditioning at least six months a year and your water heating bill is $500 or more. Generally, an investment of $2,000 to $4,000 in equipment and controls, plus costs of any structural improvements needed to accommodate the equipment, will provide you with a system that lasts up to 20 years and an ROI of five years or less.

Benefits include lower energy bills, extended refrigeration compressor life, and reduced compressor loads, scale buildup, and maintenance. What you decide is the best system for you will depend upon the heat available from the refrigeration system, the amount of hot water you use, the efficiency of appropriate heat recovery units, and the cost effectiveness of the installation.

Start by reviewing the available literature, then contact your local energy utility or state energy extension service for advice and referrals to heat recovery specialists.

Cogeneration

Heat recovery leads into a short discussion of cogeneration, where waste energy or materials can be used to produce electric power and steam.

At its best, cogeneration marries two energy-producing processes, power generators and boilers, to recapture and use as much as 80% of the available energy in their fuels. Any fuel is usable: natural gas, biogas (methane), fuel oil, municipal solid waste, wood waste, and methanol or ethyl alcohol from agricultural residues.

Cogeneration is primarily an option for large manufacturers.

Generally, the larger the plant, the more likely cogeneration will be cost effective. It is not a new idea, and plant managers may dismiss it as not being cost effective. Reconsider cogeneration, because electricity costs are rising dramatically, and this presents a low-cost means of generating alternative power from otherwise discarded waste. Again, to start the ball rolling, contact your local energy utility or state energy extension service for advice and referrals to power planning engineers. Items to consider include:

- Availability, quantities, and costs of recapturable waste heat and fuel.
- Space constraints, water quality, and availability.
- Life cycle costs and generating capacities of cogeneration technologies, and purposes for waste energy — water heating, steam, or electricity production.
- Emission limitations and control system characteristics.
- Thermal load duration (including daily swings, peak requirements, and weekly profiles) and power plant turndown or part-load characteristics.

If you can successfully cogenerate electricity at your plant, you can turn it to profit by selling the excess to your surrounding community's power grid. Your plant's contribution could represent a significant source of potential conservation for the community, and a significant public relations or green marketing advantage for you. Yours might be a source of peak electrical energy for the local utility, provide baseload energy for the industry itself, or be used to heat homes or businesses in a "district heating" program.

There are two other generating options for your plant, but your ability to implement them depends upon the answers to these questions:

- Is your community located near potential geothermal resource areas, where steam or hot water can be recovered and converted into electricity, or used directly for district heating? Since the late 1800s, for example, the City of Boise, Idaho, has used geothermal hot water for city heating.
- Is your community located in a high wind area? Wind energy is already feasible, as fan blade technologies are continually improved. Development of small- and large-scale wind systems may require modifications to building and zoning codes, or establishment of a locally owned wind energy utility.

Depending on your climate and geography, alternative energy, such as solar power, may be a viable option for your business.

Alternative Energy Sources

If there was no sun, how would we heat ourselves?

This seemingly frivolous question makes one point: all heating systems are simply backups for the sun.

In the state of Israel, most buildings are topped by solar water heating panels, and in remote locations, solar electric (photovoltaic) cells power a large percentage of lighting and electrical devices. Clearly, where sunshine is plentiful or conventional energy sources are scarce or expensive, look to the sun and alternative sources.

On this side of the Atlantic, as of 1993, some 50,000 of America's 100 million households have used these technologies to disconnect entirely from electric power generating grids.[2] All also use the latest equipment for refrigeration and efficient use and storage of energy.

Alternative energy ideas are developing by the same quantum leaps as happened in the computer industry. In the 1970s, for example, there was no such thing as a portable computer. Today, there are notebook-sized laptops with 80 megabyte hard drives.

Here are some other reasons to take another look at alternative energy. First, the new federal administration supports pro-active energy policies, and it may push through more grants and tax incentives for alternative energy investment. Check with your local office of the Small Business Administration for grant and loan information.

Second, the research and development people at the National Renewable Energy Laboratory, in Golden, Colorado, are now working to help commercialize several other "futuristic" concepts, including:

- Transportation fuels to replace oil, including methanol, ethanol, hydrogen, gasoline blends, biomass fuels such as "syngas," and proton exchange membrane (PEM) fuel cells.
- Solar, wind, geothermal, and ocean thermal production for applications as small as households and as big as office blocks and industrial plants.
- Photovoltaic improvements that will drop generating prices another 75% by the year 2000.
- Solid electrolyte, maintenance-free sodium/sulfur storage batteries for electric vehicles and utilities.

Many of the solar technologies are cost effective today, but like computers, they may be more so by tomorrow. Widespread successful uses of alternative energy systems show that you can generate some or all of your own energy now, as a way to partially or completely control your energy costs.

There are several items to check for cost effectiveness before you jump into alternative energy supply equipment. These include:

- Your business' power demands;
- The designs of your offices and facilities; and
- Which technologies will work at your location.

Answers to some of these questions, and referrals to organizations that help you with alternative energy auditing, are available from sources listed in Appendix D. You can also refer to the Yellow Pages under "Contractors," "Heating," and "Solar."

Choosing the Most Efficient Energy Source

If a move into "alternative" energy for heating is not practical for your company, consider upgrading to a more efficient plant and a more appropriate energy source.

Energy source economy should be one of the first things you consider in new construction, remodels, or retrofits. This is another area you may wish to discuss with a specialist. Knowing how much you pay for different energy sources can help you decide how to reduce future energy costs. (Refer to the EUI worksheet you completed earlier.)

Your choice of energy source depends on availability. If you have limited choices, evaluate them carefully so you avoid using whatever appears most convenient to use. For example, you may only use oil now because natural gas is not available. If you and other potential customers in the area request a gas line, however, a gas supplier may be willing to extend one to you for the promise of future business.

When you consider switching energy sources in an existing building, there are also restrictions to consider. Your existing HVAC may not accommodate an energy swap. For example, you may find it difficult or impossible to switch an all-electric unitary system to oil or gas. On the other hand, it is fairly easy to convert an oil-based system to one fired by natural gas. A propane system may provide a good temporary source if natural gas is available in the near future.

When designing new systems, consider using several energy types over the life of the building. Energy costs can change substantially over time, and even though one source is best today, that doesn't mean it will be so tomorrow. Many facilities keep their options open by maintaining dual energy systems. This allows them the flexibility to choose lower rate schedules, or simply to take advantage of low energy costs when they are available.

Some dual energy systems are straightforward, such as use the same boiler and burner. Others are more complex, and may require duplication of some equipment to function.

Every energy option change will require an investment. Research the possibilities with an energy systems engineer and with your local utilities and suppliers.

Environmentally Smart Design and Construction

Factors that affect your building's energy consumption include its age, construction materials, operating procedures, mechanical systems design, efficiency of equipment, level of occupancy, and wind and chill factors. Your building impacts several environmental areas: energy generation from power plants, use and disposal of materials, absorption and dissipation of energy, air current changes, and shading.

Take into account your climate, geography, wildlife, transportation, and workforce location before selecting a site or a building, remodeling, or re-landscaping.

Whether you plan to remodel or build a new building or complex, consider the steps in the Environmental Design and Construction Questionnaire on pages 159–161 and the Environmental Design and Construction Efficiency Measures and Considerations Questionnaire on page 162 for creating an "environmentally smart" design.

Cosanti Foundation

"As a result of their sprawl, (cities) literally transform the earth, turn farms into parking lots, and waste enormous amounts of time and energy transporting people, goods, and services over their expanses. My solution is urban implosion rather than explosion. In nature, as an organism evolves, it increases in complexity and it also becomes a more compact or miniaturized system. The city, too, is an organism — one that should be as alive and functional as any living creature." This quote by architect Paolo Soleri sums up the theme of the Cosanti Foundation. In Mayer, Arizona, 65 miles north of Phoenix, Soleri created the non-profit Cosanti Foundation to fund development of a prototype ecological town for 5,000. The earth-tones structures are integrated with the surrounding environment, and the community serves as a research and study center for the social, economic, and ecological implications of development.

Refer to Appendix D for a list of resources to help you create an environmentally smart building.

Sample Energy Efficiency Statement

XYZ Company's Energy Efficiency Statement
March 15, 1994

We at XYZ Company resolve to make the most efficient use of our energy resources, and reduce our demands. We are committed to making this company a world-class competitor, and one of our industry's lowest-cost producers.

This is a team effort, in which all members of this company are equal partners in achieving successes.

In general, our company is committed to these cost-effective energy management improvements:

- Using a variety of incentives to encourage carpool, vanpool, public transport, bicycle, and foot commuting to work, and discourage commuting by one-passenger vehicle.
- Using low cost/no cost efficiency measures, such as switching off lights and equipment that aren't being used.
- Creating efficient lighting, heating and cooling systems, while maintaining comfortable working temperatures: about 65 to 68° F for heating, and to 78°F for cooling.
- Reducing energy demands for our processes and products to create more efficient operations, and a more competitive company.
- Conducting preventive maintenance programs for all equipment and systems.

Signed:

John E. Farrel

John E. Farrel
President

Sample Coordinator Announcement

XYZ Coordinator Announcement
March 15, 1994

We are happy to announce that, as the next step in our energy and water management program, we have selected Janice Holten, ext. 21, as our energy conservation management coordinator.

She will be exploring several areas to find opportunities where we can save energy, and boost our company's efficiencies. Areas include:

- Administrative and purchasing practices.
- Physical plant operations.
- Usage practices for lighting, plumbing, envelope, HVAC and landscape.

Please call or approach her at any time with ideas for cost savings and efficiency improvements here at the company. Also approach her if you find that any of the changes are creating problems for you, your colleagues, or your area. We'll announce our accomplishments and successes regularly as we implement conservation steps.

Basic Energy Efficiency Measures

Group 1: Measures You Can Do Yourself

☐ 1. Turn off or disconnect electrical items that are not in use, such as coffee makers, lights, air conditioners, heaters, radios, typewriters, computer monitors, and printers. You can shut off incandescent lights and most printers when not in use; fluorescent lights, laser printers, and computer monitors if they will be unused for 10 minutes or more. Disconnect refrigerated drinking fountains if acceptable with building occupants.

☐ 2. Tag the items that must remain on during business hours, to avoid confusion with those that can be turned off.

☐ 3. Place signs reminding people to please turn off lights and equipment when they finish with them, and keep doors and windows closed when heating or air conditioning is on.

☐ 4. Spread electrical demand over a broad period. For example, in the morning, turn on building or plant lights and electrical equipment sequentially, over an hour or more, to spread the load.

☐ 5. Block the sun's heat with light-colored or reflective window films, shades, or curtains.

☐ 6. Cover unused windows, such as those that are painted out or blocked by merchandise, with insulating material. Window glass transfers more heat per square foot than any other building material. To cover windows use roll or batt insulation, wood panels or Styrofoam board sandwiched in sheetrock.

☐ 7. Clean dirty skylights and windows to increase the amount of natural light available.

☐ 8. On hot sunny days, close windows, blinds, curtains, and doors on the sunny side of the building to keep heat out. Close them at night, too. When the day's sun has passed, open windows on both sides of the building to create cross ventilation. Also, keep curtains open on cool sunny days to let heat in.

☐ 9. Set space heating thermostats no higher than 68°F, and air conditioning thermostats no lower than 78°F. At night, set heating back to 55° or 65°, and air conditioning up to 80°F.

☐ 10. When you first switch on heaters or air conditioners, do not set them to higher or lower temperatures than what you want in the room. Playing with their thermostats won't help them work any faster.

☐ 11. Use portable heaters and air conditioners wisely. They are useful if only one part of a large area must be heated or cooled. But if there are cold spots (or hot spots) in an area that a central heating/cooling system serves, it indicates there is a problem such as air infiltration, lack of insulation, poor air distribution, or inadequate placement or calibration of a thermostat. Call your building manager, or a heating, ventilation, and air conditioning (HVAC) specialist to identify and correct it. Then, you can turn off the portable units.

☐ 12. Adjust outdoor light timers seasonally, as days get shorter or longer.

☐ 13. Cover wall and window air conditioners during cold months so cold air cannot come in and rob your building of heat.

☐ 14. Use rechargeable batteries wherever possible.

Basic Energy Efficiency Measures (continued)

☐ 15. Use pushbrooms for cleaning decks, drives, and streets, rather than gas-powered blowers or water hoses.

☐ 16. Investigate using solar thermal units for space, water, and pool heating. Also, research uses and cost-effectiveness of other energy sources, such as natural or bio-gas, geothermal, wind, and cogeneration for general or task-specific uses. Tax credits or financial incentives may also be available for alternative energy investments.

☐ 17. Reduce thermostat temperatures on domestic hot water heaters. Most applications require no more than 105°F water at the tap. Kitchens, laundries, and laboratories may require hotter water.

☐ 18. During shutdowns and vacations, set thermostats back to the minimum allowable for the season.

Group 2: Measures You May Want a Professional to Do

☐ 19. Install water heater jackets where appropriate for the model and type of heater you use.

☐ 20. Insulate hot water piping throughout the building.

☐ 21. Drain and flush sediment from water heaters regularly.

☐ 22. Change or replace filters for heating, ventilation, and air conditioning systems regularly. Dirty filters overwork fans; deteriorating filters can clog cooling coils or heat exchangers.

☐ 23. Replace broken windows with new thermal windows.

☐ 24. Caulk and weatherstrip areas, such as joints, doors, windows, louvers, flues, stacks and pipes, access hatches, unsealed utility connections, and cracks in the building's surfaces.

☐ 25. Repair damaged or missing duct and pipe insulation.

☐ 26. Evaluate operation and maintenance procedures. For many commercial buildings, setting up a program can cut annual utility costs by up to 20% with little or no capital investment.

☐ 27. Commission your building, plant, and equipment. Run your own tests to make sure specifications are met, and your suppliers, contractors, and consultants are doing their jobs.

Group 3: Industry Specific Measures

Group Three items are covered in more detail later in the chapter. These measures are listed here only to alert readers to differences in energy efficiency options between industries. Most of these measures require the help of a qualified specialist to accomplish, and should be undertaken as part of an overall energy management plan.

A: Offices, Plants, and Retail Stores

☐ 1. Audit and adjust HVAC and lighting systems — the building's primary energy consumers.

☐ 2. Lower or remove office partitions wherever possible to improve HVAC and lighting efficiency.

☐ 3. Upgrade office machines such as FAX, photocopiers, computers, and printers to the most energy efficient models available.

Basic Energy Efficiency Measures (continued)

☐ 4. Encourage building occupants to take the stairs instead of the elevator for trips of up to three floors.

☐ 5. Cut down the number of elevators in service on nights, weekends, and holidays, when the majority of occupants are not in the building.

☐ 6. Switch off the motor-generator set located in the elevator machine room when not in use.

B: Retail and Wholesale Grocery

☐ 1. Turn off HVAC air handler units in stores, food services, and storage buildings when the areas are unoccupied. This enables air to stratify and helps refrigeration equipment operate more efficiently.

☐ 2. Keep refrigerated products below marked product load lines in display cases. Overloading decreases product quality and increases energy use by 10 to 20% for each fixture.

☐ 3. Cover open reach-in refrigerated cases to reduce equipment cycling during hours the area is unoccupied. Check with your refrigeration contractor to learn if you must take precautions on your particular units to protect compressors and avoid frost build-up on products.

☐ 4. Keep refrigeration pressure and temperature controls serviced and accurate. Recommended settings are:

Ice cream chests/cases	-14° F
Frozen food cases	- 8° F
Deli cases	35° F
Beverage/dairy cases	40° F

(Check with your local health department for specific code requirements.)

☐ 5. In glass door refrigerated cases, turn off door defogger heaters during low traffic periods, such as midnight to 7:00 A.M. on weekdays, and midnight to 8:00 A.M. weekends.

☐ 6. Open cold box doors as briefly as possible, and expose refrigerated products to outside air for as short a time-period as possible during unloading and restocking.

☐ 7. Use manual timers on lights in the employee lunchroom and other infrequently used rooms.

C: Food Service, Hospitality, Laundry

☐ 1. Run dishwashers, clothes washers, and dryers with full loads only. Clean dryer lint traps regularly. Schedule laundry operations to avoid peak demand.

☐ 2. Use cold water for garbage disposal and cleaning wherever possible.

☐ 3. Upgrade to equipment that saves time and energy, such as steam cookers and kettles, and tilting skillets/braising pans.

☐ 4. Set freezer and refrigerator temperatures at maximum allowable by health codes, usually 0 to 5°F on freezers, 38 to 42°F on refrigerators. Call your local health department for limits.

Basic Energy Efficiency Measures (continued)

D: Hotels, Motels, Restaurants

☐ 1. Use manual timers for bathroom lighting and exhaust systems, and self-closing faucets at sinks.

☐ 2. Use booster heaters with dishwashers and other appliances that need high temperature or steriliz-ing water. Also, use boosters for applications remote from the main water heater or boiler if fuel used with booster is cheaper than or the same price as that used with main water heater.

☐ 3. Use automatic dimmers in open areas lit by daylight. Use manual dimmers to create atmosphere and energy savings in dining area.

E: Miscellaneous Commercial Warehouse

☐ 1. Avoid using air-curtain doors on loading docks. Instead, use swinging doors or build an enclosed staging area for loading activities.

☐ 2. Use radiant space heaters at key task locations in warehouses rather than HVAC to heat the entire area.

☐ 3. In areas with high ceilings, suspend lighting fixtures from ceiling to bring illumination closer to work, and use task lights for such specific areas as receiving desk and loading dock.

Btu Conversion Worksheet

When calculating energy consumption, costs, and projections, convert all figures to Btus, multiplying by these factors:

Electricity:	_____ kWh	x	3414	=	_____	Btus
Natural Gas:	_____ Therms	x	100,000	=	_____	Btus
Oil #1:	_____ gallons	x	136,000	=	_____	Btus
#2:	_____ gallons	x	138,690	=	_____	Btus
#3:	_____ gallons	x	141,000	=	_____	Btus
#4:	_____ gallons	x	144,000	=	_____	Btus
#5:	_____ gallons	x	150,000	=	_____	Btus
#6:	_____ gallons	x	152,400	=	_____	Btus
#7:	_____ gallons	x	143,000	=	_____	Btus
Butane:	_____ gallons	x	103,000	=	_____	Btus
Propane:	_____ gallons	x	91,330	=	_____	Btus
Kerosene:	_____ gallons	x	134,000	=	_____	Btus
Gasoline:	_____ gallons	x	124,000	=	_____	Btus
Coal:	_____ short tons	x	21,435,000	=	_____	Btus

Steam: 125 psig = 1,193,000 Btus (1.193 MBtu)

100 psig = 1,189,000 Btus (1.189 MBtu)

80 psig = 1,186,000 Btus (1.186 MBtu)

60 psig = 1,182,000 Btus (1.182 MBtu)

40 psig = 1,176,000 Btus (1.176 MBtu)

Wood pellets, sawdust	_____ tons	x	16,000,000	= _____	Btus
Hog fuel	_____ tons	x	9,000,000	= _____	Btus
Municipal solid waste	_____ tons	x	9,000,000	= _____	Btus

Every month, review and adjust EUI and CUI based on changes in weather, building use, and efficiency improvements.

Building: _____

Year: _____

Gross Area (square foot): _____

Utility Ledger — EUI and CUI

Month	Heating Degree Days	Cooling Degree Days	Electricity							Fuel						Total Energy Cost
			kWh	kW Demand		Cost				☐ Gas ☐ Coal ☐ Other			Cost			
				Actual	Billed	Total	Per Unit			Quantity		Total	Per Unit			

Energy Utilization Index (EUI)

$$EUI = \frac{\text{Total Energy Consumption Btu's per Year}}{\text{Gross Area (square foot)}}$$

$$= \underline{\qquad} \text{ Btu's per sq. ft. per year}$$

Cost Utilization Index (CUI)

$$CUI = \frac{\text{Yearly Energy Cost}}{\text{Gross Area (sq. ft.)}}$$

$$= \underline{\qquad} \text{\$ per sq. ft. per year}$$

Lighting Assessment Worksheet

Use this worksheet to count the number and type of lights in your building(s).

F = fluorescent – these ballasted lights use 5 to 15% more energy than their listed lamp wattage. Count ballasts. If you only count lamps, you will underestimate your usage.

I = incandescent (interior or exterior)

H = halogen

M = mercury vapor

MH = metal halide

S = sodium, high pressure or low pressure

Area	Lighting Type	Lamp Wattage Ballast	Number of Lamps	Hours On Per Day	Total Watt-Hours

Total lighting load in watt hours _____

Divided by 1,000 = _____ kWh

Total kWh x work days/month = _____

Basic Lighting Efficiency Measures

Measures You Can Do Yourself

☐ 1. Use posters, signs, and light switch decals to remind employees to turn off lights and conserve energy.

☐ 2. Post a small sign or chart near each switch that identifies which lights are controlled by the switch. This enables the user to be more selective while also reducing trial-and-error lighting which can consume energy as banks of lights are quickly turned on and off.

☐ 3. Campaign to use lighting only when it is needed, to use only the amount required, and to turn off lights whenever they are not being used.

☐ 4. Instead of moving lights, move desks and other work surfaces to a position and orientation that will use installed luminaires and daylighting to their greatest advantage.

☐ 5. Eliminate exterior lighting except for the purpose of identifying the building entrances or for security.

☐ 6. Leave hallway lighting off in those hallways facing the interior courtyards during daylight hours, if a foot-candle meter reading indicates the lighting level is satisfactory.

☐ 7. Use task lighting for work areas and stations. This enables you to reduce general lighting in surrounding areas.

Measures You May Want a Professional to Do

☐ 8. Start preventive maintenance programs for all indoor and outdoor lighting. Clean lights and re-lamp on a scheduled basis.

☐ 9. Measure illumination intensities around your office(s) and plant(s) with a foot-candle meter. Your goal is to achieve lighting levels that work for your employees, or are close to those recommended by the Illumination Engineering Society. As you change to new lamps, a consultant can assure that you maintain good lighting quality and color, low heat output, and use the reflective qualities of walls and ceilings to enhance lighting.

☐ 10. Reduce numbers of lamps in high-intensity fixtures, and reduce brightnesses of other lamps to save energy and ease eye strain. Indoors, replace high-wattage incandescent lights with low-wattage halogen, tube fluorescent, or compact fluorescent lights. Outdoors, use low-wattage mercury vapor, sodium vapor, metal halide, or fluorescent lamps.

☐ 11. Turn off outside lights during the day, or install timers or photocells that automatically turn them on and off. Make sure they are appropriately sized and located, and are the most efficient models for the purpose. Clean their lenses regularly.

☐ 12. In incandescent fixtures, use dimmers which enable the user to adjust illumination to a comfortable level.

☐ 13. Install efficient ballasts in fluorescent fixtures as the inefficient ones burn out. Replace unnecessary lamps with "dummy" or "phantom" tubes, which occupy the ballast but draw no energy.

Basic Lighting Efficiency Measures (continued)

☐ 14. Localize switches, so that when only one light is needed, it can be turned on separately, rather than having to light an entire area. Also, put infrequently-used, or specific-purpose lights and appliances on appropriate switches: automatic dimmers, timers, photocells, motion sensors, or trip switches. These switches save energy while they keep you from forgetting to turn things off or on.

☐ 15. Replace yellowed light diffusers with clear, non-yellowing ones or, where appearance and glare are not factors, remove the light covers entirely. If the resulting light is too intense, change to lower wattage lamps.

☐ 16. Shade skylights with reflective film during summer to minimize overheating.

☐ 17. Test out uses of solar electric (photovoltaic) cells to power outdoor lighting and electronics.

Illumination by the Hour

List the lights that must remain on during business hours in the left column. In the right column, list the hours they must be on or check the box next to 24 hours if they must remain on all the time.

Signage

_____ Hours: _____ A.M. to _____ P.M. ☐ 24 hours

Exterior Lights

Front: _____ Hours: _____ A.M. to _____ P.M. ☐ 24 hours

_____ Hours: _____ A.M. to _____ P.M. ☐ 24 hours

_____ Hours: _____ A.M. to _____ P.M. ☐ 24 hours

_____ Hours: _____ A.M. to _____ P.M. ☐ 24 hours

_____ Hours: _____ A.M. to _____ P.M. ☐ 24 hours

Side 1: _____ Hours: _____ A.M. to _____ P.M. ☐ 24 hours

_____ Hours: _____ A.M. to _____ P.M. ☐ 24 hours

_____ Hours: _____ A.M. to _____ P.M. ☐ 24 hours

Side 2: _____ Hours: _____ A.M. to _____ P.M. ☐ 24 hours

_____ Hours: _____ A.M. to _____ P.M. ☐ 24 hours

_____ Hours: _____ A.M. to _____ P.M. ☐ 24 hours

Back: _____ Hours: _____ A.M. to _____ P.M. ☐ 24 hours

_____ Hours: _____ A.M. to _____ P.M. ☐ 24 hours

_____ Hours: _____ A.M. to _____ P.M. ☐ 24 hours

Interior Lights

Offices: _____ Hours: _____ A.M. to _____ P.M. ☐ 24 hours

_____ Hours: _____ A.M. to _____ P.M. ☐ 24 hours

_____ Hours: _____ A.M. to _____ P.M. ☐ 24 hours

_____ Hours: _____ A.M. to _____ P.M. ☐ 24 hours

Showroom/retail: _____ Hours: _____ A.M. to _____ P.M. ☐ 24 hours

_____ Hours: _____ A.M. to _____ P.M. ☐ 24 hours

_____ Hours: _____ A.M. to _____ P.M. ☐ 24 hours

_____ Hours: _____ A.M. to _____ P.M. ☐ 24 hours

Workroom: _____ Hours: _____ A.M. to _____ P.M. ☐ 24 hours

_____ Hours: _____ A.M. to _____ P.M. ☐ 24 hours

_____ Hours: _____ A.M. to _____ P.M. ☐ 24 hours

_____ Hours: _____ A.M. to _____ P.M. ☐ 24 hours

Illumination by the Hour (continued)

Receiving: _____   Hours: _____ A.M. to _____ P.M. ☐ 24 hours
_____   Hours: _____ A.M. to _____ P.M. ☐ 24 hours
_____   Hours: _____ A.M. to _____ P.M. ☐ 24 hours
_____   Hours: _____ A.M. to _____ P.M. ☐ 24 hours

Warehouse: _____   Hours: _____ A.M. to _____ P.M. ☐ 24 hours
_____   Hours: _____ A.M. to _____ P.M. ☐ 24 hours
_____   Hours: _____ A.M. to _____ P.M. ☐ 24 hours
_____   Hours: _____ A.M. to _____ P.M. ☐ 24 hours

Kitchen: _____   Hours: _____ A.M. to _____ P.M. ☐ 24 hours
_____   Hours: _____ A.M. to _____ P.M. ☐ 24 hours
_____   Hours. _____ A.M. to _____ P.M. ☐ 24 hours

Deli: _____   Hours: _____ A.M. to _____ P.M. ☐ 24 hours
_____   Hours: _____ A.M. to _____ P.M. ☐ 24 hours
_____   Hours: _____ A.M. to _____ P.M. ☐ 24 hours

Shop: _____   Hours: _____ A.M. to _____ P.M. ☐ 24 hours
_____   Hours: _____ A.M. to _____ P.M. ☐ 24 hours
_____   Hours: _____ A.M. to _____ P.M. ☐ 24 hours

Garage: _____   Hours: _____ A.M. to _____ P.M. ☐ 24 hours
_____   Hours: _____ A.M. to _____ P.M. ☐ 24 hours
_____   Hours: _____ A.M. to _____ P.M. ☐ 24 hours

Lights that can go off during business hours. These will be spaces that are not continuously used during the day, such as storerooms or break rooms.

Illumination Standards

Type of Work	Footcandles
Assembly	
Rough	30
Medium	100
Fine	200-500
Auditorium	10-20
Bakeries	30-100
Chemical	30-100
Construction	
Indoor	See "Assembly"
Outdoor	See "Assembly"
Elevators	5-15
Exhibits	100-200
Food preparation	50-100
Hall, stairway, lounge, lobby,	
storage area, washroom, locker room	10-20
Laboratory	50-100
Library card files	50-100
Library stacks, reading room	20-50
Machine shops	See "Assembly"
Offices	
Bookkeeping, typing, accounting	50
Business Machine, keypunch	60-90
Conference room	30
Drafting	50-100
Filing	25-35
Lobby/Corridors	5-15
Mail sorting	50
Stenographic	50
Reading handwriting	
in hard pencil	60-90
in medium pencil or ink	40-60
School classroom	30-75
Power plants	See "Assembly"
Printing shops	See "Assembly"
Warehouses	10-30
Welding	50
Woodworking	See "Assembly"

Electrical Equipment Inventory

	Number		Wattage Use		Hours on Per Day		Total Watt-Hr	Service Date
Office Machines								
Computers	_____	X	_____	X	_____	=	_____	_____
Monitors	_____	X	_____	X	_____	=	_____	_____
Printers	_____	X	_____	X	_____	=	_____	_____
Copiers	_____	X	_____	X	_____	=	_____	_____
FAX	_____	X	_____	X	_____	=	_____	_____
Typewriters	_____	X	_____	X	_____	=	_____	_____
Coffee maker	_____	X	_____	X	_____	=	_____	_____
_____	_____	X	_____	X	_____	=	_____	_____
_____	_____	X	_____	X	_____	=	_____	_____
			Subtotal Watt Hours			=	_____	

Refrigerated Drinking Fountains

Locations:

	Number		Wattage Use		Hours on Per Day		Total Watt-Hr	Service Date
_____	_____	X	_____	X	_____	=	_____	_____
_____	_____	X	_____	X	_____	=	_____	_____
_____	_____	X	_____	X	_____	=	_____	_____
_____	_____	X	_____	X	_____	=	_____	_____
			Subtotal Watt Hours			=	_____	

Kitchen Appliances

	Number		Wattage Use		Hours on Per Day		Total Watt-Hr	Service Date
Small mixers	_____	X	_____	X	_____	=	_____	_____
Big mixers	_____	X	_____	X	_____	=	_____	_____
Slicers	_____	X	_____	X	_____	=	_____	_____
Food processor	_____	X	_____	X	_____	=	_____	_____
Coffee maker	_____	X	_____	X	_____	=	_____	_____
warmers	_____	X	_____	X	_____	=	_____	_____
Steam table	_____	X	_____	X	_____	=	_____	_____

Electrical Equipment Inventory (continued)

	Number	Wattage Use	Hours on Per Day	Total Watt-Hr	Service Date
Kitchen Appliances (continued)					
Blenders	_____	X _____	X _____	= _____	_____
Range	_____	X _____	X _____	= _____	_____
Oven	_____	X _____	X _____	= _____	_____
Microwave	_____	X _____	X _____	= _____	_____
Refrigerator	_____	X _____	X _____	= _____	_____
Freezer	_____	X _____	X _____	= _____	_____
Milk Chiller	_____	X _____	X _____	= _____	_____
Ice maker	_____	X _____	X _____	= _____	_____
		Subtotal Watt Hours		= _____	
Shop, Laboratory and Workspace Equipment					
_____	_____	X _____	X _____	= _____	_____
_____	_____	X _____	X _____	= _____	_____
_____	_____	X _____	X _____	= _____	_____
		Subtotal Watt Hours		= _____	
Other Electrics					
Television	_____	X _____	X _____	= _____	_____
Video Cameras	_____	X _____	X _____	= _____	_____
Radios	_____	X _____	X _____	= _____	_____
Monitors	_____	X _____	X _____	= _____	_____
_____	_____	X _____	X _____	= _____	_____
_____	_____	X _____	X _____	= _____	_____
		Subtotal Watt Hours		= _____	
		Total Watt Hours Used		= _____	
		Divided by 1,000		= _____ Total kWh	

Basic Motor Efficiency Measures

☐ 1. Inventory all motors.

☐ 2. Catalog motors — by short or long running times, downtime costs and efficiency losses. Motors typically lose one to three points of efficiency each time they are rewound.

☐ 3. Buy energy efficient motors: they may initially cost 10 to 30% more than standard motors, but they provide superior construction and materials, more reliability, lower slip values, better power factor, less waste heat and quieter operation.

☐ 4. Make sure motor size, drive, and controls fit the function. Life cycle costs of a bargain used motor or the wrong new one will be high. They will be more costly to operate and maintain, and will run noisier, hotter, and less efficiently than the right motor. Also, measure motor loads; upgrade to units that are more efficient, properly sized, and suited to load.

☐ 5. Create a power quality management program that fine-tunes voltage, phase balance. and power factors to assure motor efficiency and avoid system-wide electrical losses.

Motor Inventory Questionnaire

1. Take a fresh look at your process. If you were going to redesign it to achieve optimum efficiency, how would it look? Draw it in the space below.

2. Based upon your new assessment,

   a. How would you use your energy differently? _____

   _____

   _____

   _____

   _____

Motor Inventory Questionnaire (continued)

b. How would you use your air or water differently? _____
_____
_____
_____
_____

c. Which motors, drives, and controls would you use? _____
_____
_____
_____
_____
_____

d. Which areas would be state of the art, which would not, and which wouldn't matter? _____
_____
_____
_____
_____
_____
_____

3. Does your process use steam? ☐ Yes ☐ No   If yes, how many pounds? _____ Why?
_____
_____
_____
_____

4. Is this the combination of factors your process currently uses? _____
_____
_____
_____

5. If not, where would you make changes? _____
_____
_____
_____
_____

Basic Compressor Efficiency Measures

☐ 1. Put compressors in cool rooms, to help keep down temperatures on lines and pumps.

☐ 2. Operate at the lowest practical pressure, generally, at 10 psig (pounds per square inch gauge) over the highest air pressure required by the system. For every 10 psig that a system's pressure can be reduced, the energy required to compress the same volume of air will be cut by approximately 5%.

☐ 3. Repair air leaks in distribution lines and pneumatic equipment.

☐ 4. Use oversized filters and the maximum coarseness permitted when replacing intake and compressed-air filters to reduce filter pressure drop.

☐ 5. Install pressure gauges on either side of compressed air line filters, and a vacuum gauge to determine pressure drop across the inlet filter.

☐ 6. Implement a preventive maintenance program, which includes cleaning, lubrication, belt adjustments, water draining, leak repair, and parts replacements.

☐ 7. Keep a compressed-air system log, which includes manufacturer's recommended maintenance points and schedules, and your records of maintenance and repair, system air pressure, pressure drop across filters, compressed air temperature (if there is a cooler, temperatures before and after it), average cycle times, and amperage or wattage draw of compressor motor.

Basic Refrigeration Energy Efficiency Measures

What You Can Do Yourself

☐ 1. Open walk-in cooler and freezer doors briefly. For loading, stack the items outside, then open the door, and make as few trips inside as possible. For unloading, close door after you, gather what you want inside, then open door again to exit.

☐ 2. Keep areas clear around condensers and compressors for good air flow and efficient refrigeration.

☐ 3. In walk-ins, keep lights turned off. One 60-watt incandescent lamp operating continuously in a 0° F freezer increases energy consumption by about 750 kWh.

☐ 4. Check door and structural joint seals for tightness. Quick test — can a dollar bill slip through the gasket? Over time, gaskets, door latches, and hinges wear and stop sealing in the cold. The unit sucks in outside heat and robs you of energy dollars. Evidence: areas where you can feel cold, visible openings at door seals and joints, condensation on insides of doors and walls, or thin layers of ice on interior freezer surfaces. When you see these, call your maintenance person for adjustments or repairs.

☐ 5. Clean and maintain condenser coils quarterly. Dirty coils cannot dump heat, which impairs compressor efficiency.

Basic Refrigeration Energy Efficiency Measures (continued)

☐ 6. If you have a CFC-based cooling system, make certain all maintenance and repairs on it are done by qualified personnel who use CFC recapture equipment. Check their documents and references, and document and keep receipts for all work performed.

What You Will Want A Professional to Do

☐ 7. Start with a preventive maintenance program on all refrigeration equipment. This includes repairing insulation on piping between expansion valve and compressor, checking and calibrating thermometers, checking charge pressure, changing compressor oil and oil filters regularly, or on manufacturer's schedule.

☐ 8. Reduce frequency of automatic defrost cycle depending on the season. In winter, the compressor typically runs less and the humidity is lower, which requires less defrosting. Defrost the evaporator before more than 10% of the coil and fins are blocked.

☐ 9. Unplug or turn off milk coolers, chest freezers, vending machines and water coolers when not in use. Left running, these typically consume 75, 100, 150, and 100 kWh per month, respectively.

☐ 10. Operate coolers and vending machines at highest acceptable temperatures, just as for refrigerators and freezers. Raising the temperature of water coolers and vending machines by 10°F can reduce standby energy losses by 25%.

☐ 11. Defrost chest freezers when frost builds up to 1/4 inch. Although some frost is almost always present, the greater the frost thickness, the greater the amount of energy required to cool the contents.

Basic Cooking Energy Efficiency Measures

What You Can Do Yourself

☐ 1. Cover pots and pans when cooking.

☐ 2. Turn heat down to simmer when food begins to boil. Higher heat does not cook food faster once you reach boiling temperature.

☐ 3. Use flat-bottom pots, pans, and griddles on solid top and electric ranges, any shape utensil over flame.

☐ 4. Regulate burners on open-top ranges so flame tips just touch the bottom of the utensil. Cook and saute where possible with medium to low flame, then turn flame down when you reach cooking temperature. Broil at moderate temperatures.

☐ 5. On electric ranges, burners remain hot after they are turned off. To maximize heat use, turn off burners just before cooking is finished, and just before kettles boil.

Basic Cooking Energy Efficiency Measures (continued)

☐ 6. Use exhaust and hood fans only when necessary. Clean kitchen and other exhaust filters every week.

☐ 7. During shift, turn down or shut off equipment not in use. Turn off infrared warmers when no food is being warmed.

☐ 8. Convert to infrared broilers. They cut broiling time in half, preheat quickly, and can be turned off between operations.

☐ 9. Use pressure cookers and microwave ovens wherever appropriate. They use less energy than conventional cooking equipment.

☐ 10. With the exception of fryers, which need 20 minutes to warm up, do not turn on or preheat equipment until it is needed. No equipment heats up any faster if you set it at a temperature higher than the one you want.

☐ 11. Preheat ovens only for baking.

☐ 12. Plan baking and roasting so that foods requiring the same temperature can be done at the same time, and then load the oven to capacity.

☐ 13. Open an oven door briefly, insert or remove what you want, then close the door. When you're ready to load the oven, gather your pans nearby, open the door, and transfer them all in together.

☐ 14. Convection ovens use the same energy as standard ovens, but circulate the heat to reduce cooking times for certain dishes. Check convection cookbooks to determine how much cooking time and energy this style oven can save.

What You May Want A Professional To Do

☐ 15. Adjust gas range flame so that it is blue. If you cannot accomplish this by adjustment or cleaning, have the gas/air mixture adjusted.

☐ 16. Check that oven thermostat settings are accurate for the heat you get inside. Every oven cooks "hot" or "cold" that is, above or below the temperature on the dial, and every cook can get used to that. But why bother? Set a thermometer inside the oven, and if the heat isn't on the mark, call a repair person to reset it. This will reduce your wastes of energy, and of food.

☐ 17. Door and structural joint seals:

As with coolers and freezers, door latches, hinges, and gaskets wear out over time. The most obvious evidence is feeling the heat escaping. Other evidence is seeing the shot gasket, or damaged hinge. Again, call your repair person to fix it.

Basic Water Heater Energy Efficiency Measures

What You Can Do Yourself

☐ 1. Do washing and rinsing activities with cold water wherever possible.

☐ 2. If you are located in the area between 35° North and South latitude, or your area enjoys 3,000 or more hours of daily sunshine a year, strongly consider active or passive solar panels to supply hot water for your building or pool, and to supplement your current DHW system.

☐ 3. Drop thermostat settings where appropriate on heaters serving lower-temperature applications. Every 10° F setback from 160° F on DHW can cut energy demand for hot water heating by as much as 6%.

☐ 4. Check ages of your DHW units. A heater more than six years old, or one that is more than two years old running softened water, will probably need a new anode. Manufacture date is stamped on the heater name plate. For example: 0186 or A86 is January 1986; 8604 is fourth week of 1986, etc.

☐ 5. To further control heat loss, install heat traps to prevent tank heat loss to plumbing. On gas units, install flue dampers to prevent heat loss up the flue.

What You May Want a Professional To Do

☐ 6. Put heater on preventive maintenance program, keep maintenance records on a sticker on the tank itself, and maintain the heaters on manufacturer's schedule.

☐ 7. Wrap hot water pipes, and cold line three feet back from the tank, in sleeves of closed-cell foam insulation.

☐ 8. Replace wet or damaged piping insulation.

☐ 9. If heater is not insulated to at least R-11, wrap it in a 1 1/2" to 3" blanket that brings it to that level of insulation. Check with manufacturer or supplier. Do not use a sealed blanket — it can cause the tank to overheat and fail prematurely. Instead, make holes in the blanket so it does not cover (1) access panels to thermostats, heating elements, and junction box; (2) external wiring; (3) operating instructions and labels; or (4) for gas heaters, air vents on top of unit.

☐ 10. To further control heat loss: Install heat traps, or flue traps on gas units, where appropriate, to prevent tank heat loss to plumbing.

☐ 11. Check connections at hot, cold, and recirculating loop lines for rust. Replace steel connectors with dielectric unions and plastic-lined steel nipples to reduce electrolytic corrosion with copper and brass tubing.

☐ 12. Keep heater dry to protect it from external rusting; filter air to gas heaters to minimize or eliminate intake of salt, chlorine, or corrosive chemicals in combustion air.

☐ 13. Check anode rod for remaining sacrificial metal every year in locations supplied with hard, acidic, or softened water; every three years in neutral pH water areas. Replace anode if damaged, or core wire is exposed.

Basic Water Heater Energy Efficiency Measures (continued)

☐ 14. Immediately repair all water or steam leaks.

☐ 15. Remove sediment semi-annually. Sediment buildup is slow at temperatures below 130° F., fast at 140° F. and above. Indications of buildup include lower element burnout in electric heaters, noise in gas heaters, and odor in either type heater.

☐ 16. Slow sediment buildup by limiting incoming water pressure to 50 psi and checking with water heating supplier or contractor about whether water conditions in your locale merit using a low-watt density element in electric heaters, and minimum flame size in gas heaters.

☐ 17. Limit auxiliary hot water heating and water circulation pumping to periods of highest use, and pre-set the periods on timers.

☐ 18. If cost-effective, consider small booster or on-demand heaters hooked into the cold line for locations that need hot water far from the main heater or boiler. Also consider return systems such as the Hot Water Saver (see Appendix D) that automatically pushes hot water back to the heater when the tap is closed.

☐ 19. As supplements to DHW, or when you are ready to replace current tanks, consider options such as de-superheaters, high efficiency gas hot water and heat-pump water heaters.

Domestic Hot Water Tank Worksheet

Heater Serial Number: _____   Age: _____

Location: _____   Purpose: _____

1. Current temperature setting: _____° F Reset to: _____° F
   Degree setback: _____° F x 6%(.06) = maximum possible energy saved: _____

2. Insulated to R-11 minimum?   ☐ Yes   ☐ No

3. Wrapped in Insulator Blanket?   ☐ Yes   ☐ No

4. Hot water pipes wrapped in sleeves?   ☐ Yes   ☐ No

5. Cold pipes wrapped 3 ft. out from tank? ☐ Yes   ☐ No

6. Sediment flushed?   ☐ Yes   ☐ No   Date: _____

7. Anode checked?   ☐ Yes   ☐ No   Date: _____
   Replaced?   ☐ Yes   ☐ No

8. Water treatment?   ☐ Yes   ☐ No   Type: _____

Domestic Hot Water Tank Worksheet (continued)

Heater Serial Number: _____ **Age:** _____

Location: _____ **Purpose:** _____

1. Current temperature setting: _____° F Reset to: _____° F
   Degree setback: _____° F x 6%(.06) = maximum possible energy saved: _____

2. Insulated to R-11 minimum?   ☐ Yes   ☐ No

3. Wrapped in Insulator Blanket?   ☐ Yes   ☐ No

4. Hot water pipes wrapped in sleeves?   ☐ Yes   ☐ No

5. Cold pipes wrapped 3 ft. out from tank? ☐ Yes   ☐ No

6. Sediment flushed?   ☐ Yes   ☐ No   Date: _____

7. Anode checked?   ☐ Yes   ☐ No   Date: _____
   Replaced?   ☐ Yes   ☐ No

8. Water treatment?   ☐ Yes   ☐ No   Type: _____

Heater Serial Number: _____ **Age:** _____

Location: _____ **Purpose:** _____

1. Current temperature setting: _____° F Reset to: _____° F
   Degree setback: _____° F x 6%(.06) = maximum possible energy saved: _____

2. Insulated to R-11 minimum?   ☐ Yes   ☐ No

3. Wrapped in Insulator Blanket?   ☐ Yes   ☐ No

4. Hot water pipes wrapped in sleeves?   ☐ Yes   ☐ No

5. Cold pipes wrapped 3 ft. out from tank? ☐ Yes   ☐ No

6. Sediment flushed?   ☐ Yes   ☐ No   Date: _____

7. Anode checked?   ☐ Yes   ☐ No   Date: _____
   Replaced?   ☐ Yes   ☐ No

8. Water treatment?   ☐ Yes   ☐ No   Type: _____

Basic Boiler Inventory

Boiler ID number/ Age in Years	Location	Energy O=Oil G=Gas	Last P–M* Check (Date)	Combustion Effeciency Before/After	Hours Weekly Use	Boiler Down Time: Hrs/Wk	Replace? / Date Date
_____/_____	_____	_____	_____	B ___% A ___%	_____	_____	Y N _____
_____/_____	_____	_____	_____	B ___% A ___%	_____	_____	Y N _____
_____/_____	_____	_____	_____	B ___% A ___%	_____	_____	Y N _____
_____/_____	_____	_____	_____	B ___% A ___%	_____	_____	Y N _____
_____/_____	_____	_____	_____	B ___% A ___%	_____	_____	Y N _____
_____/_____	_____	_____	_____	B ___% A ___%	_____	_____	Y N _____
_____/_____	_____	_____	_____	B ___% A ___%	_____	_____	Y N _____
_____/_____	_____	_____	_____	B ___% A ___%	_____	_____	Y N _____
_____/_____	_____	_____	_____	B ___% A ___%	_____	_____	Y N _____
_____/_____	_____	_____	_____	B ___% A ___%	_____	_____	Y N _____
_____/_____	_____	_____	_____	B ___% A ___%	_____	_____	Y N _____
_____/_____	_____	_____	_____	B ___% A ___%	_____	_____	Y N _____
_____/_____	_____	_____	_____	B ___% A ___%	_____	_____	Y N _____
_____/_____	_____	_____	_____	B ___% A ___%	_____	_____	Y N _____
_____/_____	_____	_____	_____	B ___% A ___%	_____	_____	Y N _____
_____/_____	_____	_____	_____	B ___% A ___%	_____	_____	Y N _____
_____/_____	_____	_____	_____	B ___% A ___%	_____	_____	Y N _____
_____/_____	_____	_____	_____	B ___% A ___%	_____	_____	Y N _____
_____/_____	_____	_____	_____	B ___% A ___%	_____	_____	Y N _____
_____/_____	_____	_____	_____	B ___% A ___%	_____	_____	Y N _____
_____/_____	_____	_____	_____	B ___% A ___%	_____	_____	Y N _____
_____/_____	_____	_____	_____	B ___% A ___%	_____	_____	Y N _____
_____/_____	_____	_____	_____	B ___% A ___%	_____	_____	Y N _____
_____/_____	_____	_____	_____	B ___% A ___%	_____	_____	Y N _____
_____/_____	_____	_____	_____	B ___% A ___%	_____	_____	Y N _____

*P–M= preventative maintenance

Basic Boiler Energy Efficiency Measures

The following measures should be handled by a specialist.

☐ 1. Start a preventative maintenance (PM) program, and keep a boiler room log (which includes the "Basic Boiler Inventory" sheet). The PM program should include at least everything from checking oil viscosity every delivery (on oil-fired boilers) to regular temperature measurements, equipment adjustments, repairs, and cleaning.

☐ 2. Reduce blowdowns by removing light solids with automatic skimming.

☐ 3. Increase insulation on all hot water lines, and reinsulate all outside steam lines.

☐ 4. Reduce boiler pressure, and lower temperatures of the water or air delivered from the unit to reduce steam pressures, radiation and convection losses.

☐ 5. In hard water areas, use ozone rather than chemical treatment of water to help control scale and save money and energy.

☐ 6. After reducing the building distribution load, readjust boilers to accommodate the new loads.

☐ 7. In winter, reduce amount of fresh air admitted to the boiler room, but do not choke boilers.

☐ 8. If you operate the boiler seasonally, take steps to "store" it in the off-season and protect it from corrosion, sedimentation, and scale.

☐ 9. In spring and fall, adjust boiler to come on line at low fire and stay there until the heating requirement is satisfied. This will enable it to cycle less often and maintain a higher overall annual efficiency.

☐ 10. In buildings with two boilers: use the one that is capable of carrying the entire load under design conditions, and leave the other one off, or use it for backup. Eliminating a hot standby boiler will not usually cause serious hardship, and one boiler carrying the building space heating load will operate at a higher annual efficiency than two boilers dividing the load.

☐ 11. Decrease boiler fuel input rate. It operates over longer time periods at the low fire limit, and cuts off cycle losses.

☐ 12. Install a solar evaporative roof cooler.

☐ 13. Install a boiler economizer.

☐ 14. Wherever possible, retrofit old boilers with upgrades such as turbulators and firebox improvements. When boilers wear out, replace with new, high-efficiency units.

☐ 15. Use boiler stack gases to preheat combustion air or makeup water.

☐ 16. Use dual fuel boilers where possible — in retrofits or when replacing equipment. Oil can be used as a backup if the gas supply is interrupted, or low seasonal temperatures decrease pressure.

Heating, Ventilation, and Cooling Systems Worksheet

Use one of these worksheets as appropriate for every room, area, or building in which you operate.

Building/Area/Room _____ **Date** _____

Heating

1. Thermostat type? ☐ Manual ☐ Automatic

2. Thermostat day setting: _____° F

3. Thermostat night setting: _____° F

4. Central heat? ☐ Yes ☐ No

5. Type: ☐ Forced air ☐ Baseboard ☐ Water ☐ Steam ☐ Other: _____

6. Energy fuel source: _____

7. More efficient energy source available? ☐ Yes ☐ No

8. More efficient heating system available? ☐ Yes ☐ No
   Where? Name: _____ Phone: _____
   Attach Cost Figures

9. Filter cleaned? ☐ Yes ☐ No Date: _____

10. Ductwork cleaned? ☐ Yes ☐ No ☐ N/A Date: _____

11. Ductwork insulated? ☐ Yes ☐ No

12. Energy audit appointment scheduled? ☐ Yes ☐ No Date: _____

13. Current heater maintenance checked? ☐ Yes ☐ No Date: _____
    By whom? _____

14. Items that need repair/replacement::

    _____ Date: _____ Price $_____
    _____ Date: _____ Price $_____
    _____ Date: _____ Price $_____
    _____ Date: _____ Price $_____
    _____ Date: _____ Price $_____
    _____ Date: _____ Price $_____
    _____ Date: _____ Price $_____
    _____ Date: _____ Price $_____
    _____ Date: _____ Price $_____

Contractor: _____ Phone: _____

Heating, Ventilation, and Cooling Systems Worksheet (continued)

Ventilation and Cooling

1. Air conditioning? ☐ Yes ☐ No

2. Thermostat type? ☐ Manual ☐ Automatic

3. Thermostat day setting: _____° F

4. Thermostat night setting: _____° F

5. Type of A/C? ☐ Window mount ☐ Central forced air ☐ Other: _____

6. Energy fuel source: _____

7. More efficient energy source available? ☐ Yes ☐ No

8. More efficient cooling system available? ☐ Yes ☐ No
   "Swamp cooler" ☐ Yes ☐ No
   Circulating fans ☐ Yes ☐ No
   Window shades ☐ Yes ☐ No
   Structural or landscape shade to create natural air currents ☐ Yes ☐ No
   Where? Name: _____ Phone: _____
   Attach Cost Figures

9. Filter cleaned? ☐ Yes ☐ No Date: _____

10. Ductwork cleaned? ☐ Yes ☐ No ☐ N/A Date: _____

11. Ductwork insulated? ☐ Yes ☐ No

12. Energy audit appointment scheduled? ☐ Yes ☐ No Date: _____

13. Current ventilation or A/C maintenance checked? ☐ Yes ☐ No Date: _____
    By whom? _____

14. Items that need repair/replacement::

    _____ Date: _____ Price $_____

    _____ Date: _____ Price $_____

    _____ Date: _____ Price $_____

    _____ Date: _____ Price $_____

    _____ Date: _____ Price $_____

    _____ Date: _____ Price $_____

    _____ Date: _____ Price $_____

Contractor: _____ Phone: _____

Basic HVAC Energy Efficiency Measures

☐ 1. If you are a building tenant, assure yourself in your rent or lease agreement that the owner or manager you work with:

  ☐ a. Is now, or has finished retrofitting the building and its HVAC systems to meet or exceed local building codes for energy and water efficiency. You want to keep your energy and water costs low.

  ☐ b. Has correctly sized and now maintains and operates the building's HVAC system, or the components that serve your space, to function as efficiently as possible.

  ☐ c. Will negotiate rent reductions or service improvements that result from savings achieved through energy and water efficiency improvements.

☐ 2. If you own the building:

  ☐ a. Set up a preventive maintenance program in-house or on contract to keep the system running at peak efficiency as you survey and improve the efficiency of your lighting, envelope, and physical plant.

  ☐ b. Audit your system and learn what its capacity and operating efficiencies are. Contact (1) the efficiency auditors at your local gas or electric utility, (2) HVAC engineers referred by the utility or your electrical equipment supplier, or (3) people you choose from the Yellow Pages under "Heating, Ventilation, and Air Conditioning."

  ☐ c. Write into your rent or lease agreements that your tenants must employ energy efficient lighting, machinery, HVAC, and other equipment. Set forth standards based upon local code requirements, suggestions from your local utilities, or recommendations from engineering, manufacturing, and other trade groups.

  ☐ d. If you downsize your system and realize savings, you may wish to apportion those savings among your tenants in the form of lower rents or enhanced services.

☐ 3. Size any space heating, air conditioning, or fan unit to the space or area you intend to have it serve. Measure the size of the space, then shop for a unit with a rated cooling capacity that matches. If the unit's label doesn't give you the answer you want, contact your local utility or state energy extension office for advice.

☐ 4. Window air conditioners:

  ☐ a. Each has a seasonal energy efficiency rating (SEER). Select units with a SEER efficiency rating of 10 or better.

  ☐ b. When placing the units, mount them out of direct sunlight. Sun heats the unit and demands 10% more energy from it than if it runs in the shade. If you must place the unit in a southern or western exposure, provide an awning or other shade for it. Set its thermostat at 78° F, and only run it to cool rooms you are using.

☐ 5. If you work from a home office or you rent space that you cool yourself, install an exterior shade or awning that shades the window from the sun, or draw the interior shades if you are on the hot side

Basic HVAC Energy Efficiency Measures (continued)

of the building; open doors and windows on the cool sides. Provide air movement by cross ventilation with doors, windows, and small breeze fans.

☐ 6. Seal off rooms and spaces you don't use from heating and cooling systems: Close off registers, disconnect space heaters, coolers and thermostats, close window treatments and doors. For more elaborate measures, consult an HVAC expert.

☐ 7. Do not heat or cool storerooms, unoccupied spaces or buildings except to protect contents from damage. Likewise, do not heat or cool parking garages.

☐ 8. In occupied spaces, set minimum heating temperature at 65° to 68° F, cooling temperature at 78° F. If you have an automatic thermostat, adjust its settings so that your system's heating or cooling hits desired day temperature by the time people arrive for their shifts, and changes to night/weekend temperature, or shuts off 30 to 60 minutes before people leave.

☐ 9. Shut off, or remove heating and cooling units from vestibules, lobbies, and corridors.

☐ 10. Adjust room temperatures seasonally by steps to match increases and decreases in outside temperatures.

☐ 11. Set humidity at 10% below outdoor. Drier air feels cooler.

☐ 12. Use venetian blinds or draperies as interior shading devices and awnings for exterior shading.

☐ 13. Post a small sign next to each operable window that says, "Please don't open this window while the building is being heated or cooled." Place the same kind of sign next to each exterior door.

☐ 14. Shut off HVAC vents to unused areas. Make sure from your HVAC or installation person that the system will run properly when the air flow in the duct system is reduced.

Basic Heat Pump Energy Efficiency Measures

☐ 1. Put your heat pump on a preventive maintenance program — a regular program to maintain, repair, and replace components, refrigerant levels, and thermostats.

☐ 2. In heating season, if you are using an air fin pump, check for ice on coils, which indicates the defrost cycle is not working, and can lead to valve problems.

☐ 3. Do not move heat settings in large increments. Raise the thermostat setting only two or three degrees at a time in the morning to keep your winter bills down. This allows the heat pump to keep up with load and supply the heat you need without turning on the back-up heating strips

☐ 4. Set the thermostat at 68° F in winter for day, 61° to 63° at night. Set at 78°F for summer.

☐ 5. Keep outside coil and air intake clean and free of obstructions. In the growing season, cut weeds and tall grass around the unit, blow leaves and clippings away, and check the coils to make sure they are clean. In winter, clear snow away.

Environmental Design and Construction Questionnaire

Feasibility/Environmental Impact

1. What do you want the project to become in its community, and how do you want it used? _____

_____

_____

_____

_____

Exterior Design Factors

Natural Resources

2. What is the sun's path across the property, and can you take advantage of it for daylighting, water and space heating, and photovoltaic power generation? _____

_____

_____

_____

3. Can you use wind patterns for space ventilation, cooling, and energy generation? ☐ Yes ☐ No

4. Does water flow by the property, and can it support a low-head hydro unit for power generating?

_____

_____

Environmental Design and Construction Questionnaire (continued)

Local Wildlife

5. What are the local plants and animals and how will your development affect them? _____

_____

_____

_____

_____

Parking Availability and Traffic Patterns

6. How will your business affect the surrounding community and comply with new federal and state pollution reduction measures? _____

_____

_____

Effluents and Waste Materials

7. Will you provide dock space for collecting and transferring recyclable materials?   ☐ Yes   ☐ No

8. What is the current burden on your local sewer or septic system, and will your development add to it significantly? _____

_____

_____

How will you address that burden? _____

_____

_____

9. Will you or your tenants generate hazardous materials, and if so, how will you dispose of them?

_____

_____

Interior Design Factors

Daylighting

10. How will you use natural light to reduce your loads and energy needs for lighting? _____

_____

_____

_____

Water, Swimming Pool, and Space Heat

11. Can you use solar heat to supplement or replace conventional systems?   ☐ Yes   ☐ No

Environmental Design and Construction Questionnaire (continued)

General Design Factors

12. What are your projected energy costs for the next ten years? _____
_____
_____
_____

13. Do you plan to change energy sources, stick with current ones, or use a mix? _____
_____
_____

14. How will your investment in energy efficiency measures now pay back based on your future cost projections? _____
_____
_____

15. What are the toughest current code requirements for your climate area in the U.S., and can you cost-effectively meet or exceed them? _____
_____
_____
_____

    What is the payback period? _____
_____
_____

16. Does your landscaping appropriately shade the building, and reduce wind velocities to mitigate exterior R-value losses? ☐ Yes ☐ No

17. Are the building materials you plan to use environment-friendly? ☐ Yes ☐ No

18. Is the design focused and workable? ☐ Yes ☐ No

    Will it maintain or enhance the marketability of the building, and can you do it on an affordable budget? Explain: _____
_____
_____
_____

19. The small things are also important: does exterior lighting affect neighbors, night sky visibility, etc.?
    Explain: _____
_____
_____

Environmental Design and Construction Efficiency Measures and Considerations

☐ 1. Climate — refer to the Ecoregion map at the end of Chapter 8. Climate affects all of your design choices: insulation, glazing, exterior materials, water consumption, and landscaping.

☐ 2. Avoidance of sick building syndrome: ventilation, and air exchange and filtration are key factors in keeping building occupants healthy. Assure that HVAC systems are properly designed and sized to your spaces and the brands you choose have strong life-cycle performance.

☐ 3. Financing: Ask about DSM (demand side management) programs from your utility, and research other local, state, federal, and utility financial incentives that may apply to your project.

☐ 4. Evaluation: pros/cons of existing conditions, building assets, and liabilities. When you renovate, check possible problems with HVAC, fire protection systems, and hazardous materials, and know that you may be faced with unanticipated requirements, such as adding ramps and an elevator to comply with new disabled persons codes.

☐ 5. Contractors: Select your advisors, design firm, and vendors based upon:

    ☐ a. Abilities to create and supply functional, energy-efficient designs that (1) exceed existing code requirements and (2) create spaces where real people can work.

    ☐ b. On-time, on-budget track records. Beware of such design blunders as high-maintenance materials use, triangular closets, out-of-reach amenities, walls that block windows and elevation elements that don't match; and of technology elements that sound "hot" but are not proven in use.

☐ 6. General design factors: Give direction on customer/ tenant targets along with budget and design intent for design team. Check with such organizations as ACE, Electric Ideas Clearinghouse, and others (see Appendix D) for options that will make design more resource efficient.

☐ 7. Paperwork: allow adequate time for permitting, bidding and negotiation with all contractors so all hidden costs are "smoked out," and all codes are satisfied. You don't want costly, work-stopping surprises mid-project. A key is making certain the project is welcomed by the surrounding community, and what you build is the same plan you filed with the building department.

☐ 8. Schedule: create one that is realistic for completing the work with incentives to encourage faster progress.

☐ 9. Teamwork: make yourself a member of the team, so you can stay informed of every design and construction step. If anything doesn't make sense to you, ask questions until you get understandable answers. While every dollar spent comes out of your pocket, understand that renovations are expensive, and the reason you have researched and hired the team you chose is because (a) you can't do it yourself and (b) you chose them because they can.

☐ 10. Contracts: review all existing tenant leases for clauses that may require you to meet certain financial obligations when they renew.

Chapter 8

Improve Your Water Efficiency

Low-flow shower heads will cut your energy costs.

Yes, this chapter is about saving water. But, as noted throughout this book, every improvement you make in one area has positive ripple effects into others.

If you retrofit your standard showers with low-flow (2.5 gallon per minute) heads and your faucets with low-flow aerators, they can pay for themselves every three months in the energy you no longer use to heat water.[1] Anywhere you cut hot water use, your bonus is energy savings.

Anywhere you reduce water consumption, you also help aquifers recharge, save rivers from dams and wetlands from destruction, and promote healthy wildlife. Water not heated with fossil fuel means oil or gas not depleted, coal not burned, carbon not released into the atmosphere, and sulfur not deposited as acid rain.

Dramatic Commercial Possibilities

Right now, your business can cut its overall consumption by up to 25% a year with low cost/no cost water efficiency measures. Advanced technologies, such as water recirculation systems and cooling tower retrofits, will perform even better and yield paybacks in less than three years.[2]

You don't necessarily need more water. You need the services that water provides — cleansing, cooling, processing, thirst quenching, irrigation, and recreation. You would use less water if you could be guaranteed the same or better services with it. And your water supplier would be happy to satisfy you and avoid the billion-dollar capital costs of developing new sources.

Thus, suppliers and customers nationwide are entering win-win partnerships and taking actions to make better use of this finite resource, such as:

- Water service companies (WASCOs) in Arizona, California, Florida, Colorado, and Virginia contract with apartment buildings, schools, and housing developments to retrofit them with water efficient equipment, such as ultra-low flush (ULF) toilets, low-flow showerheads, and faucet aerators. They also fix leaks for free.

- The Tucson, Arizona, water utility is using water conservation programs to cut business and industrial water use by 10%, or nearly 650 million gallons by the mid-1990s.

- Utility-financed efficiency projects in Lubbock, Texas, have reduced region-wide water use by 25 to 40% and cut the annual aquifer depletion rate in half.

- Commercial and industrial plants also realize great savings through recycling their water. The Olympia Brewing Company of Tumwater, Washington, irrigates its lush landscape and nearby golf courses with spent cooling water. The Armco Steel Mill in Kansas City, Missouri, recycles its water 16 times a day, drawing only 3.6 million gallons from city water sources to supply the 58 million gallons of water its operation uses every day.

Demand Side Management

It is faster, easier, and cheaper for you to implement efficiency programs than for your water supplier to find and develop new water sources. Your demand side actions cost less, yield significant returns, and can be implemented one at a time. Your water provider will support your efforts, because they enable the supplier to make the best possible use of current capacity.

You and your supplier thus get the greatest possible return from every molecule of water you use.

At the same time, you can build your image as a good corporate neighbor. Commercial and industrial water accounts consume up to a third of local water supplies.[3] Using less gives back to your community, makes your operations more efficient, reduces your effluents, and cuts your costs not only for water, but for treatment, sewage, and energy.

The steps to make your facility more water efficient are now familiar to you:

1. Commitment from the top, and support for employee participation, and for the coordinator or committee who will handle your efficiency efforts.

2. Eliminate obvious water waste by immediately implementing low cost/no cost methods that make use of, or eliminate, waste.

3. Water audit: review how, where, and how much water your company uses — from drinking fountains and bathrooms to space conditioning and processes. Develop a baseline water utilization index (WUI), as you did an EUI for your energy use.

4. Based on the audit, create a plan for improving water use company-wide. The plan will outline costs, benefits, and financing options for

each proposed action, and then prioritize and schedule each one. As you complete each action, plug the savings into your WUI to mark the improvement. Periodically review, revise, and update your plan.

5. Market your green image to suppliers, customers, and the public.

Step 1: Create a Company-wide Commitment From the Top

With company-wide input, develop a water management declaration, post it on the bulletin board, and add a copy to your mission statement notebook — if you have more than one statement now (refer to previous chapters for models).

Again, to win company-wide participation, your statement must answer two questions: "Why are we doing this?" and "What do we expect to accomplish?"

You can answer the "Why?" with "Our company is committed to creating a water-efficient operation that stands as one of the most forward-thinking, and lowest-cost producers in our industry."

You can answer "What do we expect to accomplish?" by listing actions from the low cost/no cost Basic Water Efficiency Measures on page 175 or by setting water reduction goals in gallons or percentages of weekly or monthly use. After you have begun the basic actions, you can set more complex goals, such as recapturing process water for reuse or landscaping with drought-tolerant plants.

Keep your people informed of their achievements and challenges through memos, E-mail, bulletin boards, or newsletters. Celebrate their achievements.

Reassure employees that:

- You will maintain comfort levels as you develop the program;
- Their efforts are needed, appreciated, and recognized; and
- The program is not a means of singling out people who waste water.

Step 1B: Select a Water Efficiency Coordinator or Committee

Choose a coordinator or a committee to oversee your water efficiency program. Announce your selection to the company. The coordinator or committee may be the same individual(s) in charge of energy, recycling, or hazardous materials.

Step 2: Implement Basic Efficiency Measures

Water, just as energy, is not a fixed cost. You can control how you use it, and what you pay for it. Reduce the amount and cost of water you use, and you free up resources you can use somewhere else.

How much water your company consumes each year can vary from the hundreds of gallons to tens of thousands, depending upon your business activity. Most offices use water only for drinking and for bathrooms; artists, painters, and cleaning services use additional water; and car lots, food processors, diaper services, and metal plating shops go far beyond that.

Use the Basic Water Efficiency Measures on pages 175–177 to reduce the amount of water you waste. When you need advice and answers, call your water utility first, pursue other local resources, then move further afield — see Appendix D for more resources. Whenever you don't understand something, ask questions until you get straight, understandable answers.

Cautions

Whenever you encounter a water efficiency claim for a technique or piece of equipment, get documentation and testimonials from people you trust. So much good equipment and advice are now available to you, there is no reason you should have to waste money on any unproven option.

Also, don't make any change until you have examined its life-cycle effects. Here are two examples of pitfalls:

- Converting cooling systems from water to air: It saves water, but it can boost electricity consumption, cut cooling capacity, and reduce condenser life by forcing them to cycle more often and work at higher temperatures.
- Eliminating "obvious" water waste areas: in an attempt to save water, a Northeastern hot dog manufacturer almost eliminated a post-cooking spray of cooling water. Line people stopped the move when they saw that the spray also de-greased and cleaned the hot dogs, making them attractive to consumers. Without the spray, the hot dogs would look dirty and lose their appeal.

Step 3: Conduct a Water Audit

This step assumes your company is already implementing Group 1 of the Basic Water Efficiency Measures and you are ready to conduct a water audit to determine what further improvements are necessary.

You start by surveying where, how, and how much water you use and what it all costs you. Complete the Real Annual Water Cost Worksheet on page 178. This will show you what your water cost is.

If yours is a production business, use the Water Ledger on page 179 to record your monthly and annual usage and real costs for water. The ledger enables you to create two indexes: a Water Utilization Index (WUI) of your water quantity use per unit produced, and a Water Cost Index (WCI) of your water cost per unit produced.

Even if you don't run a factory, the Water Ledger is helpful. It enables you to see your real costs and uses of water every month. No matter what type of business, your entries on it will show you the effects of efficiency improvements and waste problems on your bottom line.

Your water efficiency goal is to reduce your usage and real cost of water. All your water costs are based upon quantities of water used and processed. The less water you draw and send down the drain, the less you will have to pay for.

There is no right amount of water to use. For example, at a paper plant, a good WUI is 1,500 gallons per ton of paper output. At a soft drink plant, a good WUI is 2.5 gallons per case of 24 12-ounce cans, where 2.25 gallons go into the product and .25 gallons are process water released as waste.

The best WUI figure for you is simply the lowest one you can achieve.

Use the Water Usage Inventory worksheet on page 180 to list where and what equipment and processes use water in your company. Complete a copy of the Water Process Analysis Questionnaire on pages 181–182 for each process. These worksheets will provide you with a starting place to begin efficiency improvements.

Step 4: Create Your Water Management Plan

At this point you are taking steps to eliminate your company's obvious water wastes by implementing the Basic Water Efficiency Measures and you have a clear sense of how much water your business uses, how much it costs you, and where you need to make further improvements.

You are now ready to work specifically on improving the water-consuming equipment and processes in your business. Many of them are noted in the Basic Water Efficiency Measures, but they will be covered in more detail here.

In many cases, these improvements are complex and should be done by specialists from plumbers to process engineers. The areas to consider are noted here so you can be well-informed and able to ask key questions and get straightforward answers.

Process Improvement Possibilities

You can now incorporate reclamation technology in most plant processes. The benefits: continuous savings in reduced demands and costs for water and sewage and short payback periods. There are two types of reclamation technology:

1. Recirculation, or water recycling within a process. This option is feasible when water remains clean, and quality is constant throughout. Heating and cooling water are good examples.

   You can also recirculate low quality water, but only if it is treated and neutralized before it is recycled into the process.

2. Sequential reuse or using a given water stream for two or more processes or operations before disposal. An example of this process is when dishwashers recycle rinse water from each outgoing load as wash water for each incoming load.

   In process batches, treatment may or may not be necessary between each process. The determinant is your minimum water quality specifications for the processes.

Rinse Options

The following options may require additional floor space, tanks, piping, valves, and controls but offer strong payback opportunities:

1. Standing or drag-out rinses for plating and etching baths, etchers, washers, and similar processes. Rinses are dumped periodically instead of running all the time. This technique reduces water needs for succeeding rinses and minimizes pollution problems.

Standing or drag-out rinses, extra tanks for cascade rinsing, and countercurrent rinsing are three rinse options that offer strong paybacks.

2. Extra tanks for cascade rinsing. A double rinse can save 65 to 75% of water required for single rinsing; a triple rinse can save 85 to 90%.

3. Countercurrent flow rinse baths, which run water flow from tank to tank in a direction opposite to the process sequence. This process enables you to use one stream of water for more than one rinse bath. In some cases, converting from a single rinse tank to two countercurrent tanks can reduce water consumption by half.

Cooling Towers

Cooling towers can consume up to 60% of the water used in large facilities.

In facilities with large cooling loads, such as industrial plants, office buildings, or hospitals, cooling towers can consume up to 60% of the water.

The towers use evaporation to cool water that is circulated through hot equipment, such as air conditioning compressors. Once the circulating water is cooled, it is returned to remove more heat from the equipment. Cooling capability is expressed in tons. A ton of cooling capacity is the ability to remove 12,000 Btu of heat from water per hour.

The evaporating spray, and the discharge (bleed-off) of sediment-laden water left behind, are the places where the tower loses most of its water. The key places to cut cooling tower water consumption are boosting concentration ratios and cutting bleed-off.

Options for making the towers more efficient are listed in the Basic Cooling Tower Efficiency Measures on page 183. Investigate and calculate the costs on each one before choosing to implement the option. For more advice, call your water utility.

Evaporative Coolers

Evaporative coolers and air washers are used to increase the humidity and lower the temperature of air being drawn into a building. Most evaporative cooling equipment is used for space cooling. Efficiency measures are similar to those of cooling towers:

1. Reduce the amount of contaminant bleed-off water to the minimum required for safe operation.
2. Equip coolers with water recirculating pumps.
3. Check recirculation pump and reservoir level controls at least once a year for proper operation.
4. Replace worn pads as necessary.

Humidifiers

Use only where and when needed. Periodically check level controls and water supply shut-off valves for proper operation to avoid excessive bleed-off.

Single Pass Cooling

This is a wasteful practice, in which water is discarded after one pass through a process or piece of equipment. It is typically employed in degreasers, rectifiers, hydraulic equipment, x-ray processors, condensers, air conditioners, air compressors, welding machines, and vacuum pumps. Most of this equipment could be modified to operate using a closed-loop cooling system which would consume very little water. If you are using this method, refer to the Single Pass Efficiency Measures on page 186.

Single pass cooling is very inefficient. Try to switch to a closed loop cooling system.

Boilers and Steam Generators

The key efficiency measure on these is to recover steam condensate for reuse as system makeup water. A condensate return system can cut operating costs in half as it reduces water use, boiler feedwater pretreatment requirements, and energy consumption.

Equipment Cooling

1. Don't overcool process equipment. It wastes water in both single pass and recycling cooling systems. Install temperature modulating or controlling valves on the outlets of the machines. These valves will let enough water through to permit a pre-set temperature rise.
2. Turn off the cooling water to machines during weekends and no-production hours. This will save 45 to 50% of cooling water used in single-pass systems.
3. Replace or modify single-pass cooling systems to allow water recycling

Improve Efficiency of Simple Plumbing

There is a simple side to water consumption. That is the improvement of standard plumbing equipment and water appliances: faucets, toilets, showers, dishwashing machines, and others. If your office is in your home, or in a small office building, you can compare your supply quantities and make retrofits yourself or with a plumber. Some of the items are covered here to give you examples of how to make your calculations. If you own a larger facility, consult a specialist.

Piping Flow Rate Calculations

To learn the flow rate of your supply line:

- Find a container of an exact volume, or with volume markings on it, such as a four-cup measure, a one-gallon jug or a five-gallon bucket.
- Get a stopwatch or a wristwatch that displays the seconds.
- Set the container under the tap or faucet and turn on the water full blast.
- Time how long it takes to fill the container.

If, for example, it takes 30 seconds to fill a five gallon bucket, your flow rate per minute is:

$$\frac{2 \times 5 \text{ gallons}}{2 \times 30 \text{ seconds}} \quad = \quad \frac{10 \text{ gallons}}{60 \text{ seconds}} \quad = \quad 10 \text{ gallons per minute (gpm)}$$

To learn how much water each piece of equipment or appliance uses, you must refer to the specification sheets, or get the brand and model number of the item and call your supplier.

Tank Toilets

Tank toilets can be one of the biggest water wasters in your company. Those in business and institutional establishments may be flushed from as few as five to more than 100 times per day. If your business falls in the latter category, consider replacing your current units with more efficient units.

To calculate how much water you use in each size unit, use this formula:

Number of Tank Toilets	Tank Size	Number of Flushes per Tank per Day	Total Daily Use
_____ x	_____ gals. x	_____ =	_____ gallons/day

Total Daily Use	Business Days per Month	Total Use Per Month	
_____ gals. x	_____ =	_____ gallons/month	

Use the following formula to calculate how much your current units cost you in terms of water usage.

Total Gallons Used Per Month	Cost Per Gallon	Total Cost Per Month
_____ gals. x $ _____	= $ _____ per month	

Your water rates are usually charged by the hundred cubic feet (ccf or hcf). One ccf equals 748 gallons.

No More Leaks

To save water with current tank toilets, eliminate leaks. Check for leaks by dropping a dye tablet or a few drops of food coloring into the tank. If the color shows up in the bowl within five minutes, you have a leak. Check the ballcock (float controlled valve that lets water into the tank), chain and flapper valve (the black rubber disk at the bottom drain inside the tank) for wear, proper closure, and adjustment.

If water is flowing into the overflow tube, it may be because of one of the following reasons:

- The chain connected to the flapper valve may be too long and lodge under it, keeping the valve open. Shorten the chain.
- The flapper may be worn out. Replace the flapper.

- The ballcock may be causing the leak. Bend the arm down a little into the tank water. The water will lift the float higher and put more pressure on closing the valve.

ULF Toilets

If none of these measures work, you could install a water displacer, but since you must invest labor in displacers, anyway, you may wish to go the extra distance and replace the entire standard toilet models (3 to 7 gallons-per-flush) with low-gallon or ultra-low-flush (ULF) tank toilets. These units use 1.6 gallons or less per flush, reduce your toilet water consumption by 60 to 80% below standard models, and can pay for themselves in water cost savings within a year.

In some areas, your municipal government or water company may pay you a subsidy for making this changeover. *Consumer Reports,* your water utility, and plumbing supplier can provide you with information on the best brands of ULF toilets.

To calculate your water savings from installing ULF toilets, use this formula:

Number of ULF Toilets		Tank Size		Number of Flushes per Tank per Day		Total Daily Use
_____	X	_____ gals.	X	_____	=	_____ gallons/day

Total Daily Use		Business Days per Month		Total ULF Gallons Used Per Month
_____ gals.	X	_____	=	_____ gallons/month

Previous Total Gallons Per Month		Total ULF Gallons Per Month		Total Savings Per Month
_____ gals.	−	_____ gals.	=	_____ gallons saved/month

To calculate your dollar savings from installing ULF toilets, use this formula:

Total ULF Gallons Used Per Month		Cost Per Gallon		Total ULF Cost Per Month
_____ gals.	X	$ _____	=	$ _____ per month

Previous Total Cost Per Month		Total ULF Cost Per Month		Total Savings Per Month
$ _____	−	$ _____	=	$ _____ saved/month

To calculate how many months it will take for the savings to pay for the investment, use this formula:

Number of New ULF Toilets	Cost Per Toilet	Total Cost	Total Savings Per Month	Payback Period
_____	x $ _____	= $ _____	/ $ _____	= _____ months

You can also use these simple formulas, with minor modifications, for calculating your savings in gallons and dollars with other plumbing efficiency equipment.

Business Specific Water Usage Improvement Options

This section explains ways specific types of businesses can improve their water usage.

Laundry Facilities

Investigate the following options:

- Use continuous batch washers for new facilities or major expansions of existing operations (60% savings over conventional washers).
- Laundry water reclamation systems (rinse only — 20 to 30% savings; rinse/wash — up to 50% savings).
- Launder full loads only, whenever possible.

Users of Steam and Ethylene Oxide Sterilizers

Steam units consume water as steam, water to cool the steam discharged, and to create a vacuum in the unit to help dry sterilized items.

Ethylene oxide units use water to carry off spent gas and create a drying vacuum.

For increased efficiency, start with the measures below.

For steam units:

- Eliminate water use to cool sterilizer steam. Instead, use a small expansion tank to hold released steam until cooled enough for discharge into the sanitary sewer system. Contact the unit's manufacturer or the service contractor about making this modification.

In both steam and ethylene oxide units:

- Eliminate or reduce the flow of water to the minimum acceptable level.
- Install solenoid operated valves to shut off the flow of water whenever the sterilizer is not in operation.
- Install a pressure regulator on the supply line, and operate the system at the lowest pressure feasible.

Manual Cleanups

Wash with water only where necessary. Where water must be used, such as in grocery store meat cutting rooms, commercial kitchens, or medical facility supply rooms, use high-pressure, low-flow spray units. They can reduce the amount of water used for cleaning by as much as 40%.

For cleaning equipment, utensils, tools, walls, and counter surfaces, wash with one bucket of water, and rinse with another. Do not leave water running. For floor areas, sweep first, then use a bucket of wash water to work on difficult spots.

Restaurants, Commercial Kitchens, and Other Food Services

The main water consumers for these types of businesses are:

- Dishwashers;
- Garbage disposers;
- Ice makers; and
- Ice cream and frozen yogurt machines.

Refer to the Basic Food Services Water Efficiency Measures on pages 186–188 for suggestions to improve the efficiency of your operations.

Outdoor Water Use and Landscape Management

Half the water that passes through a company during the watering season can go to irrigating its landscape. Some companies have extensive grounds, some have little or none at all, and some limit themselves to indoor plants.

Small or large, your planted areas consume water. This section covers how to minimize that use and still keep the plants healthy.

Reduce What You Water

Increase the plants that don't need water, and decrease the ones that do. Ultimately, you create a landscape with drought-tolerant, climate-appropriate plants. This is "xeriscaping" (also known as "zeriscaping"). Use hardy grasses and ground-hugging shrubs, such as wild strawberry, ivy, legumes, and flowering plants, like transportation departments use along highways.

Xeriscaping can cut your landscape water use in half or better. For example, when the city of Mesa, Arizona, recently ran a water efficiency improvement program, citizens who reduced the turf areas and boosted the xeriscaped ones in their yards used up to 40% less water than their turf-intensive neighbors.

For advice on making your landscape climate appropriate, call your nursery, city or county arborist, or agricultural extension agent.

Reduce the Amount of Water You Use to Irrigate

Remember, your irrigation is only a backup to natural rainfall and soil moisture. Most established plants don't need frequent irrigation. Fluctuating soil moisture brings oxygen to the root zone. It is vital for root health. Constant dampness promotes root rot and disease in many plants.

Plant growth varies with changes in environmental conditions. This enables you to cut water costs simply by working with the weather and flexing the irrigation schedule to your plants' needs.

When you have opportunities to add or replace plants or to re-landscape, shift to drought-tolerant plant species that are native to your ecoregion. To determine which ecoregion your business is located in, refer to the Ecoregion Map of the Continental United States on pages 184–185.

For more tips, refer to the Basic Landscape Water Efficiency Measures on pages 188–190.

Greywater Recycling Systems

"Greywater" is water already used for non-toxic purposes such as cooling, non-detergent washing, and food rinsing. Coolant water, for example, can be piped directly to the next purpose. Wash and rinse water, however, must be pumped into a holding tank and filtered before it can be recycled.

The system will require investment in piping, tanks, and controls. Savings depend upon how much original water you can replace with recycled. One indication of possible savings is in the pricing structure for recycled water in the Los Angeles basin.

Los Angeles-area sanitation districts supply more than 63 million gallons per day of reclaimed water to local customers, at rates from 15 to 55% below the cost of potable water, for every sort of agricultural, commercial, and recreational purpose, as well as for groundwater recharge.

For answers and advice on codes and regulations, contact your local water utility, building, and health departments. They can refer you to agricultural extension agents, and irrigation and grey water experts.

Swimming Pools, Fountains, and Shallow Ponds

Of all decorative outdoor water uses, fountains and shallow ponds lose the most water to evaporation. During hot or drought periods, shut fountains off and cover or drain shallow pools.

If you cannot make those changes because business exterior design depends on running water, shut off fountains during the evening and low-use periods, and cover open areas of water to reduce evaporation losses.

By comparison, evaporation losses from swimming pools are small. To reduce water and vapor loss further:

- Cover the pool whenever it is not in use. Arrange the cover so that one lap lane, or half the lanes can be uncovered for low-use periods. Then, recover to block evaporation and heat loss.
- Adjust the filter backwashing timer cycle to meet actual needs.

Basic Water Efficiency Measures

Group 1: No Cost/ Low Cost Actions You Can Do Yourself

☐ 1. Fix leaks and running problems at all drinking fountains and eyewash stations, on water lines, joints, tanks, sprinklers, etc. In tank toilets, check for leakage with dye tests every six months.

☐ 2. Manually shut off water taps and faucets between procedures, and when appropriate, during pauses.

☐ 3. Carry a cup to the drinking fountain and fill it, rather than leaning over for a drink and wasting 50% of what comes out of the spigot.

☐ 4. Use budgeted amounts of water for each type of job, where appropriate.

☐ 5. Use less water for mopping. "Spot" clean or damp mop where possible, and lengthen times between full cleanings.

☐ 6. Audit your water consumption. Use the "Water Usage Inventory" worksheet to create a checklist of your equipment and appliances that use water. Check each regularly and test, repair, or replace as needed.

☐ 7. Ask employees to report leak problems promptly. Offer incentives for suggesting ideas that can improve company water efficiency. Rewards for implemented ideas can range from a gift certificate to a percentage of the cost savings.

☐ 8. Make the duties of the facility maintenance staff or security personnel include regular checks for water leaks in restrooms, fountains, and other water using appliances and equipment.

☐ 9. Post water conservation stickers and signs in every area where faucets and hoses are used:

☐ 10. Install low-flow (2.5 gallon per minute or less) or laminar flow aerators at all sink faucets and low-flow shower heads with on-off flow interruptors. These devices also cut hot water consumption and can pay for themselves in energy savings in as little as three months.

☐ 11. Use positive shut-off nozzles on all hoses.

☐ 12. Have your food services and restaurants serve water only on request.

☐ 13. Use spare water for plants: catch water that is left to run from a faucet until it gets hot, or left over from pitchers, mugs, or drinking glasses and water plants with it. You can safely use diluted cleaning water, or "grey water," on outdoor plants, if it only contains biodegradable soaps. Alternate grey water with fresh water use. Do not use grey water on any leaves, trunks or exposed roots. Also, do not use it on potted plants. The soaps will concentrate in the pot and kill the plant.

☐ 14. Cover or garage vehicles to keep them clean longer and spread time between washings.

☐ 15. As you achieve each goal, update your water efficiency statement and your "Water Utilization Index" to show savings in dollars, earnings per share, annual consumption per household, or other plain terms.

☐ 16. Take advantage of available water efficiency information:

    ☐ Circulate news about conservation achievements by other companies in your industry and challenge your employees to do the same;

    ☐ Create a lobby display about water conservation;

Basic Water Efficiency Measures (continued)

- ☐ Bring in outside water efficiency speakers and show audio visual programs; or
- ☐ Send your conservation coordinator or committee to community resource efficiency seminars.

Group 2: Actions You May Want A Professional to Do

- ☐ 17. Make efficient water use a company policy, a criterion in purchasing, and in designs of facilities and processes.
- ☐ 18. Install toilet dams in tank- type toilets with 5.5 gallon or greater flush. On flushometer- type toilets, check with your plumber to see if each valve has (a) a pressure reducing valve or flow restrictor to keep incoming pressure below 80 psi, and (b) a reversible conserving ring.
- ☐ 19. When replacing toilets, purchase effective 1.6 gallon ultra-low flush (ULF) or flush valve types.
- ☐ 20. Check timing cycles and volumes for automatic water flushing systems in urinals and toilets. All automatic systems should be tied to work hours and should not run 24 hours a day, seven days a week.
- ☐ 21. Walk through your facility during working hours to locate broken pipes, faulty hoses, or leaks.
- ☐ 22. Locate and identify each water meter and record numbers. Record the destination and use of the water from each meter.
- ☐ 23. Check water meters during process and plant shutdowns for indications of leaks. Log meter consumptions monthly.
- ☐ 24. Install flow meters on pipes feeding individual processes to measure the actual water each one consumes. To effectively manage water use at your business, you must examine where it enters, and how it passes through your facility.
- ☐ 25. When replacing sink faucets, consider using metering valves (these gradually close and deliver a preset volume of water) self-closing (spring-loaded auto-shutoff) valves or infrared light controlled valves. For showers, consider metering and self-closing valves; for toilets and urinals, infrared.
- ☐ 26. Change your window cleaning schedule from a periodic to an on-call, as required basis.
- ☐ 27. For space cooling and air conditioning systems, minimize blowdown water volume, and set up valves so water shuts off when condenser is not running.
- ☐ 28. Xeriscape — landscape with drought-tolerant trees, shrubs, flowers, and ground cover that require little or no artificial irrigation. Minimize lawn areas. Cover exposed ground with mulch or compost. For advice, call your local arborist, nursery, or agricultural extension agent.
- ☐ 29. Place signs on brown lawns stating that you are conserving water, with a tag line such as, "Brown is beautiful," or "Goodbye green, hello blue!" Also, place signs to indicate drought-tolerant landscaping and plants, and how much water your business is saving.
- ☐ 30. If you landscape with lawns, use hardy turf grasses and annually thatch, aerate, and sand as appropriate, to improve penetration of rainfall.
- ☐ 31. Check with your local arborist or nursery on the most water-efficient outdoor irrigation equipment, timers, and techniques for your landscape.

Basic Water Efficiency Measures (continued)

☐ 32. To wash drives, walks, and stairs: (1) sweep area with broom; (2) isolate the dirty/greasy areas and wash those individually with a bucket of soapy water and brush, broom, or mop; (3) rinse the area afterwards, sparingly, with a hose that has a positive shutoff nozzle.

☐ 33. To wash garbage cans: (1) pour a bucket of soapy water into the garbage pail; (2) swirl around the side and bottom of the can with a mop or brush; (3) if water is not too dirty, re-use the same water for the next garbage can; (4) rinse each can sparingly using a hose with a positive shutoff nozzle.

☐ 34. Switch from wet or "steam" carpet cleaning methods to dry powder methods.

☐ 35. Minimize the water used in cooling equipment, such as air compressors, in accordance with manufacturer recommendations.

☐ 36. Avoid excessive boiler and air conditioner blow-down. Monitor total dissolved solids levels and blow-down only as needed.

Real Annual Water Cost Worksheet

1. Assemble your bills for the past year: 19_____

2. Add the total cubic feet or units of water your business used during the year (1 ccf= 748 gallons):

   _____ ccf total

3. Add the total dollar amount your water supplier charged on your bills for the 19_____ year, including commodity, sewer, seasonal, and other surcharges: $_____ cost

4. Now, divide the total annual cost by the ccf total of water used, to get your average cost per ccf:

   $_____ total annual cost / _____ ccf total = $_____ average per ccf

5. Tally annual totals of additional water-related costs:

   a. Treatment: $_____

   b. Pumping: $_____

   c. Water heating/refrigeration: $_____

   d. Disposal/treatment cost: $_____

   e. Sewer: $_____

   d. Other : $_____

6. Total additional costs: $_____

7. Now, add the total additional costs to your billed annual total:

   $_____ additional costs + $_____ billed total = $_____ real annual cost

8. Divide the real annual cost by total ccf of water used in your business. You now have your **real water** cost per ccf:

   $_____ real cost / _____ ccf total = $_____ real cost per ccf

Water Ledger

Use a separate sheet for each production facility.

Building/Facility: _____

Units Per Year: _____

Month	Water Costs						Commodity Cost Per ccf	Total Water Cost	Gallons Used	Total Units Produced
	Treatment	Pumping	Water Heating & Refrigeration	Disposal Treatment	Sewer	Surcharge				
Totals										

1 ccf = 748 gallons

$$\text{Water Utilization Index (WUI)} = \frac{\text{Total ccf}}{\text{Total units produced}}$$

$$\text{Water Cost Index (WCI)} = \frac{\text{Total water cost}}{\text{Total units produced}}$$

Water Usage Inventory

Company: _____   Date: _____

Purpose/Process	Water Consumption Per Week (if known)
Landscape watering	_____
Toilet leaks & flushing	_____
Faucets	_____
Drinking fountains	_____
Laundry	_____
Dishwashing	_____
Other: _____	_____
_____	_____
_____	_____
_____	_____
_____	_____
_____	_____
_____	_____
_____	_____
_____	_____
_____	_____
_____	_____
_____	_____
_____	_____
_____	_____
_____	_____
_____	_____
_____	_____
_____	_____
Total Gallons Consumed Per Week:	_____

Water Process Analysis Questionnaire

Use a separate questionnaire for each process.

1. Where, specifically, and in what quantities is water used in the process? Draw a diagram of the process:

   Input:: _____ gallons   Output:: _____ gallons

2. For what purposes is the water used in the process?

   ☐ Wash   ☐ _____

   ☐ Rinse   ☐ _____

   ☐ Deposition   ☐ _____

   ☐ Make-up   ☐ _____

3. When equipment is not operating, can you shut off water flow?   ☐ Yes   ☐ No   Explain: _____

   _____

   _____

4. Can you convert from deionized water to city or soft water in this process?   ☐ Yes   ☐ No

   Explain: _____

   _____

   _____

5. Can you decrease water inputs? For example, do equipment specifications allow for a lower water flow rate?   ☐ Yes   ☐ No   Explain: _____

   _____

   _____

6. Can you use flow reduction devices to deliver the lower rate over a range of pressures?   ☐ Yes   ☐ No

   Explain: _____

   _____

   _____

Water Process Analysis Questionnaire (continued)

7. Can you decrease water outputs? For example, can water be recirculated and reused? ☐ Yes ☐ No
   Explain: _____
   _____
   _____

8. Can you improve rinse tanks? ☐ Yes ☐ No   Explain: _____
   _____
   _____
   _____

9. Can you meter the flow into the tank, and set it to the minimum amount acceptable for the process?
   ☐ Yes ☐ No   Explain: _____
   _____
   _____

10. Can you change processes to find less rinse-intensive production sequences? ☐ Y ☐ N   Explain:
    _____
    _____
    _____

11. Can you agitate rinse tanks to improve efficiency? ☐ Yes ☐ No   Explain: _____
    _____
    _____

12. Can you use conductivity probes on rinse tanks to improve accuracy of make-up water you add to
    spent process water? ☐ Yes ☐ No   Explain: _____
    _____
    _____

13. Are you running individual items or batches in this process? ☐ Individual ☐ Batch   If individual
    items, can you redesign the process to run batches? ☐ Yes ☐ No   Explain: _____
    _____
    _____
    _____

14. Does the process require water cooling where air cooling will work? ☐ Yes ☐ No   Explain:
    _____
    _____

Basic Cooling Tower Efficiency Measures

☐ 1. Create an inventory of each cooling tower, its cooling capacity, and the equipment or process it serves.

☐ 2. Keep a record of the amount of makeup water added to each tower and the amount of blow-down water discharged from each tower. Review this information and use it to adjust bleed-off rates.

☐ 3. Inside the facility, use thermostats to widen the "comfort zone" band (75 to 78°F). This change will reduce the demand on cooling towers and decrease their evaporation rate.

☐ 4. Periodically check float controls on evaporative cooling equipment. They often get stuck.

☐ 5. Use blow-down water for lower grade non-potable applications.

☐ 6. Reduce the blow-down rate on the towers and water-cooled air conduits.

☐ 7. Improve operation of conventional treatment systems. Call a water treatment vendor that specializes in water efficiency.

☐ 8. Use a healthy skepticism whenever you deal with chemical vendors. The major ingredient in most chemicals used to treat recirculating cooling tower water — is water. You may be able to save significant amounts of money by purchasing dry chemicals and adding the water yourself. Ask your chemical vendor to do the following:

- Explain the purpose, effects, and ingredients of each chemical he or she wants to sell you. Require them to submit projections of quantities and costs of treatment chemicals and volumes of bleed-off water, so that you or the facility manager can make a comparison more closely based on the true cost of cooling tower water treatment.

- Comply with your company's performance-based specification and commit to a predetermined level of water-efficiency based on projections of annual water use, chemical consumption, and costs.

- Demonstrate competence in water conservation options, awareness of your facility's water efficiency program, and willingness to participate in alternative programs that could increase the cycles of concentration in the towers by reducing the amount of bleed-off water.

☐ 9. Consider using:

☐ Ozonation: This can eliminate the need for chemical treatment and help the tower operate at high cycles of concentration more efficiently. Many system manufacturers offer leasing agreements, which removes the capital investment and maintenance burdens from your company. Ozone has limited effectiveness over 90°F and need energy input, raising energy costs. Payback approximately four years.

☐ Magnets: Alter the surface charge of particles and hinder them from bonding to cooling equipment surfaces and piping. They can reduce or eliminate the need for chemical treatment, but may require additional energy costs.

☐ Electrostatic field generators: same principle as magnets. Low maintenance, reduced fouling, more energy, and need for chemical treatment.

☐ Reclaim make-up water: use only certifiably clean water, or water may need additional treatment, increasing energy costs and dangers of contamination.

Ecoregion Map of the Continental United States

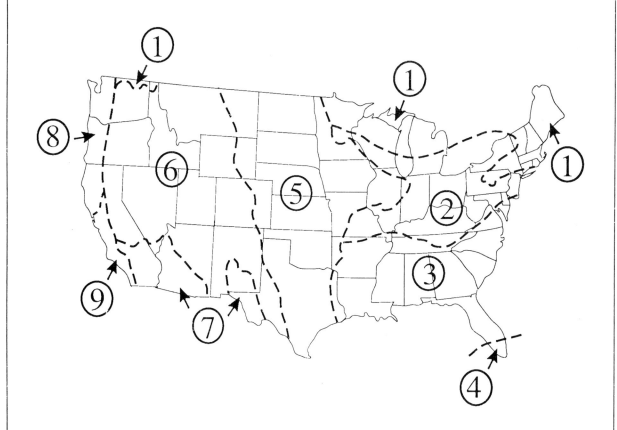

Hawaii: Rainforest — coldest month is above 64° F, annual variation less than 37° F. Rainfall is heavy with a minimum of 6 cm (2.36") per month. Vegetation is dense forest, heavy undergrowth.

Alaska: (Northern portion and Western coast) Tundra — mean temperature of warmest month is less than 50° F. Water is deficient during the cold season. Vegetation is moss, grasses, and small shrubs.

(Central and Southern) Subarctic — mean temperature of summer is 50° F, of winter 27° F. Rainfall is even throughout the year. Vegetation is forests and parklands.

Legend

Region	Temperature	Rainfall	Vegetation
1. Warm Continental	Coldest month below 32° F, warmest month less than 72° F	Adequate throughout the year	Seasonal forests, mixed coniferous-deciduous forests
2. Hot Continental	Coldest month below 32° F, warmest month above 72° F	Summer maximum	Deciduous forests
3. Subtropical	Coldest month between 64° and 27° F, warmest month above 72° F	Adequate throughout the year	Coniferous and mixed coniferous-deciduous forests
4. Savanna	Coldest month above 64° F, annual variation less than 54°F	Dry season with less than 6 cm (2.36") per year	Open grassland, scattered trees
5. Prairie	Variable	Adequate all year, excepting dry years, maximum in summer	Tall grass, parklands
6. Steppe	Variable, winters cold	Rain less than 50cm (19.69") per year	Short grass, shrubs
7. Desert	High summer temperature, mild winters	Very dry in all seasons	Shrubs or sparse grass
8. Marine	Coldest month between 64° and 27° F, warmest month less than 72° F	Maximum in winter	Coniferous forests
9. Mediterranean	Coldest month between 64° and 27° F, warmest month above 72° F	Dry summer, rainy winters	Evergreen woodlands and shrubs

Single Pass Efficiency Measures

- ☐ 1. Eliminate all pass-through uses, unless the passed water is reused elsewhere for a beneficial purpose.
- ☐ 2. Replace water-cooled equipment with air cooled units. Candidates include air compressors, vacuum pumps, ice makers, and ice cream and frozen yogurt machines. Assure yourself beforehand that an increase in energy operating costs and decrease in cooling capacity are not significant factors.
- ☐ 3. Many large facilities run a closed loop chilled water system which often has sufficient extra capacity to cool small equipment. Investigate this use to boost cooling efficiencies and reduce water and energy costs.
- ☐ 4. Pipe used cooling water to rinse tanks (the water is already preheated), or to air conditioning cooling towers.
- ☐ 5. Reuse cooling water from plant machinery, such as compressors, fans, or vacuum pumps. Vacuum pump recycling systems can save up to 75% of your water use.
- ☐ 6. Recycle spent cooling water. In plants where single pass cooling is the biggest water user, the huge water savings offset the investment in equipment and energy costs.
- ☐ 7. Reduce cooling water temperature one of three ways:
    - Using spray systems;
    - Evaporative cooling towers; or
    - Evaporative condensers.
    Evaporative condensers are the most water-efficient of these three systems.
- ☐ 8. Use spent cooling water for irrigation if it is of sufficiently good chemical quality. Use this water only after first testing for salts and concentrates inappropriate for landscape use.

Basic Food Services Water Efficiency Measures

Dishwashers — What You Can Do Yourself

- ☐ 1. Reduce the number of dishes, side dishes, underliners, and saucers you use. This reduces numbers of dishwasher loads. Serve the coffee cup without the saucer; put the "side" order on the main dish plate, if possible.
- ☐ 2. Wash only full loads of dishes.
- ☐ 3. Instead of using a sprayer to clean dishes and utensils, use a scraper and dip them in a tub of water to pre-clean. Dump tub water when dirty and refill.

Dishwashers — What You May Want a Professional To Do

- ☐ 4. Turn water off to dishwashers when dishes are not being processed, and limit water flow rates

Basic Food Services Water Efficiency Measures (continued)

according to manufacturer specifications.

☐ 5. Install pressure and flow regulators which limit supply line flow to 60 to 80 psi during periods of high water supply pressure.

☐ 6. Set up dishwasher so waste water can be used for low-grade purposes such as garbage disposals and flushing trash troughs.

☐ 7. Change to low-flow, high-pressure spray heads.

Garbage Disposals — What You Can Do Yourself

☐ 8. Minimize or eliminate the use of a garbage disposal — it typically consumes 5 to10 gallons of water per minute. Dump food waste directly into garbage can or, ideally, collect it for composting.

Garbage Disposals — What You May Want a Professional To Do

☐ 9. Shut off water when disposer motor shuts off, manually, or with a solenoid switch.

☐ 10. Regularly check operation of water supply lines to assure they are in order and not stuck open.

☐ 11. Install water supply line flow regulators.

☐ 12. Gradually reduce water flow through disposer to find minimum rate at which it will operate properly.

☐ 13. Replace garbage disposer with a garbage strainer. These pass a recirculating, two gallon per minute stream of water over food waste held in a basket, and reduce waste volume by as much as 40%. Use waste dishwasher water to supply the unit, instead of fresh water.

☐ 14. Eliminate plate cleaning troughs. Instead, dump waste in the garbage, or collect it for composting. If you must use the system, set water flush or conveyor to operate only when dishwasher is in use.

Ice Making Machines — What You Can Do Yourself

Depending on design, cube machines use 20 to 90 gallons of water to produce 100 pounds of ice; flake makers use 15 to 20 gallons. If either machine uses water to cool its refrigeration condenser, it may consume another 20 to 90 gallons for cooling.

☐ 15. Minimize or eliminate use of ice machines. Serve chilled water from soft drink fountain head.

☐ 16. Adjust ice machine to dispense less ice.

☐ 17. Use flake instead of cube machines wherever possible.

Ice Making Machines — What You May Want a Professional to Do:

☐ 18. Where softened water is available, the soft water could be used to produce clear cubes with less bleed-off.

☐ 19. Eliminate the use of single pass cooling.

☐ 20. Consider replacing water-cooled ice makers with air-cooled units. These use slightly more electricity for operation and do not produce as much ice as water-cooled units.

Basic Food Services Water Efficiency Measures (continued)

Wash, Rinse, and General Cleanup — What You Can Do Yourself:

☐ 21. Do not leave water running to thaw foods, melt ice, wash vegetables, or while washing bar glass.

☐ 22. Plan ahead so you can thaw foods in the refrigerator. If that is not possible, thaw under a slow hot water stream of 0.5 gpm or less.

☐ 23. Fill a sink or tub for washing and cleaning operations, and a second tub of clean water for rinsing.

☐ 24. Clean bar glass as part of a full load in the dishwasher.

☐ 25. Use water from the steam table instead of fresh to wash down the cooking area.

☐ 26. Use a bucket of soapy water and brush, broom, or mop for the floor mats in the kitchen.

☐ 27. Use a pitcher of water to wet down potted plants, or dip them in a tub or full sink of water, and set them by to drain.

Basic Landscape Water Efficiency Measures

Watering/Irrigation

☐ 1. Water only when needed, as infrequently as possible. Outside of arid zones, once a week should be plenty. Check first to see if soil is dry to an inch below the surface. Also, check for wilt and color change in leaves, and for turf that doesn't spring back when you press on it. These indicate a need for watering.

☐ 2. Time waterings for early evening and morning hours, and overcast days, and water areas only when they are in the shade on sunny days. These minimize evaporation losses from solar heat and winds. In southerly climates, where temperatures remain high even at night, you may be able to water at night without promoting mildew, moss or rot. If you or your landscape person need answers, refer to your local nursery people, city or county arborist, or agricultural extension agent.

☐ 3. During a drought period, budget irrigation. Do not intensively irrigate for part of the drought period then miss several weeks.

☐ 4. Water for as long as it takes to irrigate the four- to six-inch root zone. Check the depth of watering periodically with a soil corer or trowel, or use a tensiometer to measure soil moisture.

☐ 5. To keep lawns healthy in summer, allow a half-inch to three-quarters inch of water a week to soak into the ground. For winter watering, you can generally manage with half the summer water quantity.

Basic Landscape Water Efficiency Measures (continued)

Sprinklers and Control Systems

☐ 6. Avoid runoff and obstacles. Make sure that sprinkler heads aim at landscaping, not at buildings, fences, trees, poles, sidewalks, streets, driveways, or other objects.

☐ 7. To save up to 50% of lawn watering costs, adjust sprinkler timers monthly or weekly from May to October to accommodate varying weather conditions.

☐ 8. Match the sprinkler head to the area, size, shape, and types of plants it covers.

☐ 9. Use a sprinkler that can irrigate slowly, or in pulses with pauses between, so the soil has a chance to soak up the water. If the soil doesn't absorb water as fast as the sprinkler applies it, it will accumulate puddles or run off your landscape, both wasteful and harmful to turf and planted areas.

☐ 10. Heads within the same irrigation zone should have matched precipitation rates and minimum spray overlap.

☐ 11. Use the proper attachment and control device for the specific purpose on hoses. Attachments include bubblers, single hole screw nozzles, and watering wands. Control devices including: thumb, screw, or gate valves.

☐ 12. Check your automatic sprinkler system frequently for leaks, faulty heads, spray pattern overlap, general condition, and operating efficiency. It should deliver water evenly. Place cans around to check its distribution; you may be surprised to find some areas get more water than others.

☐ 13. On automatic systems, install soil moisture overrides or timers so that they water landscaping only when needed. If you want automatic sprinkler results without investing in the whole system, use an electronic faucet meter (approximately $100.00, plus 9-volt battery), on which you can preset watering days and times, or a mechanical faucet meter (about $30.00) or measuring sprinkler, both of which can be preset to run a fixed amount of water, then switch off.

☐ 14. For trees, woody plants, and planting beds that require watering, use an automatic, soaker hose or drip irrigation system.

☐ 15. Design decorative ponds, fountains, and waterfalls with recycling water systems and shut them off when not in use.

Plant/Landscape Management: Turf, Lawns, and Grassy Areas

☐ 16. Where possible, keep grass and trees separate. Grass needs frequent moderate watering, trees need less frequent, deep watering. If you combine the two, start the grass area far from the tree trunk, as close as possible to the tree "drip line," or furthest extension of its branches.

☐ 17. Use turf only where necessary. Otherwise, use ground cover, drought tolerant trees and shrubs, and mulch. Where you do use turf, grow a variety with low water needs, such as fescue rather than a thirsty one, such as bluegrass.

☐ 18. Keep lawn areas small and on level grades where water won't run off. Circular and rectangular lawns are easiest to water without overspray. Avoid turfing narrow strips and odd shapes, such as along driveways, walkways, or building edges. Instead, fill in with pebbles, wood chips, or decorative

Basic Landscape Water Efficiency Measures (continued)

ground cover and water with drip or soaker hose irrigation lines.

☐ 19. If any returfing needs to be done, wait to do it until after the hot months or water shortage period is over.

☐ 20. In dry weather, let the lawn go brown, as natural grassland does during the hot season, or practice grass cycling: Cut it high, and let the clippings settle in and die to create a mulch among the live stalks. This reduces yard waste. If your policy is to rake the grass up, you can use it as green material for composting.

☐ 21. For play- and ball-fields and golf courses, turf will need water to remain attractive, though it will remain playable, and will survive, if left to go brown.

☐ 22. Annually, aerate soil and thatch turf.

Plant/Landscape Management: Woody Plants, Trees, and Shrubs

☐ 23. Xeriscape. Growing plants outside their climate zones begs for problems — pests, diseases, inappropriate toil, and too much water. Deciduous trees do not grow naturally in a desert, just as Suguaro cactus do not grow naturally in the Northwest. Don't plant pines with willows; or cactus with ferns. Your local nursery, arborist, or agricultural extension agent can supply you or your environmental coordinator a list of grasses, flowers, woody plants and trees that fit well, give all-season ornamentation, and after their roots are set the first season, require no more water than the natural climate provides.

☐ 24. Mulch. On all planting beds and around trees and woody plants, you can conserve water, slow evaporation, and control insect pests and weeds by laying down a layer of compost, chipped woody yard wastes, leaves, or grass clippings. Some trees may be harmed by having mulch around their bases, because it can harbor parasites that damage the crop. Ask your nursery, arborist, or extension agent for advice.

☐ 25. Build the soil's ability to hold water. Work in compost to improve the soil before planting or laying down turf. You can also use wetting agents, water-absorbing soil additives, sand, leaves, and other materials to improve water penetration.

☐ 26. Where possible, provide shading to block sunlight from plants and help slow evaporation from ground areas.

☐ 27. Avoid stimulating plant growth, and promote drought hardiness. Decrease fertilizers, increase potassium levels. Remove plants that are unhealthy so that other plants can benefit from water saved.

☐ 28. Postpone landscaping additions or alterations until the dry season or water shortage period is over. New landscaping needs large amounts of water to get established. Drought-tolerant varieties, however, will only need setting water the first season. Thereafter, requirements will be minimal.

Chapter 9

Transportation Options and Alternatives

You and your employees may be your business' biggest polluters.

The days are gone when Americans took trolleys, walked, or bicycled to work at large factories. Today, most of us drive to light industry or service jobs, and that makes employee and company motor vehicles your business' one greatest source of pollution, energy consumption, and land use impacts.

Every year, 26% of the country's energy resources are burned by the transportation sector, three-quarters of it in road vehicles, the other quarter by ships and airplanes. Vehicle exhaust accounts for 25% of air pollution, and over half of America's developed urban land is devoted to roads and parking space.[1]

Money, resources, and space are devoted to automobiles because they are considered the most convenient means to reach work, carry goods to market, and deliver services to customers.

Since this is a people problem first and a transportation problem second, the challenge is to make vehicles, and the use of them, more efficient. If this can be accomplished, then the problems associated with vehicles, such as those listed below, will be reduced.

- Air pollution;
- Fossil fuel consumption;
- Traffic congestion and noise;
- The space devoted to lots, roads, and highways; and
- Hazardous waste — 40% of America's hazardous materials and waste are used and generated by the automotive industry.[2]

"Population is pollution spelled inside out."

David Brower, Founder, Friends of the Earth

New technology is not a "magic pill" to end transportation problems.

- Electric cars pollute. Their batteries are full of hazardous materials such as lead, cadmium, and lithium. They must be charged with electricity from hydroelectric, nuclear, oil- and coal-burning power plants — the same grid that supplies your company's lights, HVAC, and equipment. And they won't keep traffic off our roads.
- Shifting to propane or natural gas fuel only offers a new energy source for the same old problems.
- Expanding road systems and transportation options only invites more traffic, noise, accidents, and land development.
- Telecommuting is a two-edged sword. It reduces traffic, but encourages people to move to and develop land even further from work.

You need a transportation efficiency program. Use the now familiar steps to create your program.

Step 1: Create Commitment From the Top

State your intention to create more efficient transportation methods for your business. You are both an employer of employees, and a fleet owner, even if your "fleet" has only one vehicle.

Create a statement, and commit to efficiency goals such as these:

1. Minimize total driving. There are two ways to do this:
   a. Through modes other than one-passenger vehicles, such as public transit, carpools, bicycles, and walking.
   b. Through work schedules, such as compressed work weeks or telecommuting.
2. Maintain company vehicles so they have minimum environmental impacts.
3. Select the most environmentally responsible vehicles.
4. Locate your offices and facilities near established population centers.

Step 1A: Announce Your Program

Post the message or transportation statement on the bulletin board, put commuting information on E-mail, in memos, and in your employee newsletters. Invite a transit agency representative to your next staff meeting.

Step 1B: Support the Program

Provide a bulletin board for carpoolers, a rack of current bus schedules, routing information, and bicycle maps. Offer to work with those who seek commuting alternatives. Then do practice runs. As you and your employees learn the new system, allow for late arrivals and missed connections at first.

To handle your program, you may wish to select a transportation coordinator. If this is a different person than your environmental program coordinator, be sure they work closely together. He or she is the liaison between employees and management to develop workable policies, address problems, provide information, and manage activities to promote more efficient commuting habits. The person must learn what local resources are available and what, if any, commute trip reduction requirements apply to your business.

Step 2: Start with the Basics

Begin implementing the items listed in the Basic Transportation Efficiency Measures on pages 204–205. The most obvious solution to traffic problems is to eliminate them. Items 1–4 of the Basic Measures provides ways to do just that.

If you must use vehicles for your business, explore the other options provided in the Basic Measures. Throughout this chapter, "vehicles" means over the road cars, vans, trucks, and buses; vehicles also include "materials handling units," such as forklifts, tractors, donkeys, and electric carts.

Step 3: Create a Transportation Utilization Index

What do your vehicles cost you, and where do you use them? As with energy and water, you can create a Transportation Utilization Index (TUI) for your vehicle use.

Assemble your vehicle logs, fuel and maintenance bills, payment and other records, and tally them together. Vehicle inventory software is available for this accounting. If you don't have software, use the Transportation Utilization Index worksheet on page 207 to establish a baseline TUI.

Factor out for seasonal peaks and valleys, and this simple TUI gives you a baseline for examining:

- Problems and improvements in vehicle performance;
- Effects of maintenance and repair; and
- Effects of using different types of vehicles.

It also raises some questions:

- Are you getting full use out of your current vehicles?
- Are you paying more than necessary for the service you get?
- Are you using the best vehicles for your tasks?
- Are you carrying optimum loads?

For example, regularly review any tools or materials that are kept in vehicles to insure that they are needed. You may be carrying unnecessary weight.

Small Business Fleets

If yours is a small business with five or less vehicles traveling in the local area where high speeds and powerful engines are not requirements, consider:

- Using electric, natural gas, or propane-fueled vehicles;
- Using small vehicles with high fuel-efficiency; or

- Reducing the number of vehicles you own, and instead, consolidating trips and using bicycles or local services for pickups and deliveries.

Consider purchasing a range of vehicle sizes and use the smallest, most efficient model suitable for each trip. If you only occasionally need a large vehicle, such as a full-size van, truck or bus, consider renting rather than buying. This avoids carrying excess size and weight that is seldom needed.

Vehicle minimum gas mileage and emission standards are coming to all states. When you have an opportunity to purchase a new vehicle, invest in the most fuel (and combustion-) efficient, or those that meet California Transitional Low Emission Vehicle standards. You benefit from fuel savings and encourage automobile manufacturers to continue improving vehicle designs.

Medium-sized and Larger Fleets

If yours is a medium-sized business with five or more vehicles, again, review how well you have matched each one to its intended purpose. You wouldn't use a two-door, subcompact car to make large-quantity deliveries, nor a panel truck for inter-city long hauls. If your company runs several routes:

- Review how well your vehicles match their purposes; and
- Consider investing in route-planning software. By making the most efficient use of driver time and rolling stock, these convenient distribution programs, which can be run or a personal computer, can save you 8 to 35% in costs for fuel, maintenance, replacement parts, and labor. They automatically select the best routing on your map for the tasks and times you enter. For routing software resources, please refer to Appendix D.

Small or large, if your business involves a large quantity of driving, consider installing trip computers or manual tachygraphs to track driving speeds, fuel consumption, and other vehicle data. Mandatory in several countries, and in some U.S. cities, their benefits prove out in reduced fuel consumption, wear and tear on vehicles, and improved driver performance.

Delivering these advantages enables the units to pay for themselves in relatively short order. For example, the Cicero, Illinois, Police Department has doubled the life of their cars and boosted brake job life by 50%; Howmet Turbine Component Corporation of La Porte, Indiana, saved $30,000 on its 19 vehicles in their first year of use.

Minimize Your Vehicles' Environmental Impacts

After you choose the correct vehicles for each job, keep their environmental impacts low by maintaining them.

A defective vehicle is both a general and environmental hazard. It gets poor fuel efficiency, its crankcase can leak oil and pollute surface water and endanger wildlife, it can exhaust off-spec pollutants, and it can cause accidents.

Make your drivers partners in maintaining your vehicles. When your equipment is on the road, your driver is legally responsible for its condition and performance.

Preventative Maintenance

Preventative maintenance is what keeps motor vehicles operating efficiently, reliably, and safely. To properly maintain your vehicle and the environment as well:

- Check your vehicle owner's manuals and ask your mechanic for advice on optimum maintenance scheduling. Since business vehicles often operate under heavy service conditions, consider increasing your maintenance schedule over what the manufacturer recommends.
- Be sure that your mechanics dispose of waste oil, CFCs, used tires, and other environmentally hazardous materials correctly. When a vehicle air condition system fails, investigate replacing it with a non-CFC unit, if available.
- Instruct mechanics to allow dirty oil to drip from each oil filter before the filter is thrown out, or recycled with scrap steel.
- Use re-refined oil. Test it in one or more different vehicles to gauge its performance before committing to it for your fleet.

After the maintenance is handled, there are more items to check before taking your business vehicle on the road.

1. Require drivers to inspect their vehicles before starting runs each day. They should check lights, brakes, turn signals, tire inflation, and note any accident damage. About 80% of vehicle defect accidents can be traced to brakes, tires, or wheels. Take your cue from rental car agencies — most now furnish drivers with a simple diagram of the car and instruct them to mark on the diagram any damage they see on the car body. This allows the rental agency to determine if any new damage occurred. Likewise, have your drivers document their inspections and sign and date them.

2. At the end of the day, have drivers update their morning inspection report with notes on the general condition of the vehicle and any specific maintenance or safety items that must be corrected. Encourage them to promptly report problems, including low tire pressure, smoky exhaust, and dripping oil.

3. Require all mechanics to check the vehicle maintenance history record before performing any repairs. That way, they learn the cause of a failure and correct it, rather than just removing and replacing parts. After repair, require the mechanic to sign off that he or she has corrected the defect and road-tested the vehicle.

4. Select parts suppliers that carry product liability insurance, and will stand behind you if you are involved in a parts-related lawsuit. Price is not so much the issue as service and long-term costs per mile.

Basic workups on vehicle maintenance are available from a variety of sources, including the Commercial Vehicle Safety Alliance, the Association of Fleet Managers, the American Automobile Association, and most auto maintenance books.

If you do not wish to handle these details, contract for services with a local garage that guarantees its work and uses certified mechanics. The garage should also have all necessary local and state licenses and certifications to conduct inspections, CFC system maintenance, and authorized repairs. Remember, you are hiring this shop to do work for you. Inspect it carefully, interview its principals, and get referrals.

If you do wish to handle basic inspection matters, you can cover the key points with the Basic Vehicles Maintenance Checklist on page 206. The checklist will also serve as a maintenance history for the next maintenance period.

Step 4: Create an Employee Commute Trip Reduction Program

Potential benefits from a commute trip reduction (CTR) program include:

- Avoided costs for real estate, parking, energy, vehicles, and insurance;
- Reduced air pollution and land use impacts;
- Reduced employee tardiness and absenteeism; and
- An improved, environment-friendly business image.

In a recent survey of private employers who manage ridesharing programs, 50% indicated that they helped reduce employee tardiness and improved public relations, and a third believe that it reduces absenteeism and helps retain valued employees.

Setting Up Your CTR Program

The CTR options will work for two groups of employers:

- Small businesses in commercial clusters, such as malls and central business districts; and
- Larger businesses, with 50 or more people.

The success of a program depends upon employees' abilities to either commute on their own by an alternative means or pool together in a single vehicle from a central location.

Thus, a large company can organize an in-house carpooling program. A small company, mall manager or business district Chamber of Commerce can create a commute trip reduction program by sponsoring a lunchtime transit fair, inviting other nearby employers to participate, and assembling a shared ride network among workers of different employers.

CTR Commitment From the Top

Your transportation efficiency statement has already declared your commitment to efficient commuting. Continue to stress that management will work with employees to develop effective and fair policies that encourage more efficient commuting.

Your company should be willing to spend as much money per employee on alternative commuting modes as you do now on parking facilities. This gives alternative choices, both to employees who can and cannot drive or afford their own cars.

Be flexible — each employee has unique needs. In the beginning, many can only give up their car commute a few days each month. Even an employee who shifts commute habits one day a month is worth encouraging. Understand that change is difficult, and workers need to know you support them as they learn new ways to commute.

Outline the Program and Assemble Components

Use the Commute Trip Reduction Questionnaire on page 208 to determine the structure of your program. After determining the structure, you can use the CTR Options Checklist on page 209 to begin assembling the components of your program.

As options become available and acceptable to employees, they'll learn to use and enjoy them. The programs will only continue to be effective, however, as long as they respond to changing needs and enjoy your continuing commitment.

Promote the Program and Encourage Participation

An increasing number of local urban governments require that employers encourage CTR programs to reduce traffic congestion and air pollution problems.

Promotion and education are important. Be sure that employees are aware of your company's transportation policies and explore all available resources, such as transit schedules, rideshare matching services, and bicycle facilities. Publicity can include desktop distribution of brochures and flyers, articles published in a company newsletter, brochures or flyers attached to paychecks, and posters mounted on bulletin boards. Information should be changed, updated, and distributed frequently. For example, during a year, your company might:

- Distribute an updated employee transportation policy statement each time there is a change, or at least once a year.
- Distribute transit and ridesharing information directly to each employee twice a year.
- Post information on a bulletin board in the lunch room.
- Sponsor one Commute Information fair.
- Include a commute information column in your monthly employee newsletter.
- Offer transit schedules and rideshare-matching applications at the reception desk.
- Provide transportation information to each new employee.
- Let all employees know when an in-house Commute Trip Reduction committee or task force is being convened to create or modify company policy, and how employees can submit their ideas and comments.

- Sponsor a transportation fair or exhibit in a main lobby or staff room. Invite transit agencies, bicycle clubs, and even computer vendors (for telecommuters) to provide information and advice. If your company has too few employees, organize events and activities with other nearby companies.
- Organize a contest to see which offices, divisions, or businesses can have the most employees commute using efficient travel modes.

Commute Trip Reduction Case Study

State Farm Insurance, of Costa Mesa, California, implemented a Commute Trip Reduction program for its 980 employees as required by State Regulation XV. The program started in 1987 with a ridesharing program which includes a company sponsored carpool, preferential parking and free coffee in the morning for carpoolers, and promotion. Within a year the company's ridesharing rate was 20%, achieving an average vehicle occupancy rate of 1.22.

In 1989 State Farm began to subsidize one third of the cost of vanpools and added a direct subsidy for employees who shift to efficient modes. Upon arrival at the company's parking lot in the morning, each employee is issued coupons according to the following formula:

Mode	Coupon Value
2-person carpool	$ .50
3-person carpool	$1.00
4-person carpool	$1.50
Bicycle, bus, walk	$1.50

Employees attach their coupons to their time sheets for cash reimbursement at each pay period. Maximum monthly payment is $30, with lower amounts depending on the number of days and mode that each employee uses. This approach is very flexible, and employees can choose whichever mode and schedule they want.

These steps increased State Farm employee's average vehicle occupancy rate to 1.55, placing State Farm in compliance with Regulation XV. The vehicle trip generation rate was reduced from 82.4 monthly trips per employee to 63.4, eliminating 190 trips per month.

Commute Options for Your Transportation Efficiency Program

The remainder of this chapter discusses the options available for your transportation efficiency program.

Public Transit

What can you do to promote your employees' use of public transit? You can:

- Provide free or discounted transit passes to employees.
- Post and distribute bus schedules at your business.

- Check with your local transit agency, they may have programs and resources such as displays, workshops, and contests that your company can sponsor.

Carpooling

You can help employees find carpool partners by posting a ride board in a staff room or placing notices in an internal newsletter. There may be a free carpool matching service in your community that can help employees from different companies find partners. Provide carpoolers with preferential parking spaces. If your company charges for parking spaces, allow carpool vehicles to park for free. If several employees live in the same area, your business can sponsor a carpool.

Guaranteed Ride Home

A concern of employees who may want to carpool is that, without their own car, they will have trouble responding to domestic emergencies during the day, such as a child becoming sick. Employers can allay this concern by offering employees a guaranteed ride home in emergencies. This is typically provided by the employer paying taxi fare, with reasonable limits on the travel distance, and frequency that any employee can use this option. The experience of employers who offer this option is that it is seldom used but greatly appreciated.

On-site Daycare

Parents with small children drive extra distances delivering and picking them up from childcare, and they state this as a reason they must drive their own cars to work. As part of promoting efficient transportation, and as a way to retain valued employees and get public relations points, you may wish to consider establishing an on-site daycare center. Setting one up will, of course, depend on many factors, including the demand for such service at your business and development and management costs.

Bicycling

Bicyclists need a safe place to store their bicycles, protected from the weather and secure from theft. Ideally, this is in a locked storage room, or a spot located in a public place (bicycle thieves love privacy). Either space must have some means to support and lock each bicycle. This can be a commercially produced or custom-made bike rack, or simply an eye-bolt or railing attached to a wall that bicycles can lean on. Be sure that any rack design is approved by the users,

You will need enough protected bicycle parking for year-round riders and an overflow area for fair weather riders.

Bicyclists also need a place to shower and change into work clothes and lockers for storing their bicycling clothes during the day. If showers exist in your facility, let potential cyclists know that they are available for use. If not, consider adding them or arranging to use showers in nearby buildings or at a nearby YMCA or gym.

If employees are enthusiastic about bicycling, consider sponsoring a company bicycle club or team.

Flex-time

This provides employees discretion on work hours. It can simply mean they arrive a few minutes before or after 8:00 A.M., or that they take significantly different shifts, such as 6:30 A.M. to 4:00 P.M., or even four ten-hour days. Flex-time helps reduce rush hour traffic congestion and supports other options, such as riding transit and telecommuting.

Telecommuting

Telecommuting means working from home or from a neighborhood office. While some professions, such as consultants, salespeople, writers, and artists have often worked at home, telecommuting has become increasingly common for many more types of jobs as portable computers, modems, faxes, and telephone voice mail enable electronic communication to replace physical movement. It is now possible to do at home many of the tasks previously done in offices.

Many workers enjoy telecommuting — the privacy and comfort of working at home, and the time and dollar saving from reduced commuting. Telecommuting is not usually a full-time arrangement; most telecommuters choose from one to four days a week to work at home. They schedule their work week to take advantage of the blocks of undisturbed time allowed by this arrangement.

As an intermediary step, a few larger employers have established neighborhood or satellite offices. Employees use the work site closest to their residence. The satellite office includes common office tools such as computers, fax machines, and copiers. This facility may be shared by several different employers.

Not every employee can or wants to work at home. Some are uncomfortable without the office or plant structure. Some jobs require tools and other resources that are not available at home. The best candidates for telecommuting are those who enjoy independence, are self-starters, and prefer to work by objective rather than by timeclock.

Likewise, supervisors who are self-reliant and "manage by objective" are most comfortable with this arrangement.

Telecommuters need a comfortable and undisturbed work space at their home. So, this is not a substitute for childcare, and you must make that clear to potential telecommuters.

Other issues must be resolved around this, too:

- Equipment — a computer, copy machine, and fax may be needed for jobs. Some employers provide a fully equipped home office, while others require telecommuting employees to invest in their own equipment. Most telecommuting programs are somewhere between, with employers supplying some equipment, perhaps offering a pool of portable computers or fax machines that employees can check out the days that they telecommute. Many professional employees already have a computer and may only need software that is compatible with that used at the main office; check your software licensing agreement to determine whether it allows employees to have a copy of the software on a home computer.

- Compensation — a company may also need to reimburse employees for long-distance telephone calls. Better yet, obtain a business long-distance telephone card. Voice mail and E-mail systems also provide considerable assistance to telecommuters, allowing them to receive telephone calls at the office and send messages to colleagues while working from home. An E-mail system that can be assessed by modem even allows employees to distribute computer files between office and home.

- Management style — You can't oversee an employee who is working at home the same as somebody working in your office, so telecommuting requires a high level of trust and cooperation. Managers must learn to use the end product as a gauge of how productive their telecommuters are, rather than simply measuring hours in the office.

- Insurance — Some employees may be concerned about their workers compensation or other employee insurance coverage while working at home. In most cases, employee insurance covers employees no matter where they work, but you may want to clarify this issue under your state law to reassure potential telecommuters.

- Scheduling — One of the keys to successful telecommuting is careful planning and scheduling. Most telecommuters develop a file of work that is appropriate for work at home, such as writing and telephone calls. In-office days are used for activities that require face-to-face communication. Telecommuters should schedule their office days in coordination with other people in their work group. Some managers choose one or two days of the week that all employees must work in the office to allow for staff meetings.

Rethink Your Parking Spaces

People don't expect their employers to provide free gasoline. But a free parking space is actually more valuable than the fuel most commuters use getting to work.

A typical parking space is worth $25 to $100 per month in land and maintenance costs, yet about 90% of employees who drive to work receive free parking.[3] Free parking only subsidizes people who drive, most of them in single passenger vehicles, the least efficient form of transportation. Workers who use other forms of transportation to work don't usually receive a comparable benefit.

Now, you may believe parking is a sunk cost. Your company already owns the parking spaces, so they are free.

This may be true in the short term if your company owns a building with parking spaces. But some time in the future, your company will probably either need more parking spaces or could use the land currently in parking for something more profitable. The cost then of those "free" parking spaces could be very high.

For example, say your company wants to build another building to expand its current facilities. Perhaps you would need to spend $30,000 to acquire a small piece of adjacent land.

Instead you might want to implement new policies that reduce parking demand and use land that is current parking spaces for the building. You should be willing to spend at least $30,000, perhaps more to keep your facilities close together and to reduce parking demand by the required amount.

Perhaps you are experiencing an increase in employment that will require more parking spaces. Instead, you can use a CTR program to help reduce or eliminate your company's need to build parking facilities, again saving money and additional environmental impacts.

Success Story

Vanpool-parking facility tradeoff: By creating a successful vanpool program, 3M Corporation of St. Paul, Minnesota, was able to avoid the need and cost of building 1,500 new parking spaces. Total savings: $2.5 million. Often, a pool commute program can more than offset its costs.

Traditionally, employers were expected to provide one parking space for each employee. But successful Commute Trip Reduction efforts enable employers to cut this amount in half. Reduced parking subsidies are one of the most effective measures for promoting efficient commute habits. Even a parking charge that only represents a portion of the total cost of the parking space can have a significant effect:

- When the Los Angeles area's ridesharing agency phased in market rates for employee parking, the number of solo drivers declined from 42% to 8%, while the number of carpoolers rose from 17% to 58%.
- When charges equal to half of prevailing commercial parking rates were imposed at several federal buildings in Washington, D.C. in 1979 and 1980, the number of employees driving alone declined by as much as 40% in some sites.

Most of the effective Commute Trip Reduction programs nationwide include aggressive parking pricing combined with strong ridesharing, transit, and bicycle encouragement. Of course, the impacts of reduced parking subsidies will also depend on the availability of free parking near your business.

Cash Out Free Parking

If your company offers free automobile parking, be sure to provide an equally valuable benefit to those who use more efficient forms of transportation.

Some companies provide a free transit pass, although that is seldom as valuable as a parking space.

The best approach is to "Cash Out" free parking: simply give all employees a transportation subsidy, say $40 per month that they can spend however they wish. Then charge that same amount for each employee parking space. Workers who continue to drive alone to work are no better or worse off. But employees who carpool, ride a bus, or bicycle can pocket their savings. Be sure to structure this policy to provide incentives to workers who drive alone part-time.

Company sponsored bicycle teams increase employee enthusiasm for bicycling.

Basic Transportation Efficiency Measures

Basic Low Cost/No Cost Measures

☐ 1. If you don't need a vehicle, don't use one.

☐ 2. Commute by foot or bicycle. If the distance is too great, use public transportation, or a carpool.

☐ 3. Work as much as possible from your home via telephone, computer modem, FAX, regular and E-mail, and messenger services.

☐ 4. For errands and deliveries, go by foot, bicycle, or public means; use in-place services, such as messengers (bicycles, taxis, overnight, and air), the post office, and vehicle rental agencies.

☐ 5. Make fuel efficiency, low pollution output and low life- cycle costs priorities when you select vehicles for personal and business use.

☐ 6. Keep a log for each vehicle. Include mileage, fuel intake and cost, repairs and maintenance. This enables you to track performance of your vehicle and identify problem areas.

☐ 7. Minimize uses of company vehicles and consolidate errands, pickups, deliveries, and transportation to meetings in single vehicle trips.

☐ 8. Encourage employees to commute by other transportation means than single-occupancy vehicles. Set up a carpooler and errand consolidation bulletin board. Provide a rack of current bus schedules and bike route maps to entice people out of single-passenger cars.

☐ 9. If you want a carpool employee to work late, inform them ahead of time and provide them an emergency ride home if they miss their shared ride.

☐ 10. Do not let gas or light diesel vehicles idle for more than one minute. After that point, it takes less gas to shut them off and restart them, than to let them continue idling.[4]

☐ 11. Implement preventive maintenance and repair programs for all vehicles. Sample benefits: (a) A tuned gas-powered or light diesel vehicle with a clean fuel filter uses 9% less gas than one without (b) Most blowouts are caused by under-inflated tires. Fully-inflated tires reduce rolling resistance, and can give you 5% better gas mileage (c) Fewer accidents — the U.S. Bureau of Motor Carrier Safety reports that, nationwide, defective vehicles account for between 9% and 12% of reported accidents.

☐ 12. Make aerodynamics a priority for any vehicle that will travel at highway speeds (50 mph or greater) for periods of 30 minutes or more. On long-haul trucks, consider aerodynamics of hood, cab, side mirror, bumper and sleeper, use of air shields and extenders, side farings and between-wheel skirts. On flatbeds, place loads close to the cab; on boxes, travel with side curtains down.

☐ 13. Minimize large diesel idling. It leads to engine overheating, and burns 3/4-gallon of fuel per hour. Large diesels may need up to four minutes of start-up idling to charge an air system, and two minutes of pre-shutoff idling to cool down a turbocharger. If these are not concerns, shut the diesel off.

☐ 14. Keep highway speeds for large diesels at 55 mph. Every mile per hour over that costs the truck 1/10 mile per gallon (mpg) of fuel. At 55, the typical over-the-road truck gets 6 mpg, at 65 it gets 5 mpg.[5]

☐ 15. Explore uses of alternative vehicle types and fuel or power sources for specific purposes in your business.

Basic Transportation Efficiency Measures (continued)

☐ 16. Join an automobile or fleet managers' trade group to keep abreast of the latest developments in vehicle management, regulations, and improvements.

The next group of options are more expensive; analyze their costs and benefits for your specific business.

Moderate Cost/High Cost Measures

☐ 17. As company "perks,"
- Offer employees monthly bus passes for free or at reduced rates;
- Allot free space for carpools near your building;
- Charge for parking single-occupant vehicles there; and
- Install in-house showers (with low-flow heads) and lockers, and encourage employees to bicycle and walk to work.

☐ 18. Develop a fleet of bicycles or tricycles for errands around large plants, campus facilities, and downtown areas where employees often make short trips. Equip them with locks to guard against theft. Often faster than automobiles for short distances, bicycles are also appropriate for multi-stop work, such as utility inspection and light delivery.

☐ 19. Equip all long-haul vehicles with aerodynamic farings.

☐ 20. If any of your vehicles has an air conditioner, avoid CFC leaks by taking it to an authorized dealer for regular system checks. If the system is in disrepair, have it replaced with a non-CFC system, or taken out entirely.

☐ 21. Equip every vehicle with appropriate area maps to avoid driver delays and excess mileage.

☐ 22. Invest in mapping and routing software to streamline driving on delivery, distribution, and merchandising routes and decrease vehicle fuel consumption and wear and tear. Software programs can reduce vehicle costs and driving time by 8 to 35% and are tailored to specific businesses.

☐ 23. Provide driver's training to employees who will use company vehicles. This improves safety, reduces vehicle wear, saves fuel, and can reduce insurance costs.

☐ 24. Install computerized trip recorders or manual tachygraphs in all vehicles to record driving speeds, fuel consumption, periods in and out of service, etc. Offer to split resulting fuel and maintenance savings with your drivers.

☐ 25. Operators of large fleets will find it worthwhile to invest in computerized vehicle logs, preventative maintenance and inventory control software.

Basic Vehicles Maintenance Checklist

Use a separate checklist for each vehicle.

Vehicle: _____ **Date:** _____

License number: _____ **Purchase date:** _____

Mileage at purchase: _____ **Current mileage:** _____

Fuel type: _____ **Miles per gallon:** _____

Last emission test date: _____ **Results:** _____

Last tune-up date: _____ **Miles:** _____

Last oil change/lube date: _____ **Miles:** _____

1. Oil level: □ OK □ Low □ Quarts added   How many? _____

2. Oil filter changed? □ Yes □ No

3. Air filter changed? □ Yes □ No

4. Radiator level: □ OK □ Low

   Hoses OK?   □ Yes □ No   Replaced: _____   Date: _____

   Leaks?   □ Yes □ No   Where: _____

   Repaired?   □ Yes □ No   Date: _____

   Winterized?   □ Yes □ No   Date: _____

5. Battery installed?   Date: _____   Warranty life: _____

   Condition: □ OK □ Problem

   Repair/replacement: □ Yes □ No   Date: _____

6. Tires   Condition   psi   Repair/Replace   Date

   Right front   _____   _____   _____   _____

   Right rear   _____   _____   _____   _____

   Left front   _____   _____   _____   _____

   Left rear   _____   _____   _____   _____

7. Fluid levels:

   Windshield   □ OK □ Add   Date: _____

   Brake   □ OK □ Add   Date: _____

   Transmission   □ OK □ Add   Date: _____

8. Emissions test:

   □ CO_2 Date: _____

   □ CO   Date: _____

   □ No

Transportation Utilization Index

Use a separate worksheet for each vehicle.

Vehicle: _____ Year: _____

Make: _____ Model: _____

License Number: _____ Date: _____

Month	Lease/Loan Payment	Mileage	Fuel Cost Per Gallon	Gallons Used	Insurance	Maintenance Repair	Total Monthly Cost
January							
February							
March							
April							
May							
June							
July							
August							
September							
October							
November							
December							
Totals							

Calculations:

Total Btu consumed = Total gallons of fuel x 125,000

Transportation Utilization Index (TUI) = $\dfrac{\text{Total Btu consumed}}{\text{Total vehicle mileage}}$

Commute Trip Reduction Questionnaire

1. How will alternative commuting benefit the company? _____
_____
_____
_____

2. Have any of our people expressed interest in alternative commuting? ☐ Yes ☐ No

   Can we raise interest? ☐ Yes ☐ No   Contact the transit authority for information.

3. Where do our managers and employees live? _____
_____
_____

   Are there two or more in each area who can pool rides? ☐ Yes ☐ No   If so, how often? ____
_____

   Are there enough employees in a given area to merit using a van? ☐ Yes ☐ No   If yes, call the
   transit authority for information.

4. Do we have shower and locker facilities for employees who wish to commute by bicycle, or walk?
   ☐ Yes ☐ No

5. Can we work out a bus-pass incentive with the transit authority? ☐ Yes ☐ No

6. Can we reduce or eliminate the money we pay for reserved parking spaces, and use it to help fund a
   bus-pass or other alternative commuting incentive program? ☐ Yes ☐ No   Explain: _____
_____
_____
_____

7. Can we network with other employers in the mall or business district, and enable ourselves and our
   employees to pool rides? Perhaps we can (1) sponsor a transit fair, with the help of the transit authority, or (2) create a map of where everyone lives, trade phone numbers and addresses, and let everyone
   make their own arrangements. Explain: _____
_____
_____
_____

8. Can we offer incentives to our customers who use transit, carpools, bicycles, and other alternative
   modes for shopping at our store, and at the stores of other merchants in the mall or business district?
   ☐ Yes ☐ No   Explain: _____
_____
_____
_____

CTR Options Checklist

This checklist provides options you can do yourself and who to contact for other options.

☐ 1. Drop parking space payments, and invest them either as direct disbursements that pools can use to pay for parking, or as indirect investments in ride-sharing incentives.

☐ 2. Install or find showers and lockers for bicycle commuters and walkers.

Contact the following:

☐ 3. State transportation or energy office:

    ☐ CTR program guidelines

    ☐ CTR technical assistance for program setup

☐ 4. Transit authority:

    ☐ Rack of current bus schedules

    ☐ Bus pass information and incentive arrangements

    ☐ Carpool arrangements

    ☐ Ride-sharing/carpooling information

    ☐ Transit fair assistance

    ☐ CTR speaker for meetings

☐ 5. City or county planning or engineering department:

    ☐ Bicycle path maps

    ☐ Ride-sharing/carpooling information

☐ 6. Local stores for a large map of the area. You can post this for potential commute pool planning and ride sharing.

☐ 7. Small businesses in your neighborhood or mall, with whom you can network ride-sharing commuters.

☐ 8. Building manager.

Appendix A

Hazardous Materials — Laws & Governing Agencies

There are specific substances to avoid today, and specific solutions for handling them. The basic avoidance/solution list includes the following:

Toxics Now Restricted or Banned
- Coatings:
  - Penta
  - Creosote
- Pesticides:
  - DDT
  - 2,4,5-T
  - Chlordane
  - Silvex

Solutions to Handling Restricted Toxics
If you don't have these specific products, you may find them included in the ingredients lists of other gardening and maintenance products. Call your waste management company, county extension agent or municipal or county solid waste department for advice on how best to dispose of them.

Highly-publicized Toxics
The next group consists of the highly-publicized toxic substances. Of this group, the only item that cannot be regulated is radon, a naturally-occurring

element which is present to some degree in most parts of the country and must be dealt with where you find it.

Formaldehyde: Used as an ingredient in carpeting, foamed-in-place structural wall insulation, particle board adhesives and other products, and released from them as a toxic gas. Many people appear to be adversely affected by this gas, and medical agencies are now collecting and assessing allergy data. The results may lead to restrictions on the use of this chemical and reformulation of products in which it is used.

PCBs: Oily dielectric fluids used to insulate distribution transformers; as ballast for fluorescent light fixtures; and in some carbonless copy papers; banned after 1979.

CFCs such as freon: Widely used in coolant liquids for refrigerators, freezers, and air conditioners; in aerosol propellants for Silly String and party, boat, and sports horns; and in cleaners for circuit boards and office equipment. Harmful to the earth's ozone layer, because CFCs are stable for several decades, and rise into the high atmosphere where ultraviolet light bombardment breaks them apart, releasing their chlorine molecules to combine with free oxygen atoms in the ozone. Due to be banned as of 12/31/95.

Halons: CFC relatives that contain bromine, chlorine, or fluorine and are more harmful to the ozone layer than CFCs; used in fire suppressant systems for airplanes and moisture-sensitive environments such as computer rooms, and in fire extinguishers; due to be banned 12/31/95.

Methyl chloroform: A CFC relative used as an active ingredient in aerosol degreasers and solvents, adhesives, coatings, inks, vapor degreasing for metals and electronics, and the manufacture of fluorocarbons; ozone harmful, due to be banned 12/31/95.

Carbon tetrachloride: A carcinogenic and ozone harmful compound used in the production of pesticides, fluorocarbons, pharmaceuticals, and other chemicals; due to be banned 12/31/95.

Radon: As uranium decays into lead, it gives off an odorless, colorless, tasteless radioactive gas called radon. Uranium and radon occur in trace amounts in all soils and rocks. Granite, shale, and phosphate contain more than dark volcanic rock. Dry, porous, and permeable soils, and fractured or faulted rock transport it easily; wet, tight clay soils don't.

Researchers have discovered that radon can accumulate inside closed spaces, such as homes and buildings. There, it gets attached by static charge to dust and vapor, humans can inhale it and expose their lung tissue to small bursts of radiated energy as the radon continues to decay.

Risk of radon cancer is small, partly because it decays to lead in 3.8 days. There may be a risk, however, if it is contained in a closed space and you're exposed to it over a long period of time. This is possible in offices and homes, where people spend long periods of time in the same space. Otherwise, radon just percolates through the earth's surface and mixes with the outdoor air, and is usually too diluted to be harmful.

Infectious and other medical waste: Contaminated dressings, bodily fluids and wastes, and sharps (needles and blades). Risks can result from contact with these items.

Everyday Toxic and Hazardous Materials

The toxic substance category, unfortunately, goes far beyond these chemicals. A host of everyday items must be included in the list:

Fuels: Including gasoline, diesel, white gas, methane, propane, natural gas, lighter fluid and charcoal briquet fluid. All evaporate at room temperature, giving off fumes that are flammable and harmful to health.

Vehicle and machinery lubricants and fluids: All are harmful or fatal if swallowed and can irritate skin. Animals particularly love the sweet taste of antifreeze, and will lap it up where it spills on the ground, which kills them.

Pesticides: Used for killing insects; liquids and vapors harmful or fatal to humans and animals.

Herbicides: Used for killing plants; liquids and vapors harmful or fatal to humans and animals.

Most dishwashing detergents: Contain phosphates and arsenic. The phosphates contribute to cancerous algae growth that chokes the fish in lakes and streams. The arsenic is a heavy metal that helps render sewage sludge unusable as fertilizer.

Oil-based and metallic inks, dyes, paints, and coatings: Including the mineral spirits, thinners, solvents and degreasers used to thin and clean them up. They all put off fumes that are harmful to humans and animals.

Solutions to Handling Toxics

Now that you know the problem items, look over the solutions below. The best way to handle these items is not to buy them. But if you must buy them, get the smallest amount(s) you need for the job, and use them up.

To handle them, use heavy duty neoprene or other compatible industrial-grade gloves, and protective clothing as necessary. Don't use latex dish-washing gloves; solvents dissolve them. You can find the gloves and other protective clothing at building supply, hardware, and safety-supply stores. Check the Materials Safety and Data Sheets (MSDS) for handling precautions.

If you spill hazardous materials, the quantity of the spill determines the reporting and response procedure. The "reportable quantities," or RQs, are listed under 40 CFR. If you don't have these resources handy, call your hazardous materials or EPA hotline, or your local fire department for advice and response.

Penta, creosote, DDT, chlordane, 2,4,5-T, silvex: If you find these items on site, contact your municipal or county solid waste management authority, or state ecology or environment department for procedures on how to handle, use and dispose of them.

PCBs: Less than 50 parts per million is considered a safe level. Your local electric company will have handled the transformers, and you are probably not using 1979 carbonless forms. However, the ballast in your fluorescent light fixtures may be another matter.

Depending on the manufacturer, the ballast may be at one end, run the length of the fixture in plain sight, or be tucked inside the fixture. If the ballast is not apparent, find the manufacturer's brand, call an electrical supply house, and ask where it is on that fixture. The ballast should either have a date or be stamped "No PCB."

If you find a tar-like substance on the fixture, and ballasts break down after 10-15 years, check the floor underneath it for drips. Open a window, or otherwise ventilate the area. If the floor is a hard surface, wipe up the drips with a paper towel; if carpet, cut out the drip patch. Get two plastic garbage bags; place one inside the other. Remove the fixture and wrap it with the dirty towel or carpet in the double bag, and take it to the garbage. Federal law allows disposal of up to four fixtures in the local garbage. For more than four fixtures, you must contact a disposal company for handling as hazardous waste.

CFCs: These mostly fall within the scope of the air conditioning and refrigeration industries, which are specifically regulated by federal and other statutes. However, CFCs have been, and still are, used in some Styrofoam products. The compound replacing most CFCs in foam containers is HCFC, which has one tenth the harmful punch of CFC, but is still due for banning in the year 2030.

The two items about which you should be alert are (1) to avoid buying disposable Styrofoam products, unless no other item will fit the purpose and you can recycle the Styrofoam trash, and (2) anytime your refrigeration units are serviced, make certain the technician is certified, and that he or she is using certified recapture equipment to recycle the refrigerant. None should be released or "vented" into the atmosphere during servicing. Keep a record of each service call, too.

Halons: The ban on these fire suppressants has been extended until an equally effective and safe alternative is found. Meanwhile, if you have a halon system, retain it until its expiration date, then replace it with a non-halon system. If you are in the market for a fire extinguishing system, choose one that employs another type of suppressant.

Methyl chloroform (1,1,1 trichloroethylene): Used in degreasing solvents, it is aromatic and must be used in ventilated areas. Handle with rubber gloves and protective clothing, store in a sealed container, dispose of as a hazardous waste.

Carbon tetrachloride: Virtually unavailable for anything other than industrial applications. If you find it as its own product, or included in the ingredient list of any of the products you have on site, dispose of it as a hazardous waste.

Radon: As noted above, risk of radon poisoning is small, unless the gas becomes contained in a closed space where people spend a lot of time.

Radon gas seeps into buildings mostly through cracks in cinder-block and foundation floors. It can also enter around loose-fitting drainage pipes, through sump pumps, tap water and building materials, and due to pressure differentials between the building foundation and surrounding soil.

Researchers still don't understand radon's migration patterns. Construction and soil characteristics are factors, but radon concentrations can vary enormously among neighboring buildings over similar soil, or among seemingly identical buildings.

So the first step in radon control is to test your buildings with a radon detector. These are generally available for about $20.00 through hardware, grocery, and other retail outlets. If you can't find them there, call your regional EPA office for a referral to other sources.

According to the EPA, less than 4 picocuries per liter (pCi/L) is not considered a harmful level; 4-20 pCi/L indicates a need to correct the situation within a year; a 20-200 pCi/L level means correct things within a few months; more than 200 pCi/L means get to this within weeks. If this isn't feasible, increase ventilation to the space, or relocate temporarily while the problem is resolved.

Each building is unique, so a radon reduction technique that works in one may not work in another. If you find high levels in one or more of your structures, it would be wise to have an inspection done to pinpoint radon sources and make your reduction program more effective. Again, your regional EPA office will be able to give you directions to inspection services, or you can look them up under "Radon Testing" in the Yellow Pages.

After you find high levels of radon and isolate sources, use one or all of the following four ways to cut radon levels. In each case, make sure the one(s) you choose become a permanent part of your building.

1. House ventilation — this is a temporary solution; basically, opening windows and doors, which works in good weather, not in bad, and not over the long term. Use it until you set up a permanent solution.

2. Soil-gas suction — a preventative system that reduces air pressure under the foundation to a level less than that in the house. This draws the radon away into the air.

3. Sealing — basically, sealing cracks and around plumbing and electrical openings in walls and foundations to prevent the entry of radon. If the gas is still present after using this mode, refer to (1).

4. Pressure control — higher pressure in the soil than in the building's substructure can draw in radon gas. This method increases substructure pressure, and in effect, pushes the gas away.

Fuels: Keep tanks and containers sealed unless they are in use, and then use in well-ventilated areas, taking care not to spill. Most fuel handling will be done by authorized personnel, such as your oil or gas company driver or representative. If you are pumping gas for vehicles on site, equip your pump nozzle with a collar that prevents fumes from escaping into the air when you fill. Any spilling of fuel on water must be reported if it causes a "sheen, slick, sludge, or emulsion" on the surface or below. Check with your local EPA or Coast Guard hazardous materials hotline to make sure. If you spill fuel on land, reportable quantity varies. Again, check with your fire department or local hazardous materials authority.

For barbecues and picnics where you will be using charcoal briquets, avoid lighting fluid. It burns dirty, like diesel fuel, and should not be used. Instead, start the fire with paper under the charcoal in a metal or tinfoil charcoal chimney. Or use an electric starter, a gas grill, charcoal fire-starting gel, paraffin sticks or treated wood chips.

Caustics, corrosives, and reactives: Avoid using them if possible. Otherwise, purchase only as much as you plan to use, use it all up in a well-ventilated area, protecting yourself with industrial-grade neoprene gloves and other appropriate clothing. Check the MSDS, HMIS label or other guide for safety precautions. Dispose of the excess or the empty container as hazardous waste.

NEVER pour toxics down the drain. They damage sanitary sewage and septic treatment systems, and ruin sludge for use as fertilizer.

Vehicle and machinery lubricants, fluids, and degreasers: These are necessary to run the machinery on which our lives depend. The main caution here is, don't spill them. Store them in sealed containers, use them in ventilated areas, and dispose of them properly. Most lubricants can be recycled, and your municipal or county solid waste management department can direct you to recyclers.

Pesticides: Don't use these unnecessarily. They are dangerous, mutagenic poisons. Most insect problems can be solved by using integrated pest management to recreate the natural system of "checks and balances." On plants, for example, introduce insect predators such as ladybugs and preying mantes or use one of the safe citrus or soap solution products now on the market. For slugs in garden beds, plant sacrificial flora such as marigolds, repellent buds of garlic and onion, or drown them in bowls of beer. Indoors, remove or seal up food and other items that attract insects; find and fill holes they use to enter buildings; put screens on doors and windows; remove their nests from buildings and activity areas.

Use your ingenuity to control the insects, rather than calling an exterminator. For more advice, call:

National Coalition Against the Misuse of Pesticides
(202) 543-5450

or

Bio Integral Resource Center
(405) 524-2567

Pesticides should only be used as a last resort, for example, in case of structural infestation by carpenter ants or termites, or garden orchard infestation by predatory, debilitating insects.

Warning: No pesticide label explains its potency against each type of insect, what minimum quantity it takes to get the job done, nor how often to re-apply it. Thus, people routinely overuse these poisons, foul living areas, and contaminate plants, utensils, and foods. A further danger is pesticides that are washed or leached from fields into wells and waterways, killing fish and contaminating drinking water.

At the very least, keep records of when you use pesticides, and of what you have in stock.

Herbicides: As with pesticides, don't use these unnecessarily; they are dangerous, mutagenic poisons. Most weed and plant problems can be solved by other means. Dig them out, rototill them under, prune or chop back fast-growing plants. As a last resort, in the case of blackberry and other invasive vine plants, for example, chop them back to the roots, then brush an herbicide, full strength, on the end of the exposed root. This effective method is slower, but it minimizes use of the poison.

When you do use a poison, select one with a short effective life, such as 3-6 weeks. Ask your nursery or agricultural extension agent for advice.

Again, the herbicide problem is the same as the pesticide problem, noted above. Refer to the warning above about pesticides for more information on herbicides.

Wear protective clothing and gloves when handling pesticides and herbicides. Store the toxics in sealed containers and dispose of them as hazardous waste.

Oil-based and metallic inks, dyes, paints, solvents, and coatings: Avoid using them if possible. If not, purchase only as much as you plan to use, use it all up in a well-ventilated area, and dispose of it as a hazardous waste.

Solvents and thinners (mineral spirits) can often be reused by filtering them through paper coffee filters, doubled-up cheesecloth, or other fine mesh screens.

Wherever possible, eliminate oil- and lead-based paints, toxic dyes, inks and coatings, and substitute water-based products instead. For example, latex enamels can be thinned with water, shellac can be thinned with alcohol, and woods can be finished with linseed oil, lemon oil, and bees wax. Also, find out how to make dyes and tints from local forest and farm products — red from strawberries, yellow/orange from tomatoes or dandelion blooms, brown from bark — and how to get clay from local earth.

Dishwashing and other detergents: Ask your supplier about the ingredients in the detergent you use, and find substitutes if you are using products that contain phosphates or arsenic. Among the new products to try are dish detergents from such companies as Mountain Fresh Products, Bi-O-Kleen, and Life Tree.

Household degreasers, solvents, and cleaners: To clean most surfaces, white vinegar, baking soda, lemon juice, and even Coca Cola work with a little "elbow grease." Coke is great for chrome. A number of more powerful products are available, too, such as Clean Green and citrus-based cleaners.

Medical wastes: Package scalpels, needles, and other sharp items in impervious containers, and cap and tape them before disposal. Flush fluids down the sanitary sewer; contact your health district about sterilization and disposal requirements for infectious medical wastes, and about whether non-infectious materials can be thrown out with regular garbage. Generally, the districts require health care providers to autoclave or disinfect dressings before disposal, or hand them over to a certified medical waste contractor for treatment and disposal. Check with your sewer district about disposing of pharmaceuticals. Some will permit flushing them down the sanitary sewer, some require other methods.

Laws, Information, and Governing Agencies

The remainder of this Appendix lists the various laws pertaining to hazardous materials, and the agencies to contact for more information. Because each city, county, region, and state has its own name for hazardous materials laws, the generic subjects are listed in these sections. For the federal level, laws are cited by name.

Hazardous Waste Information and Governing Agencies

Law, Requirement, Code, and Areas Covered	Information or Enforcement Agency
Level: Local/Regional	
1. Requirements and standards for handling hazardous, "special," and "hard to handle" materials and wastes.	City, town, or county health or solid waste management department
2. Handling procedures for hazmats and hazwastes.	City, town, or county health or solid waste management department
3. Disposal procedures for hazardous wastes.	City, town, or county health or solid waste management department
4. Operating rules and disposal fees for transfer stations, landfills, and other disposal sites.	City, town, or county health or solid waste management department
5. Codes on sewage systems, septic tanks, cesspools, seepage pits, grease traps, etc.	City, town, or county water or health department
6. Conditional use permits for hazardous materials use and disposal.	City, town, or county health or solid waste management department
7. Codes and standards for manufacture, storage, on-site transport and use of hazardous materials, and requirements to inform emergency response personnel about them.	Local fire marshal and health department
8. Comprehensive emergency response plan.	City, town, or county health and solid waste management departments, and fire marshal
9. Nonpoint source pollution in watersheds.	County or state health or environment department, or regional water quality authority
10. Underground tanks.	Local or county health and solid waste management department, or fire marshal

Hazardous Waste Information and Governing Agencies (continued)

Law, Requirement, Code, and Areas Covered	Information or Enforcement Agency
Level: State	
11. Creation of regional authorities to set and enforce water and air quality standards.	State legislature and state environmental department
12. Exceptions to hazmat and hazwaste standards and procedures, i.e., low-quantity generators such as households, or generators that recycle them, such as farms that churn wastes into the ground.	State environmental department, and EPA
13. Hazardous materials control act, which may impose taxes to help fund hazwaste prevention and cleanup efforts, establish liable attorney general parties and cleanup procedures, exempt certain parties from regulation (see 12 above), set up a ranking system for hazwaste sites, prohibit industrial property from sale unless hazwastes are cleaned up, etc.	State environmental department, revenue department, and attorney general
14. Solid waste management code, which creates a statewide program for solid waste handling, recovery and recycling, and requires local governments to develop long-term action plans for state approval.	State environmental department
15. Hazardous waste disposal act, sets state priorities for hazwaste management, usually: (1) waste and source reduction, (2) recycling, (3) physical, chemical, and biological treatment, (4) incineration, (5) solidification and stabilization and finally, (6) landfilling. Also, sets zoning guidelines for hazwaste facility siting, defines hazardous waste terms, requires public and media participation in management plan development (see 14 above).	State environmental department
16. Minimum standards for solid waste handling, which covers all waste handling facilities and procedures, permitting requirements and hazardous materials processing restrictions.	State environmental and labor and industries departments
17. Dangerous waste regulations, which list, define, and set testing criteria for hazardous materials and wastes, for generators of the materials and wastes, and for treatment, storage, and disposal facilities. May also cover disposal site permitting, and rules for recordkeeping, waste manifesting, facility operations and closure, and groundwater protection.	State environmental and natural resources departments

Hazardous Waste Information and Governing Agencies (continued)

Law, Requirement, Code, and Areas Covered

Information or Enforcement Agency

Level: State (continued)

18. Safety and health administration and emergency response regulations. These are generally OSHA Hazardous Waste Operations and Emergency Response Safety Regulations (see below).

State labor and industries department

19. Solid waste planning guidelines, which may amend and/or supplement other ordinances (see 4–7).

State environmental department

20. Water pollution control act, which sets state water quality standards, creates a state discharge permit system, and prohibits pollution of state waters.

State environmental or natural resources department, or water quality authority

21. Waste discharge permit program for any operation that discharges into ground and surface waters, and municipal sewerage systems. Excludes point source discharges into navigable waters that are regulated by the National Pollutant Discharge Elimination System (NPDES) permit program (also see above, and 35 below).

State environmental and natural resources or water quality department

22. Water quality standards for surface and ground waters — defines types of and quality and testing standards for surface and ground waters.

State environmental and wildlife departments and regional water quality authority

23. Water pollution control law — prohibits discharge of polluting matter into any state water.

State environmental department

24. Worker right to know law — requires employers to provide workers with information on all hazardous materials present and used in the workplace, and with safety training and protective gear for handling those materials.

State environmental or labor and industries department

25. Environmental liability law — enables individual citizens and organized parties to bring legal action for redress of grievances arising from environmental pollution, and to recover cleanup costs from potentially responsible parties (PRPs).

State attorney general's office and environmental department

26. Hazardous substance information law — requires a state office to provide public information and education about household hazardous wastes in cooperation with local governments.

State environmental or health department

Hazardous Waste Information and Governing Agencies (continued)

Law, Requirement, Code, and Areas Covered

Information or Enforcement Agency

Level: State (continued)

27. Oil recycling law — requires business selling more than a certain quantity of oil, i.e. 500 gallons, to post signs indicating the location of the nearest oil recycling site, and requires a state office to provide public oil recycling education.

State environmental department

28. Solid fuel burning device standards — restricts the types of fuels that can be burned in a wood stove or fireplace to reduce releases of toxic fumes.

State environmental department, county fire marshal

Level: Federal

29. National Environmental Protection Act (NEPA, P.L. 91-190 of 1970). Created the Environmental Impact Statement (EIS), and is our basic national charter for protecting the United States environment.

Environmental Protection Agency (EPA) Hotline: (202) 260-5053. Also, call your regional EPA office.

30. Resource Conservation and Recovery Act (RCRA). Promotes environmental health and natural resources conservation. Key components include:

EPA and other federal departments and agencies: (800) 424-9346

Subtitle C — requires EPA to create and update lists of hazardous materials and wastes; rules for transporting, handling, storing, using, treating, and disposing of them; definitions of users and generators.

Subtitle D — requires EPA to identify specific state and local responsibilities for solid waste planning and management; authorizes federal financial assistance for these activities.

Subtitle I — defines underground storage tanks and lists those that are exempt; specifies owner and EPA responsibilities; authorizes and requires tank inspection, monitoring, reporting, and testing programs.

Hazardous & Solid Waste Amendments (HSWA) to RCRA — prohibits land disposal of dioxins and other toxic materials; sets landfill design standards and requires corrective action for waste facility toxic releases.

31. Comprehensive Environmental Response, Compensation and Liability Act of 1980 (CERCLA or "Superfund"). Now includes

EPA and other federal departments and agencies: (800) 424-9346

Hazardous Waste Information and Governing Agencies (continued)

Law, Requirement, Code, and Areas Covered	Information or Enforcement Agency

Level: Federal (continued)

the Superfund Amendments Reauthorization Act (SARA) of 1986. Key SARA titles are:

I — authorizes federal government to respond to the release of contaminants into the environment.

II — establishes Superfund.

III — pre-empts state corporate dissolution statutes, so former shareholders may be held liable for hazardous waste cleanup costs if they received corporate assets at the time of dissolution. Requires governments at all levels, and users and generators of "extremely hazardous substances" to prepare emergency plans and report accidental release of the substances. Requires facilities that handle and use hazardous materials to post Material Safety Data Sheets (MSDS). Provides for citizen lawsuits, demonstration and R&D programs.

IV — federal policies on pollution insurance, and radon research program.

V — funding elements, including a trust fund for leaking underground storage tanks.

32. Toxics Substances Control Act (TSCA, P.L. 94-496 of 1976) — gives EPA authority to regulate manufacture of toxic chemicals not regulated under the Federal Insecticides, Fungicide and Rodenticide Act (FIFRA, P.L. 92-516 of 1972). Requires EPA to review each new chemical now marketed for potential danger to environmental health. Requires manufacturers of new chemicals to provide EPA with premanufacturing notice (PMN). EPA makes determination, and can prohibit chemical from reaching market.

    EPA: (202) 554-1404

33. Hazardous Materials Transportation Act (HMTA, P.L. 93-633, 1975) — governs all transport of hazardous materials and wastes, including classification, description, packaging, marking and condition of transport. Quantities of consumer

    Department of Transportation (DOT): (202) 366-4488

Hazardous Waste Information and Governing Agencies (continued)

Law, Requirement, Code, and Areas Covered	Information or Enforcement Agency

Level: Federal (continued)

commodities under five gallons (such as paint and paint-related products) are exempt. HMTA also covers specific reporting requirements for discharge or spill during transport.

34. Occupational Safety & Health Act (OSHA, 1970) has specific regulations for protection of employees engaged in hazardous waste and emergency response operations.

OSHA, U.S. Department of Labor: (202) 219-8151

35. Federal Water Pollution Control Act (WPCA, P.L. 92-500, 1972) — expands the role of federal government in water pollution control and construction funding for waste water treatment works. Requires uniform, technology-based effluent standards (National Standards of Performance) coupled with a National Pollutant Discharge Elimination System (NPDES) permit system for all point source of waste water discharges.

EPA/NPDES Hotline: (703) 821-4823

36. The Clean Water Act — amendments to WPCA (1977 and 1988). Regulates pretreatment for existing and new sources of pollution; sets and requires implementation of national water pretreatment standards for all governments, publicly-owned waste water treatment works (POTW), and industries.

The Act also includes: The National Oil and Hazardous Substances Pollution Contingency Plan, which defines organization, operation, and communication elements needed for evaluation and response to environmental incidents.

Call your EPA Regional Office (see Appendix E)

37. Safe Drinking Water Act (P.L. 93- 523, 1974) — covers pollutants in and sets standards for drinking water, controls on underground injection of hazardous waste, and provisions for citizen suits and civil penalties.

EPA Hotline: (800) 426-2791

38. Clean Air Act (P.L. 84-159, 1955 and amendments through 1991) — policies, planning authorities, standards and enforcement for all matters relating to air quality in the U.S. and air affecting the U.S. Covers such areas as visibility, ozone (CFCs and VOCs), waste combustion, noise, acid rain, and trading pollution credits.

EPA: (919) 541-2777

Hazardous Waste Information and Governing Agencies (continued)

Law, Requirement, Code, and Areas Covered	Information or Enforcement Agency

Level: Federal (continued)

39. Endangered Species Act (P.L. 93-205, 1973 and amendments through 1988) — sets forth standards and actions to protect endangered plant and animal species and their habitats.

U.S. Department of Interior

40. Marine Mammal Protection Act (P.L. 92-522, 1972 and 1988 amendments) — extends endangered species protections (see 39) to plants and creatures of the seas.

National Oceanic and Atmospheric Administration (NOAA) and EPA

41. National Ocean Pollution Planning Act (P.L. 92-573, 1978 and 1988 amendments) — creates a five-year federal monitoring program for ocean, Great Lakes, and estuarine waters.

NOAA

42. Marine Protection, Research and Sanctuaries Act (P.L. 92-532, 1972 and 1988 amendments) — regulates ocean dumping to protect the marine environment.

NOAA

43. Noise Control Act (P.L. 93-205, 1972, and 1978 amendments) — coordinates research and control activities, sets standards and disseminates information on noise that is considered dangerous to the population from vehicles, equipment, machinery, and appliances.

OSHA, U.S. Departments of Labor and Commerce: (202) 219-8151

Appendix B

Green Marketing

The news media and public are always hungry for good news, excitement, and innovation. If you can supply any one of these, you have a green marketing opportunity.

Basically, your company, process, or product qualifies if it is taking some environment-friendly action. If your new product is made with 10% recycled content, put that on the label. If you are running vehicles powered by natural gas, paint it on the side of the truck, or put it on a bumper sticker. If you donate 1% for peace, or a portion of your revenues to a pet environmental cause, such as "Saving the Bay," mention in your ads that you are "a partner in Saving the Bay."

Leverage

You get the most leverage for your expended effort, however, from the free publicity newspapers and magazines can provide. Journalists are wary, however, of publicity-hungry people, so you must have a message that is targeted, newsworthy, and of general interest.

Before contacting the media, you must determine a publicity goal. Do you want to promote a new program, an environmentally-friendly process, the recycling of a formerly wasted package? Do you want to highlight an innovation with far-reaching benefits, or an accomplishment by the company or one or more employees? Possibilities include:

- An employee carpooling program that significantly reduces traffic congestion, air pollution, or gasoline consumption;

- A hazardous materials reduction program that saves money and improves the safety of your workers; or
- Any innovation or invention in energy or water efficiency, reclamation, or other area that has positive impacts on your business, your business district, mall, or surrounding community.

Reporters and editors only cover subjects that are interesting to a broad base of people — their readership or listening or viewing audience. They avoid stories that appeal only to a select group.

Some newsworthy angles include "This is the first time this has been done," "an innovative partnership with the community," "partnership with suppliers and customers," "a new job-skill program," or "an employee-initiated program that any company can do successfully."

Once you decide on your news angle, your next step is to contact the media. Look in your local newspaper for the telephone number of the "Business," "Features," or "Managing Editor." Call the number and ask for the editor's name and confirm the address of the newspaper.

Next, write a brief letter — no more than one page — explaining to the editor why your story is important. Suggest one or two story angles. In the last paragraph, set a time and date that you will call the editor to answer questions and to see if the paper is interested in covering the story, then follow up. For television and radio stations, follow the same procedure, but ask for the name of the Assignment Editor at the station. In both cases, send your letter about two weeks before you want coverage.

The Event

If the media agrees to visit and do a story, be sure to tell people at your company when and where reporters might appear. When they do arrive, make sure you or a designated representative meets them and answers any questions they may have. Keep reporters away from proprietary equipment and restricted areas, but otherwise, avoid suffocating them. Let them do the story their way, interviewing participants and shooting pictures as they need. Get signed releases from those they photograph.

If the story contains a lot of detail, you may ask the reporter if you can review it for facts. Reporters are extremely sensitive about the styles in which they write, and about their own views. Your function is only to guarantee that what they write is true. Present it to them as a win-win situation: their accuracy makes you both look good.

Afterward, watch the newspaper, listen to the radio or watch television stations, as appropriate, for coverage of your event. Be sure to clip articles, tape the radio, or use the VCR to tape the television stories.

More Mileage

Always alert employees, partners, and directors to your company's media coverage. You might also contact your local city and county representatives, including the mayor and your district's state representatives and U.S. Congresspeople about your efforts. Be sure to display any congratulatory letters from these sources for your board, employees, and stockholders to see.

Public recognition raises the company's status in everyone's eyes.

Beyond the Media

Since your employees make your programs happen, they want to know how well they did. Post the story, or show the video. Supply them with a review of their achievements in newsletters, bulletin boards, or E-mail.

Let other members of your industry know about your company's work through the local, regional, and national trade press and trade associations, and your daily journal of commerce.

A Green Marketing Checklist is provided on pages 228–229 for your convenience.

Success Story

REI is committed to environment-friendly business practices. In keeping with this commitment, each REI retail store dedicates space for an "Environmental Center." These centers provide customers with information and learning opportunities relating to environmental issues. Retail stores also organize and fund annual service projects in the communities where they are located. These and REI's many other programs provide excellent green marketing opportunities. REI's programs demonstrate the company's commitment to the environment, so environment-conscious consumers can feel good about purchasing REI products.

Green Marketing Checklist

Advertise your company's "green" message

☐ Present the message in print and broadcast ads.

☐ Paint it on vehicles.

☐ Print it on bumper stickers, t-shirts, hats, jackets, mugs, matchbooks, shelf or table talkers.

☐ Rent space on billboards, or paint on side of buildings.

☐ Print the message on cards, stationery, invoices, receipts, and envelopes.

☐ Record a message on answering machines and other message systems. Slogan ideas include:

    ☐ "Make every item/electron/drop count."

    ☐ "Squeeze that electron!"

    ☐ "Squeeze that water molecule!"

    ☐ "Do the "Five R's: Rethink, Reduce, Reuse, Recycle and get Results."

    ☐ "Use just what you need."

    ☐ "Hello efficiency, goodbye waste."

Public Relations

☐ Make certain you or your public relations person is well-versed on:

    ☐ The environmental issues facing your industry in general, and your company in particular.

    ☐ The impacts your company has on the community and region.

☐ Keep a list of positive things your company does, which it can use in replies to letters and media inquiries: "we use rechargeable batteries"; "our people drive CNG-fueled, low-polluting vehicles"; "our packaging reduction program has cut waste by __-percent, or ___ thousand tons a year."

☐ Sponsor or partner on a "green" event with another business, non-profit organization, or school: beach, road, or lake shore litter cleanup, then, call the news media for coverage.

☐ Give away items to your customers with recycling, energy-saving, water-saving, and other ecological tips on them.

☐ Produce public service ads for local papers about your model environmental practices.

☐ Stage a weekly contest at your company, mall, or business community for environmental improvements, i.e., least total garbage produced, most packaging reduced, hazardous material substitute discovered, etc. Pay bonuses for or award prizes for greatest savings generated to the company.

☐ Network with other businesses in your office park, mall, or block to consolidate recyclable materials output in one location. You will generate a surprisingly large collection, which is attractive to any recycler.

☐ Sponsor an environmental program on public radio or television, donate office equipment to an environmental group, or donate a portion of property as a public gardening plot.

☐ Donate to school environmental programs, non-profit environmental groups, garden clubs, and other organizations that work in partnership with businesses and citizens to improve environmental health.

Green Marketing Checklist (continued)

☐ Work with a youth organization on a community based environmental project, such as plastics recycling, or a hazardous waste or litter clean up day. Alert media to your participation.

Getting Into the News Media

☐ Call the media any time you sponsor an event. Have the facts ready. Give concise answers to reporters.

For stories you want done:

☐ Choose the news angle

☐ Send a one-page letter to the business or features editor of the newspaper, or to the assignment editor at the radio or television station, summarizing your company's accomplishment.

☐ Place a follow-up call within a week.

If the station or newspaper decides to cover your company:

☐ Have the facts handy.

☐ Plan the reporter's route through your company before he or she arrives.

☐ If you agree to meet a reporter, do not treat him or her as your enemy. They are professionals. Offer to help them with any details they may not understand in the story. Offer to review the story for facts. If you don't know a particular answer, tell them you don't know, ask them their deadline, and then tell them you'll get the information to them before deadline.

In-House at Your Company

☐ Encourage employees and staff to report any resource wastes and environmental concerns.

☐ Place efficiency posters, stickers, or balloons where energy, water, and materials are used. Use conservation slogans or messages, change locations to keep up interest. Post in places like bathrooms, employee lounges, cafeterias, and kitchens.

☐ Place articles about conservation and efficiency in company newsletters or on bulletin boards.

☐ Attach resource and efficiency messages to employee paychecks and invoices.

☐ Print fact sheets or brochures about good resource management practices to place in waiting areas.

☐ Have your manager or CEO write a letter to all employees about using company resources more efficiently.

☐ Conduct employee workshops on efficient resource use and management.

☐ Hold staff meetings to communicate your company's conservation philosophy, and progress toward an achievement of efficiency goals.

☐ Reward employees for improved efficiency in resource uses.

☐ Provide your employees with discount coupons to local nurseries and hardware, electrical, and building supply stores for drought-tolerant plants, reusable and durable goods that save materials and reduce waste, and equipment that saves energy and water.

Appendix C

Dealing Successfully with Urban Wildlife

The chapters of this book dealt exclusively with the "built environment" and the landscapes around them: That is, the structures and technologies people create to enhance their lives and work on this planet.

This is carved out of the "natural" environment, subdividing habitats of plants and animals for farms, pastures, housing tracts, and industrial parks. Animals and plants simply work around us. These living things have survived for thousands or millions of years by adapting to changes on this planet. The built environment simply represents another in the long line of changes.

Face to Face

"People take personal offense when an animal invades their territory. They don't want to give them food or share space unless that animal is tamed," explains Guy Hodge, data and information services department director for the Humane Society of the United States (HSUSA), and co-author of the *Pocket Guide to the Humane Control of Wildlife in Cities & Towns.*[1]

Despite the unease with animal "intruders" on our property, however, people are reintroducing native species to areas where they have been dispossessed, relocating others to better habitats, and introducing predatory insects such as ladybugs and praying mantes to control other insect pests.

Today, game wardens are handling wild animals that appear in town with kid gloves. In Denver they catch foxes; in Dallas, herons; in Pennsylvania, black bears. They also catch raccoons, opossums, and beavers. All of them are carefully conducted back to the wilds.

Hodge asserts this may not be the best solution. "There are not many studies on this, but those few showed that over 50% of small animals didn't survive three months after relocation because the new environment was at carrying capacity. They were in town because they had found a niche, and in the wilds, the newcomers were driven off by resident animals, or there was inadequate range. If they weren't killed by a predator or car on the highway, they would wander back and take shelter in another urban situation and start the problem all over again. We consider relocation a course of last resort."

Meanwhile, bird specialists are reintroducing peregrine falcons from Boston and Baltimore to Minneapolis-St. Paul to control populations of pigeons and other "nuisance" birds. The raptors treat high-rise buildings and bridges just like the cliffs they naturally call home. They are teaching us another lesson about the food chain, according to Dr. Lowell Adams of the National Institute for Urban Wildlife in Columbia, Maryland.

"We find peregrines die from eating rats or pigeons poisoned with bait," he laments. "They get hit by cars in these cities, too." Remarks another wildlife biologist, "People in town are unnerved when a falcon swoops down and nails a pigeon right in front of them, and then carries it off. They're not used to life in the wild."

Hodge also cites a vixen (fox) recently discovered raising her litter of kits in Arlington National Cemetery, and pumas wandering northern Virginia. As the environment is studied and people find more and more animals under their noses, the connections of species and habitats are becoming more obvious:

- As U.S. agriculture moved south and west, Midwestern hardwood forests were replaced with plains that coyotes could cross. Now they have moved east from their ranges in the southwest, and have established themselves from New England into the mid-Atlantic states;
- Waterfowl are now appearing to rest and nest at industrial parks throughout the country which landscape with man-made lakes and reflecting pools;
- On the West Coast, gulls and California sea lions gather wherever easy food can be found, from San Francisco's Pier 39 to the Ballard Locks in Seattle;
- Moose regularly find winter eats in the shrubbery of northern towns from Maine to Alaska;
- Eastern black bears are being fed well by Pennsylvania residents and are reappearing in Ohio after a century's absence; and
- Now that big predator cats are largely gone, deer populations are burgeoning in parks and preserves from Long Island to Cleveland and Seattle.

Animal Evolution

Often, more wildlife can be accommodated in a community's open spaces and residents' backyards than in pristine areas, according to Dr. Adams.

How is this possible? People garden and landscape with food bearing plants, leave food out, and their structures and plantings provide numerous nesting opportunities.

A century ago, most birds in the U.S. were migratory. Now, fewer than half are, notes University of Waterloo, Ontario, urban planner Robert Dorney.

The U.S. Fish and Wildlife Service records steep declines in species of field-loving songbirds such as meadowlarks and mourning doves. They have been displaced by pigeons, starlings, and sparrows that are better adapted to nesting in human structures.

In the mid-1980s, University of Maryland research ecologist Vagn Flygler studied grey squirrels in Washington, D.C., and found striking differences from rural squirrels. The urban squirrels' coats showed a variety of colors rarely found in the wild — blacks, whites, ivories, and russets. In the city, more animals lived in a single nest, they were more aggressive, and females waited longer to breed — sometimes up to two years, versus 11 months by their country cousins. Also, the city squirrels suffered from a pox-like disease not found in the country.

University of California, Los Angeles, ecologist Michael Recht discovered that roof rats in the city have significantly larger ranges — 10 to 20 acres, and they are active during the day, as well as at night.

Uneasy Truce

Human myths, fear, and territoriality complicate people's attitudes toward urban wildlife, and may make it impossible for people to live in perfect harmony with animals. In fact, the animals with which people are most uneasy are most often harmless, according to Hodge. "Misinformation is the enemy," he says.

For example, people fear being bit by a rabid wild animal, yet few ever are. Nationwide, out of 4,809 rabies cases reported in 1989, there were only two deaths, according to Dr. Iyorlumum Uhaa of the Centers for Disease Control (CDC) in Atlanta. He credits massive veterinary inoculation programs and a variety of treatments for humans. Barbara Snow of the Fairfax County, Virginia, Department of Animal Control, also credits leash laws.

"We haven't had a dog-bite rabies case here in 30 years, but we have had cases from cats, because they tend to roam and attack small wild animals," she reports. "Your best protection against rabies bites is to not let your cat run loose."

People fear salmonella and tuberculosis from pigeons. Again, human salmonella poisoning results almost exclusively from eating undercooked meat, TB from close contact with TB-infected humans.

Bats eat up to half their weight in insects every night, and, in some countries, are key pollinators for cash crops such as bananas. Yet, people fear them even more than snakes, mice, and rats.[2] They fear that bats will fly into their hair and grab on.

The radar-equipped bat can easily avoid a target as big as the human head, Hodge asserts. But, heads give off heat. Insects like heat. So, bats that want insects may have to swing in close to catch them.

Urban Pets, Rural Enemies

The seminal study of urban attitudes to wildlife was done by Michael O'Donnell and Larry VanDruff in 1982 in metropolitan Syracuse, New York. The report states that, "In a rural environment, labeling an animal as a pest is based on economic considerations. In the urban environment, it depends upon individual experience, attitudes, and aesthetic values. Urbanites without rural backgrounds tended to be more emotionally attached to animals than those with rural backgrounds." Overall, "an animal that is a nuisance to one household may be a joy to watch for another household."

The two researchers found that about a third of suburban households reported problems with wild animals, as opposed to a quarter of urban households. The most common complaints were general nuisance, yard and vegetable garden damage, stealing feeder food, and animals inside the house. Squirrels were the most pesky critters, followed by rabbits, skunks, pigeons, mice, raccoons, moles, and woodchucks.

The more problems people had with a species, the less they liked it and the more they wanted it controlled. Attitudes varied from area to area, depending on where problem-causing animals were distributed. So geography, and specifically, habitat conditions favorable to a species, had more to do with people's perceptions of animals than socioeconomic factors.

It is noteworthy how many people landscape and garden, and then are surprised that animals come there to live and eat.

"There's a good number of people who don't perceive themselves as being part of the ecosystem," shrugs Hodge. The solution to this obtuseness, say he and Dr. Adams, is education.

Adams cautiously cites findings in the National Survey of Hunting, Fishing and Wildlife-Associated Recreation as evidence that awareness may be improving. The survey is sponsored every five years by the U.S. Fish and Wildlife Service and U.S. Bureau of the Census.

"There's some question of whether there's an actual increase in interest, or we are just measuring it better," Adams tempers. "But the 1980 survey was the first one that included questions dealing with non-game species and wildlife near peoples' homes. In 1985, half of the 80 million people surveyed said they take some interest in animals —feeding, photography, and activities such as tree and shrub-planting to enhance property for animals."

Another indication of public interest is all the media and school programs now devoted to the environment. Complaints and inquiry calls to officials are another. The HSUSA's humane wildlife control book helps people learn to coexist with animals rather than eliminate them.

Here and there, wildlife departments across the country are coming to rely more on education than violent action. Trapping is becoming a last resort. In at least 30 states, citizens can contribute some of their income taxes to nongame wildlife programs that enhance urban and suburban habitats.

In the field, news is mixed.

- Boulder, Colorado, overrun with hundreds of geese in 1990, found a solution in shipping about 350 of them via special "goose-moving trailers" to the honker-deprived state of Kansas. Fewer than 100 returned by 1991.

- Another Boulder problem, deer that eat gardens and shrubs, may have abated either because there are fewer deer now or people have resigned themselves to having deer in their yards.

- In Los Angeles, packs of coyotes and feral dogs still roam the hills, eating cats and other small animals. The public regards them as a menace.

- In Seattle, Washington, every spring, California sea lions show up for free meals on steelhead passing through the Ballard Locks on their way to spawning grounds in the Cascade Mountains. The sea lions can decimate the run by 60% (a sea lion eats 10% of his average 600 pound weight in fish each day).

  Since the lions are covered by the Marine Mammal Protection Act, wildlife officials trap, tag, and transport them out of the area, hoping that by removing experienced predators, they may buy time for the steelhead run to get through. Though other sea lions show up, in the time it takes them to become efficient, many more fish may be saved.

All these experiences underline just one thing: the best way to coexist with animals is "think like they do," says Guy Hodge. "If we create attractive habitats for them, they will come. If we don't, they won't."

Urban Wildlife Coexistence

When animals damage property, "Our traditional solution has been to kill them," says Guy Hodge. "We wanted to insure sterile environments around our homes and offices. In the right circumstances, anyone can regard any animal as a pest."

If you learn about the habits and habitats of wild animals, however, you will see how easy it is to coexist with them. The key points are listed in the checklist on pages 236–237.

Once you know what attracts an animal to your property, you can control its access. Then, you can set up attractants where you want them, and treat yourself to hours of enjoyable observation.

Wildlife Coexistence Checklist

☐ Think like a wild animal: Most wildlife is territorial. An individual animal remains in an area — its home range — because that site meets its requirements for food and shelter.

☐ If you have a problem with an animal, your first challenge is to identify what attracts it. Animals concentrate in areas where they can be fed or pilfer food, and where they can hide and safely nest. Then you can take corrective action.

To counteract problems with animals that range and scavenge:

☐ Put out your garbage in the morning rather than at night, or anchor the garbage can to a solid object

☐ Set an infrared motion sensor near garbage cans or bird feeders that will switch on a floodlight when a nocturnal intruder approaches. The sudden light will generally frighten away secretive, nighttime animals.

☐ Clear away brush or raise piles of wood or other materials off the ground to eliminate cover and nesting places for small animals.

☐ Set up physical barriers that block an animal's access.

To counteract problems with animals that nest in or want to enter buildings:

a. Make simple repairs to building structures:

☐ Replace or board up broken windows, mend torn screens, tightly fasten floor drains, and patch holes in outer walls.

☐ Block or screen all holes and openings larger than a quarter-inch, with building materials resistant to gnawing or prying, such as galvanized sheet metal, or heavy gauge hardware cloth.

☐ Patch cracks in concrete and masonry with mortar.

b. Make changes outdoors:

☐ To thwart birds attempting to roost on level surfaces, change the angles of those surfaces to 60-degrees where possible so they can't get a foothold. Where that is not possible, attach anything from prickly porcupine wire to Slinky toys along ledges, railings, and rooftops; use weatherproof, synthetic bird netting to cover fruit and vegetable plants, and to block eaves.

☐ In ponds and pools where waterfowl collect, run your pool cleaning unit, or get a solar-powered toy boat, and set its rudder to sail in circles. These items will harmlessly drive the fowl away.

☐ Use repellents. For moles, Hodge suggests stuffing old sweat socks down their burrows. Hang a bag of human hair to keep deer, rabbits, and other wild animals away from ornamental trees and vegetable gardens. Animals associate the human scent with danger. Nylons are also a good repellent.

Wildlife Coexistence Checklist (continued)

☐ To reduce the possibility of bringing animal-borne diseases into your home or business, keep pets on a leash, or otherwise controlled. Warn children away from playing around bat and bird nesting areas, or handling wild animals, even if they look injured. In injury cases, have them notify an adult for action. Also, discourage them from bringing little wild animals home as pets. They grow up to have big teeth and claws, and invariably will bite or scratch, raising fear again.

Development Issues:

☐ Check wetlands status of area;

☐ What streams, plants, animals and insects are native to the area? Can you incorporate them in your development, or enhance them in existing property?

☐ Declare your property a "backyard wildlife refuge." Requirements are simple. Contact your state wildlife department.

Appendix D

Resources

Many government and private organizations provide additional information and publications on the subjects discussed in this book. For your convenience, these resources are listed in this appendix under the appropriate subject headings. The listing here is not an endorsement of these companies by the author or publisher of this book.

Alternative Energy

Information and Research

Backwoods Home
1257 Siskiyou Boulevard, #213
Ashland, OR 97520
(503) 488-2053

Conservation and Renewable Energy Inquiry and Referral Service
P.O. Box 8900
Silver Spring, MD 20907
(800) 523-2929

Cutter Information Corp.
37 Broadway
Arlington, MA 02174
(617) 641-5118

Publishes *Energy Design Update, Demand Side Management Report*, and other environmental newsletters and reports for businesses and utilities.

Home Energy
2124 Kittredge Street, #95
Berkeley, CA 94704
(510) 524-5405

Home Power
P.O. Box 130
Hornbrook, CA 96044-0130
(916) 475-3179

Jade Mountain
P.O. Box 4616
Boulder, CO 80306
(800) 442-1972

Produces a catalog on alternative energy generating, operating, and storage systems.

National Renewable Energy Laboratory
1617 Cole Boulevard
Golden, CO 80401
(303) 231-7303

Real Goods, Inc.
966 Mazzoni Street
Ukiah, CA 95482-3471
(707) 468-9292

Real Goods is a catalog supplier of environment-friendly products and equipment, and publishes the *Alternative Energy Sourcebook*. Real Goods also sells various books focusing on the environment and related issues, i.e., from Al Gore's *Earth In the Balance* to *Toxics A to Z.*

Seventh Generation
Colchester, VT 05446-1672
(800) 456-1197

This company is a catalog supplier of environment-friendly products and equipment. Publishes *Seventh Generation's Field Guide to More than 100 Environmental Groups.*

Architecture, Design, and Development

A Guide to Resource Efficient Building Elements
Center for Resourceful Building Technology
P.O. Box 3866
Missoula, MT 59806
(406) 549-7678

American Institute of Architects
1735 New York Avenue NW
Washington, D.C. 20036
(202) 626-7300

American Society of Interior Designers
608 Massachusetts Avenue, NE
Washington, D.C. 20002
(202) 546-3480

Ballantine Environmental Resources
P.O. Box 23032
Hilton Head Island, SC 29925
(803) 681-6675

The Efficient House Sourcebook
Rocky Mountain Institute
RMI Press
Snowmass, CO 81654-9199

Environmental Building News
RR1, Box 161
Brattleboro, VT 05301
(802) 257-7300

"The Greening of Interior Design" (August 1991, p. 71)
Interior Design magazine
249 West 17th Street
New York, NY 10011

Maho Bay Camps, Inc.
17A East 73rd Street
New York, NY 10021
(212) 472-9453
(800) 392-9004

Small Office Building Handbook: Design for Reducing First Costs & Utility Costs
Van Nostrand Reinhold
New York, NY

Battery Disposal

Contact your state environment or natural resources department.

Bicycle Commuting

Bicycle Federation of America
1818 R Street, NW
Washington, DC 20009

The Bicycle Parking Foundation
P.O. Box 7342
Philadelphia, PA 19101

The League of American Wheelmen
190 W. Ostend Street, #120
Baltimore, MD 21230-3755
(410) 539-3399

Camping

Easy Green
Marty Westerman, author
American Camping Association
(800) 428-2267

Composting

BioCycle
419 State Avenue, 2nd Floor
Emmaus, PA 18049
(215) 967-4135.

Publishes monthly magazine of solid waste management, concentrating on composting.

Composting Toilet Systems
Route 2
Newport, WA 99156-9608
(509) 447-3708

Flower Press
10332 Shaver Road
Kalamazoo, MI 49002
(616) 327-0108

Publishes *Worms Eat My Garbage* by Mary Appelhof.

Let It Rot!
Stu Campbell, author
Story Communications, Inc.
Pownal, VT

Rodale Press
33 East Minor Street
Emmaus, PA 18098
(215) 967-5171

Publishes *Organic Gardening* and other magazines and books on organic gardening. Write or call for catalog.

Solid Waste Composting Council
114 South Pitt Street
Alexandria, VA 22314
(703) 739-2401

Corporate Culture and Motivation

Dinosaur Brains
Albert J. Bernstein, Phd. and Sidney Craft Rozen, authors
John Wiley & Son
New York, NY 10158

Maritz Performance Improvement Company
1375 North Highway Drive
Fenton, MO 63099
(314) 827-4000

Seven Habits of Highly Effective People
Stephen R. Covey, author
Simon & Schuster
New York, NY 10020

Energy

Air Conditioning & Refrigeration Institute
1501 Wilson Boulevard, 6th Floor
Arlington, VA 22209
(703) 524-8800

American Council for an Energy-Efficient Economy (ACE³)
1001 Connecticut Avenue, NW, Suite 801
Washington, DC 20036
(202) 429-8873

Publishes *The Most Energy Efficient Appliances and Oil and Gas Heating Systems.*

Boiler Ratings and Efficiencies
Hydronics Institute
35 Russo Place
P.O. Box 218
Berkeley Heights, NJ 07922
(201) 464-8200

California Energy Commission Building and Appliance Efficiency Office
1516 Ninth Street, MS-25
Sacramento, CA 95814-5512
(916) 324-3383

Call or write to request "Advanced Lighting Design Guidelines."

Consumer Reports
Consumers Union of the U.S., Inc.
101 Truman Avenue
Yonkers, NY 10703

Monthly magazine of product tests, annual books.

Electric Ideas Clearinghouse
809 Legion Way SE, FA-11
Olympia, WA 98504-1211
(206) 586-8588
(800) 872-3568 (Washington only)

GAMA
C/O ETL Testing Laboratories
Route 11
Courtland, NY 13045
(607) 753-6711

Publishes *Consumer's Directory of Certified Efficiency Ratings for Residential Heating and Water Heating Equipment.*

Georgia Tech Research Corp.
Georgia Governor's Office of Energy Resources
270 Washington Street, SW, Room 615
Atlanta, GA 30334
(404) 656-5176

Publishes *O&M Guidebook for Energy Conservation*, April 1989.

Handbook of Energy Audits
Albert Thumann, author
The Fairmount Press, Inc.
Atlanta, GA

Covers HVAC, boilers, and energy and process systems.

Total Energy Management — A Practical Handbook on
Energy Conservation and Management
National Electrical Manufacturers Association
2101 L Street NW
Washington, DC 20037
(202) 457-8400

Washington State Energy Extension Service
914 East Jefferson Street, Suite 300
Seattle, WA 98122
(206) 296-5640

Publishes *Performing Heat Loss Calculations*, *Calculating Your Hot Water Costs*, *Heat Recovery From Refrigeration*, and other leaflets.

Environmental Issues

Context Institute
P.O. Box 11470
Bainbridge Island, WA 98110
(206) 842-0216

Sustainability issues in business and development.

Co-op America
2100 M Street, NW, #403
Washington, D.C. 20037
(202) 872-5307
(800) 424-2667

Membership organization. Produces *Co-op America Quarterly* magazine, covers environmental news, investments, actions, and products.

Earth Care Paper, Inc.
(608) 277-2900

Catalog of recycled papers and paper products.

The Earth Report, Essential Guide to Global Ecological Issues
Edward Goldsmith & Nicholas Hildyard, ed.
Price Stern Sloan, Inc.
Los Angeles, CA 90064

Eco-Choice
P.O. Box 281
Montvale, NJ 07645-0281
Free catalog of conservation and eco-friendly equipment and products.

Eco Source
P.O. Box 1656,
Sebastopol, CA 95473
(800) 274-7040
Free catalog of conservation and eco-friendly equipment and products.

The Environmental Directory
Stewart's Green Line
128 East 28th Avenue
Vancouver, B.C., Canada V5V 3R1
(604) 872-5498
Products, technologies, services, manufacturers, organizations.

The Green Spirit
(800) 942-4383
Free catalog of environmentally protective products by Tallmark.

INFORM
381 Park Avenue South
New York, NY 10016
(212) 689-4040
A nonprofit environmental research and education organization. Acts as an information clearinghouse, and produces pragmatic articles, papers, and books. Call for a catalog.

Island Press
1718 Connecticut Avenue, NW, Suite 300
Washington, D.C. 20009
(202) 232-7933
800-828-1302 (Catalog orders)
Complete catalog of books on environmental issues.

The Nature Company
P.O. Box 188
Florence, KY 41022
Catalog of nature products.

Rocky Mountain Institute
1739 Snowmass Creek Road
Snowmass, CO 81654-9199
(303) 927-3128
Researchers, publishers, and consultants on water and energy resources management.

Taking Sides: Clashing Views on Controversial Environmental Issues
Theodore Goldfarb, author
Dushkin Publishing Group
Guilford, CT

Worldwatch and *State of the World*
Worldwatch Institute
1776 Massachusetts Avenue, NW
Washington, D.C. 20036
(202) 452-1999

Green Marketing

Assessing the Environmental Consumer Market
EPA publication 21P-0003
April 1991

Evaluation of Environmental Marketing Terms in the U.S.
EPA publication 741-R-92-003
February 1993.

EPA publications are available from:

EPA ORD Publications
CERI
26 West Martin Luther King Drive
Cincinnati, OH 45268
(513) 569-7562

Hazardous Waste Management, Minimization, and Prevention

Environmental Hazards Management Institute
10 Newmarket Road
P.O. Box 932
Durham, NH 03824
(603) 868-1496
Publishes *Household Hazardous Waste Wheel*.

EPA Guides to Pollution Prevention — see Appendix H.

Greenpeace Action
1436 U Street NW, Suite 201A
Washington, D.C. 20009
(202) 462-8817
Publishes *Everyone's Guide to Toxics in the Home*.

Hazardous Materials Identification System (HMIS)
American LabelMark / Labelmaster
5724 North Pulaski Road
Chicago, IL 60646-6797

Heating, Ventilation, and Air Conditioning

ASHRAE
1791 Tullie Circle, NE
Atlanta, GA 30329
Standards, codes, and information on HVAC equipment and functions.

Landscape Management and Environmentally Smart Design

American Forests, Global Releaf and
 Cool Communities Programs
1516 P Street, NW
Washington, D.C. 20005
(202) 667-3300
Corporate-sponsored, citizen tree-planting. As of 1993, it has sponsored planting of more than 100 million trees in North America.

Bio-Integral Resource Center
P.O. Box 7414
Berkeley, CA 94794
(510) 524-2567

A non-profit organization geared to the technical side of managing insects, plants, and small vertebrates poison-free. Catalog of books, products, and services available.

National Coalition Against the Misuse of Pesticides
530 Seventh Street, SE
Washington, DC 20003
(202) 543-5450

Regionalization as a Tool for Managing Environmental Resources
EPA book 600/3-89/060

The Taunton Press
63 South Main Street
P.O. Box 5506
Newtown, CT 06740-5506

Publishes *Common Sense Pest Control: Least Toxic Solutions for Your Home, Garden, Pets, and Community* by William Olkowski, Sheila Daar, and Helga Olkowski.

Lighting

**Illuminating Engineering Society
 of North America (IESNA)**
345 East 47th Street
New York, NY 10017
(212) 705-7926

**Lighting Research Center
Rensselaer Polytechnic Institute**
Troy, NY 12180-3590

"Report from the Second International Power Quality ASD Conference 1990," and "Specifier Reports: Electronic Ballasts."

National Lighting Bureau
2101 L Street NW, Suite 300
Washington, DC 20037
(202) 457-8437

Real Goods, Inc.
966 Mazzoni Street
Ukiah, CA 95482-3471
(707) 468-9292

Rocky Mountain Institute
1739 Snowmass Creek Road
Snowmass, CO 81654-9199
(303) 927-3128

Researchers, publishers, and consultants on lighting management

Seventh Generation
Colchester, VT 05446-1672
(800) 456-1197

Motors

Electric Ideas Clearinghouse
809 Legion Way, SE
P.O. Box 43171
Olympia, WA 98504-3171
(800) 872-3568.

Energy Information Administration (EIA)
Department of Energy
1000 Independence Avenue SW
Washington, DC 20585
(202) 252-2363

Produces motor documents.

National Electrical Manufacturers Association
2101 L Street NW
Washington, DC 20037
(202) 457-8400

Filters

System One Oil and Air Filters
P.O. Box 1097
Tulare, CA 93275
(209) 687-1955

Oil

American Petroleum Institute
1220 L Street
Washington, D.C. 20005
(202) 682-8233

Pollution Prevention

INFORM
381 Park Avenue South
New York, NY 10016
(212) 689-4040

The following titles are available from INFORM: *Making Less Garbage: A Planning Guide for Communities*; *Environmental Dividends: Cutting More Chemical Wastes*; *Business Recycling Manual*; and *Paving the Way to Natural Gas Vehicles*.

EPA Mercury Hotline
(800) 424-9346

U.S. EPA Pollution Prevention Information Exchange System (PIES)
PIES Technical Assistance
Science Applications International Corp.
8400 Westpark Drive
McLean, VA 22102
(703) 821-4800

Recycling

See also Waste Reduction.

The Aluminum Association
900 19th NW
Washington, D.C. 20036
(202) 862-5100

American Paper Institute
(212) 340-0650

The Can Manufacturers Institute
1525 Massachusetts Avenue, NW
Washington, D.C. 20036
(202) 232-4677

Dana Duxbury & Associates
16 Haverhill Street
Andover, MA 01810
(508) 470-3044
This organization recycles fluorescent tubes.

Fibre Box Association
2850 Golf Road
Rolling Meadows, IL 60008
(708) 364-9639

The Glass Packaging Institute
1627 K Street NW
Washington, D.C. 20036
(202) 887-4850

National Recycling Coalition, Inc.
1101 30th Street NW, Suite 305
Washington, DC 20007
(202) 625-6409

National Soft Drink Association
1101 16th Street, NW
Washington, D.C. 20036
(202) 463-6732

Resource Recycling
1218 NW 21st Street
Portland, OR 97209
(503) 227-6135

Society of Plastics Industries
1275 K Street, NW
Washington, D.C. 20036
(202) 371-5200

Solid Waste Information Clearinghouse
(800) 677-9424

Provides general solid waste information, and nationwide information referral.

Steel Can Recycling Institute
680 Andersen Drive, Foster Plaza 10
Pittsburgh, PA 15220
(800) 876-7274

Small Business Research and Information

Kessler Exchange
8910 Quartz Avenue
Northridge, CA 91324-9889
(800) 648-7888

A small business membership and research firm that produces regular research newsletters.

Solar

Direct Use of the Sun's Energy
Farrington Daniels, author
Yale University Press
New Haven, CT 06520

Energy Future
Robert Stobaugh and Daniel Yergin, authors
Ballantine
New York, NY 10022

National Climatic Data Center
(704) CLIMATE

Solar Energy Research Institute
(303) 231-1000

Solar Today
American Solar Energy Society
2400 Central, Unit G-1
Boulder, CO 80301
(303) 443-3130

Transportation

Route Management

Caps Logistics Inc.
2700 Cumberland Parkway
Atlanta, GA 30339-3321
(404) 432-9955

General Programming, Inc.
Plaza on the Parkway
15770 North Dallas Parkway, Suite 1100
Dallas, TX 75248
(214) 385-0400

KeyMap and CityMap
Softkey Software Products
4800 North Federal Highway, 3rd Floor, Building D
Boca Raton, FL 33431
(407) 367-0005
Small business and personal transportation route planning.

Planning: Vehicle and Fleet Management and Safety

American Trucking Association
2200 Mill Road
Alexandria, VA 22314
(703) 838-1700

Society of Automotive Engineers (SAE)
400 Commonwealth Drive
Warrendale, PA 15096-0001
(412) 776-4841
SAE develops standards for automotive, naval, aircraft, and aerospace design, manufacture, and management.

Tachygraphs and Trip Monitor Systems

Argo Instruments, Inc.

212 Fort Collier Road	OR	7075 Tranmere Drive, Unit 8
Winchester, VA 22603		Mississauga, Ontario L5S 1M2
(703) 665-0200		Canada
		(416) 612-8387

Detroit Diesel
13400 West Outer Drive
Detroit, MI 48239
(313) 592-5000

Rockwell TripMaster
Rockwell International
2135 West Maple Road
Troy, MI 48084
(800) 874-7329

Waste Reduction

Northeast Maryland Waste Disposal Authority
25 South Charles Street, Suite 2105
Baltimore, MD 21201-3330
Publishes *Commercial Recycling.*

Xerox Documentation Subscription Service
360 North Sepulveda Boulevard
El Segundo, CA 90245
(800) 445-5554
Publishes *Business Guide to Waste Reduction & Recycling,* publication # 720P30-330.

Telephone Book Recycling

Contact your local telephone company, Boy Scout office or Lions Club. In Michigan, contact Ameritech Publishing Inc. of Troy, MI. They shred phone books into animal bedding.

Water Heaters

Elemental Enterprises
P.O. Box 928
Monterey, CA 93942
(408) 394-7077

Publishes *The Water Heater Workbook* by Larry and Suzanne Weingarten.

Metlund Resource Technology
P.O. Box 4006
Costa Mesa, CA 92628
(800) 638-5863

Produces the Water Saver system for domestic hot water.

Water Purification Systems

Ozone Research & Equipment Corp.
3840 North 40th Avenue
Phoenix, AZ 85019
(602) 272-2681

Water Resource Management

American Water Resources Association
5410 Grosvenor Lane, Suite 220
Bethesda, MD 20814-2192

Rocky Mountain Institute
1739 Snowmass Creek Road
Snowmass, Colorado 81654-9199
(303) 927-3128

Wildlife

Institute for Urban Wildlife
10921 Trotting Ridge Way
Columbia, MD 21044
(301) 596-3311

National Audubon Society
950 Third Avenue
New York, NY 10022

National Wildlife Federation
1400 16th Street, NW
Washington, D.C. 20036-2266
(202) 797-6800

Nature Conservancy
1815 North Lynn Street
Arlington, VA 22209

Sierra Club
730 Polk Street
San Francisco, CA 94109

Wilderness Society
900 17th Street, NW
Washington, DC 20006

Xeriscaping

See Landscape Management.

Appendix E

EPA Regional Offices & State Environmental Departments

Region 1
VT, NH, ME, MA, CT, RI
John F. Kennedy Federal Building
Boston, MA 02203
(617) 565-3420

Region 2
NY, NJ, PR (Puerto Rico)
26 Federal Plaza
New York, NY 10278
(212) 264-2657

Region 3
PA, DE, MD, WV, VA
841 Chestnut Street
Philadelphia, PA 19107
(215) 597-9800

Region 4
KY, TN, SC, GA, FL, AL, MS
345 Courtland Street, NE
Atlanta, GA 30365
(404) 347-4727

Region 5
WI, MN, MI, IL, IN, OH
230 South Dearborn Street
Chicago, IL 60604
(312) 353-2000

Region 6
NM, OK, AR, LA, TX
1445 Ross Avenue
Dallas, TX 75202
(214) 655-6444

Region 7
NE, KS, MO, IA
756 Minnesota Avenue
Kansas City, KS 66101
(913) 551-7000

Region 8
MT, ND, SD, WY, UT, CO
999 18th Street
Denver, CO 80202-2405
(303) 293-1603

Region 9
CA, NV, AZ, HI
75 Hawthorne Street
San Francisco, CA 94105
(415) 744-1305

Region 10
AK, WA, OR, ID
1200 Sixth Avenue
Seattle, WA 98101
(206) 553-1200
(800) 424-4EPA (outside Washington)

State Environmental Departments

In many of the states, specific functions are spread among many agencies. The address and telephone numbers listed here are the first places to call for information and referrals.

**Alabama Department of Environmental
Management**
1751 Congressman W.L. Dickinson Drive
Montgomery, AL 36130
(205) 271-7700

**Alaska Department of Environmental
Conservation**
3220 Hospital Drive
P.O. Box O
Juneau, AK 99811-1800
(907) 465-2600

**Arizona Department of Environmental
Quality**
Central Palm Plaza Building
2005 North Central Avenue
Phoenix, AZ 85004
(602) 257-2305

**Arkansas Department of Pollution
Control & Environment**
8001 National Drive
P.O. Box 9583
Little Rock, AR 72219
(501) 562-7444

California Agency of Environmental Affairs
1102 Q Street
Sacramento, CA 95814
(916) 322-9840

**Colorado Office of Health &
Environmental Protection**
Colorado Department of Health
4210 East 11th Avenue
Denver, CO 80220
(303) 331-4600

**Connecticut Department of Environmental
Protection**
State Office Building
165 Capitol Avenue
Hartford, CT 06106
(203) 566-2110 (Commissioner)
(203) 566-3489 (Information/Education)

**Delaware Department of Natural Resources
& Environmental Control**
89 Kings Highway
P.O. Box 1401
Dover, DE 19902
(302) 736-4403

**District of Columbia Environmental
Control Division**
**Department of Consumer & Regulatory
Affairs**
**Housing & Environmental Regulation
Administration**
614 H Street N.W.
Washington, D.C. 20001
(202) 727-7395

**Florida Department of Environmental
Regulation**
2600 Blair Stone Road
Tallahassee, FL 32399-2400
(904) 488-4805

Environmental Protection Division
Georgia Department of Natural Resources
Floyd Towers, East
205 Butler Street, SE
Atlanta, GA 30334
(404) 656-3500

Environmental Health Administration
Hawaii State Department of Health
1250 Punchbowl Street
P.O. Box 3378
Honolulu, HI 96801
(808) 548-4139

Division of Environment
Idaho Department of Health & Welfare
5150 Kendall Street
Boise, ID 83720
(208) 334-5840

Illinois Environmental Protection Agency
2200 Churchill Road
Springfield, IL 62706
(217) 782-3397

Indiana Department of Environmental
Management
105 South Meridian Street
Indianapolis, IN 46225
(217) 232-8162

Iowa Department of Natural Resources
Wallace State Office Building
900 East Grant Avenue
Des Moines, IA 50319-0034
(515) 281-5385

Division of Environment
Kansas Department of Health
& Environment
Landon State Office Building
900 SW Jackson Street
Topeka, KS 66612-1290
(913) 296-1535

Kentucky Natural Resources &
Environmental Protection Cabinet
Capital Plaza Tower, 5th Floor
Frankfort, KY 40601
(502) 564-3350

Louisiana Department of Environmental
Quality
Natural Resources Building
625 North Fourth Street
Baton Rouge, LA 70802
(504) 342-9103

Maryland Department of the Environment
1500 Broening Highway
Baltimore, MD 21224
(301) 631-3084

Maine Department of Environmental
Protection
State House Station 17
Augusta, ME 04333
(207) 289-2811

Massachusetts Environmental
Policy Act Unit
Executive Office of Environmental Affairs
Leverett Saltonstall Building, 20th Floor
100 Cambridge Street
Boston, MA 02202
(617) 727-9800

Michigan Department of Natural Resources
P.O. Box 30028
Lansing, MI 48909
(517) 373-1214
(800) 323-2727 (Business Ombudsman
Hotline)

Minnesota Department of Natural
Resources
DNR Building
500 Lafayette Road
St. Paul, MN 55146
(612) 296-2549 (Commissioner)
(612) 296-3336 (Information)

Mississippi Department of Environmental
Quality
Southport Center
2380 Highway 80 West
P.O. Box 20305
Jackson, MS 39289-1305
(601) 961-5002

Missouri Department of Natural Resources
Jefferson State Office Building
P.O. Box 176
Jefferson City, MO 65102
(314) 751-4810
(800) 334-6946 (Missouri)

Environmental Sciences Division
Montana Department of Health &
Environmental Sciences
Cogswell Bldg.
Helena, MT 59620
(406) 444-3948

Nebraska Department of Environmental
Quality
301 Centennial Mall South, Fourth Floor
P.O. Box 94822
Lincoln, NE 68509-8922
(402) 471-2186

Nevada Department of Conservation
 & Natural Resources
201 South Fall Street
Carson City, NV 89710
(702) 687-4360

New Hampshire Department of
 Environmental Services
Hazen Drive
Concord, NH 03301
(603) 271-3503

Office of the Commissioner
New Jersey Department of
 Environmental Protection
401 East State Street
Trenton, NJ 08625
(609) 292-2885

Environmental Improvement Division
New Mexico Department of
 Health and Environment
1190 Street Francis Road
Santa Fe, NM 87503
(505) 827-2850

New York Department of Environmental
 Conservation
50 Wolf Road
Albany, NY 12233-3500
(518) 457-4500

North Carolina Department of Environment,
 Health & Natural Resources
512 North Salisbury Street
Raleigh, NC 27611-7687
(919) 733-4984

Environmental Health Section
North Dakota State Department of Health &
 Consolidated Laboratories
1200 Missouri Avenue
P.O. Box 5520
Bismarck, ND 58502-5520
(701) 224-2374

Ohio Environmental Protection Agency
1800 WaterMark Drive
P.O. Box 1049
Columbus, OH 43266-0149
(614) 644-2782

Oklahoma State Department of Health
1000 NE Tenth
P.O. Box 53551
Oklahoma City, OK 73152
(405) 271-8056

Oregon Department of Environmental
 Quality
811 SW Sixth Avenue
Portland, OR 97204
(503) 229-5696

Pennsylvania Department of
 Environmental Resources
200 North Third Street
P.O. Box 2063
Harrisburg, PA 17120
(717) 783-8303

Caribbean EPA Field Office
Office 2A
Podiatry Center Building
1413 Gernandes Juncos Avenue
Santurce, Puerto Rico 00909
(809) 729-6920

Rhode Island Department of Environmental
 Management
9 Hayes Street
Providence, RI 02903
(401) 277-2771

South Carolina Department of Health &
 Environmental Control
2600 Bull Street
P.O. Box 11628
Columbia, SC 29201
(803) 734-4880

South Dakota Department of Water &
 Natural Resources
523 East Capitol
Pierre, SD 57501
(605) 773-3151

Tennessee Department of Health
 & Environment
344 Cordell Hull Building
Nashville, TN 37219
(615) 741-3111

Texas Natural Conservation Commission
12124 Park 35 Circle
Austin, TX 78753
(512) 908-1000

Utah Department of Natural Resources
1636 North Temple, West
Salt Lake City, UT 94116-3156
(801) 538-7200

Vermont Environmental Board
58 East State Street
Montpelier, VT 05602
(802) 828-3309

Virginia Secretary of Natural Resources
9th Street Office Building
Richmond, VA 23219
(804) 786-0044

Washington Department of Ecology
St. Martin's College Campus–Lacey
Mail Stop PV-11
Olympia, WA 98504-8711
(206) 459-6000

West Virginia Department of Natural Resources
Charleston, WV 26305
(304) 348-2754

Office of the Secretary Wisconsin Department of Natural Resources
101 South Webster Street
P.O. Box 7921
Madison, WI 53707
(608) 266-2121

Appendix F

Waste Exchanges & Trade Associations

Wastes Exchanges

Alberta Waste Materials Exchange
Alberta Research Council
P.O. Box 8330
Postal Station F
Edmonton, Alberta
Canada T6H 5X2
(403) 450-5408

British Columbia Waste Exchange
2150 Maple Street
Vancouver, BC
Canada V6J 3T3
(604) 731-7222

California Waste Exchange
Toxic Substances Control Program
Alternative Technology Division
Department of Health Services
P.O. Box 942732
Sacramento, CA 94234-7320
(916) 324-1807

Canadian Waste Materials Exchange
ORTECH International
2395 Speakman Drive
Mississauga, Ontario
Canada L5K 1B3
(416) 822-4111 (Ext. 265)
FAX (416) 823-1446

Great Lakes Regional Waste Exchange
400 Ann Street, N.W., Suite 210A
Grand Rapids, MI 49505
(616) 363-3262

Indiana Waste Exchange
Purdue University
School of Civil Engineering
Civil Engineering Building
West Lafayette, IN 47907
(317) 494-5036

Industrial Materials Exchange
172 20th Avenue
Seattle, WA 98122
(206) 296-4633
(206) 296-0188 FAX

Industrial Materials Exchange Service
P.O. Box 19276
Springfield, IL 62794-9276
(217) 782-0450
(217) 524-4193 FAX

Industrial Waste Information Exchange
New Jersey Chamber of Commerce
5 Commerce Street
Newark, NJ 07120
(201) 623-7070

Manitoba Waste Exchange
c/o Biomass Energy Institute, Inc.
1329 Niakwa Road
Winnepeg, Manitoba
Canada R2J 3T4
(204) 257-3891

Montana Industrial Waste Exchange
Montana Chamber of Commerce
P.O. Box 1730
Helena, MT 59624
(406) 442-2405

New Hampshire Waste Exchange
c/o NHRRA
P.O. Box 721
Concord, NH 03301
(603) 224-6996

Northeast Industrial Waste Exchange, Inc.
90 Presidential Plaza, Suite 122
Syracuse, NY 13202
(315) 422-6572
(315) 422-9051 FAX

Ontario Waste Exchange
ORTECH International
2395 Speakman Drive
Mississaugo, Ontario
Canada L5K 1B3
(416) 822-4111 (ext. 512)
(416) 823-1446 FAX

Pacific Materials Exchange
South 3707 Godfrey Boulevard
Spokane, WA 99204
(509) 632-4244

Peel Regional Waste Exchange
Regional Municipality of Peel
10 Peel Center Drive
Brampton, Ontario
Canada L6T 4B9
(416) 791-9400

RENEW
Texas Water Commission
P.O. Box 13087
Austin, TX 78711-3087
(512) 463-7773
(512) 463-8317 FAX

San Francisco Waste Exchange
2524 Benvenue #35
Berkeley, CA 94704
(415) 548-6659

Southeast Waste Exchange
Urban Institute
UNCC Station
Charlotte, NC 28223
(704) 547-2307

Southern Waste Information Exchange
P.O. Box 960
Tallahassee, FL 32302
(904) 644-5516
(800) 441-7949
(904) 574-6704 FAX

Tennessee Waste Exchange
226 Capital Boulevard, Suite 800
Nashville, TN 37202
(615) 256-51541
(615) 256-6726 FAX

Wastelink Division of Tencon, Inc.
140 Wooster Pike
Milford, OH 45150
(513) 248-0012
(513) 248-1094 FAX

Industrial & Trade Associations

Air-Conditioning Contractors of America
1513 16th Street NW
Washington, DC 20036
(202) 483-9370

Air Movement and Control Associations, Inc.
30 West University Drive
Arlington Heights, IL 60004
(708) 394-0150

Air-Conditioning and Refrigeration Institute (ARI)
1501 Wilson Boulevard, #600
Arlington, VA 22209
(703) 524-8800

Air-Conditioning and Refrigeration
  Wholesalers Association
6360 NE Fifth Way, #202
Ft. Lauderdale, FL 33309
(305) 771-1000

American Boilers Manufacturers Association
950 North Glebe Road, Suite 160
Arlington, VA 22203
(703) 522-7350

American Consulting Engineers Council
1015 Fifteenth Street, NW, Suite 802
Washington, DC 20005
(202) 347-7474

American Gas Association (AGA)
1515 Wilson Boulevard
Arlington, VA 22209
(703) 841-8400

American Institute of Plant Architects
1735 New York Avenue, NW
Washington, DC 20006
(202) 626-7300

American Institute of Plant Engineers (AIPE)
8180 Corporate Park Drive, Suite 305
Cincinnati, OH 45242
(513) 489-2473

ASHRAE
1791 Tullie Circle, NE
Atlanta, GA 30329
(404) 636-8400

National Association of Photographic
Manufacturers, Inc.
550 Mamaroneck Avenue
Harrison, NY 10528
(914) 698-7603

United Engineers Center
345 East 47th Street
New York, NY 10017
(212) 705-7000

The following organizations are located
at the United Engineers Center:

American Society of Mechanical Engineers

American Institute of Chemical Engineers

American Institute of Mining, Metallurgical,
  and Petroleum Engineers

American Society of Civil Engineers

Institute of Electrical and Electronics
  Engineers (IEEE)

Association of Energy Engineers
4025 Pleasantdale Road, Suite 340
Atlanta, GA 30340
(404) 447-5083

Building Owners and Managers Association
  International
1201 New York Avenue, NW
Washington, DC 20005
(202) 408-2662

Commerical Refrigerator Manufacturers
  Association
1101 Connecticut Avenue, Suite 700
Washington, DC 20036
(202) 857-1145

Edison Electric Institute
Conservation and Energy
  Management Division
701 Pennsylvania Avenue, NW
Washington, DC 20036
(202) 508-5000

Electricity Consumers Resource Council
1333 H Street, NW
Washington, DC 20036
(202) 682-1390

Illuminating Engineering Society of North
  America (IESNA)
120 Wall Street, 17th Floor
New York, NY 10005
(212) 705-7000

Cogeneration and Independent Power
  Coalition of Ameria
2715 M Street, NW
Washington, DC 20036
(202) 965-1134

National Association of Energy Service
  Companies
1200 G Street, NW
Washington, DC 20036
(202) 347-0419

National Association of Plumbing-Heating-
  Cooling Contractors
P.O. Box 6808
Falls Church, VA 22040
(703) 237-8100

National Electrical Contractors Association
  (NECA)
7315 Wisconsin Avenue
Bethesda, MD 20814
(301) 657-3110

National Electrical Manufacturers
  Association (NEMA)
2101 L Street, NW., Suite 300
Washington, DC 20037
(202) 457-8400

Sheet Metal and Air-Conditioning Contractors' National Association, Inc. (SMACNA)
8907 Georgetown Pike
McLean, VA 22102
(703) 759-6852

Solar Energy Industries Association, Inc.
777 North Capitol Street, NE., Suite 805
Washington, DC 20002
(202) 408-0660

Appendix G

Waste Minimization Programs

Alabama

**Hazardous Material Management and
  Resources Recovery Program**
University of Alabama
P.O. Box 6373
Tuscaloosa, AL 35487-6373
(205) 348-8401

Alaska

Waste Reduction Assistance Program
Alaska Health Project
431 West Seventh Avenue, Suite 101
Anchorage, AK 99501
(907) 276-2864

Arkansas

**Arkansas Industrial Development
  Commission**
One State Capitol Mall
Little Rock, AR 72201
(501) 371-1370

California

Alternative Technology Division
Toxic Substances Control Program
**California State Department of
  Health Services**
714/744 P Street
Sacramento, CA 94234-7320
(916) 324-1807

Connecticut

**Connecticut Hazardous Waste
  Management Service**
900 Asylum Avenue, Suite 360
Hartford, CT 06105
(203) 244-2007

Florida

Waste Reduction Assistance Program
**Florida Department of Environmental
  Regulation**
2600 Blair Stone Road
Tallahassee, FL 32399-2400
(904) 488-0300

Georgia

Environmental Health and Safety Division
Hazardous Waste Technical
  Assistance Program
Georgia Institute of Technology
Georgia Technical Research Institute
O'Keefe Building, Room 027
Atlanta, GA 30332
(404)894-3806

Environmental Protection Division
Georgia Department of Natural Resources
Floyd Towers East, Suite 1154
205 Butler Street
Atlanta, GA 30334
(404) 656-2833

Illinois

Illinois Department of Energy and
  Natural Resources
1 East Hazelwood Drive
Champaign, IL 61820
(217) 333-8940

Illinois Waste Elimination Research Center
Pritzker Department of Environmental
  Engineering
Illinois Institute of Technology
Alumni Building, Room 102
3200 South Federal Street
Chicago, IL 60616
(313) 567-3535

Indiana

Environmental Management and
  Education Program
Purdue University
Young Graduate House, Room 120
West Lafayette, IN 47907
(317) 494-5036

Office of Technical Assistance
Indiana Department of Environmental
  Management
105 South Meridan Street
P.O. Box 6015
Indianapolis, IN 46206-6015
(317) 232-8172

Iowa

Center for Industrial Research and Service
205 Engineering Annex
Iowa State University
Ames, IA 50011
(515) 294-3420

Air Quality and Solid Waste
  Protection Bureau
Iowa Department of Natural Resources
Wallace State Office Building
900 East Grand Avenue
Des Moines, IA 50319-0034
(515) 281-8690

Kansas

Bureau of Waste Management
Kansas Department of Health
  and Environment
Forbesfield, Building 730
Topeka, KS 66620
(913) 269-1607

Kentucky

Division of Waste Management
Kentucky Natural Resources and
  Environmental Protection Cabinet
18 Reilly Road
Frankfort, KY 40601
(502) 564-6716

Louisiana

Office of Solid and Hazardous Waste
P.O. Box 44307
Baton Rouge, LA 70804
(504) 342-1354

Maryland

Maryland Hazardous Waste Facilities
  Siting Board
60 West Street, Suite 200 A
Annapolis, MD 21401
(301) 974-3432

Maryland Environmental Service
2020 Industrial Drive
Annapolis, MD 21401
(301) 269-3291
(800) 492-9188 (Maryland)

Massachusetts

Office of Technical Assistance
Massachusetts Executive Office of
  Environmental Affairs
100 Cambridge Street, Room 1094
Boston, MA 02202
(617) 727-3260

Source Reduction Program
Massachusetts Department of
  Environmental Protection
1 Winter Street
Boston, MA 02108
(617) 292-5982

Michigan

Resource Recovery Section
Michigan Department of Natural Resources
P.O. Box 30028
Lansing, MI 48909
(517) 373-0540

Minnesota

Solid and Hazardous Waste Division
Minnesota Pollution Control Agency
520 Lafayette Road
St. Paul, MN 55155
(612) 296-6300

Minnesota Technical Assistance Program
1313 5th Street SE, Suite 207
Minneapolis, MN 55414
(617) 627-4555
(800) 247-0015 (Minnesota)

Missouri

Missouri State Environmental Improvement
  and Energy Resources Agency
P.O. Box 744
Jefferson City, MO 65102
(314) 751-4919

New Hampshire

Waste Management Division
New Hampshire Department of
  Environmental Sciences
6 Hazen Drive
Concord, NH 03301-6509
(603) 271-2901

New Jersey

New Jersey Hazardous Waste Facilities
  Siting Commission
28 West State Street, Room 614
Trenton, NJ 08608
(609) 292-1459
(609) 292-1026

Hazardous Waste Advisement Program
Bureau of Regulation and Classification
New Jersey Department of Environmental
  Protection
401 East State Street
Trenton, NJ 08625
(609) 292-8341

Risk Reduction Unit
Office of Science and Research
New Jersey Department of Environmental
  Protection
401 East State Street
Trenton, NJ 08625
(609) 984-6070

New York

New York State Environmental Facilities
  Corporation
50 Wolf Road
Albany, NY 12205
(518) 457-3273

North Carolina

Pollution Prevention Pays Program
North Carolina Department of Natural
  Resources and Community Development
512 North Salisbury Street
P.O. Box 27687
Raleigh, NC 27611
(919) 733-7015

Governor's Waste Management Board
325 North Salisbury Street
Raleigh, NC 27611
(919) 733-9020

Technical Assistance Unit
Solid and Hazardous Waste
 Management Branch
North Carolina Department of
 Human Resources
306 North Wilmington Street
P.O. Box 2091
Raleigh, NC 27602
(919) 733-2178

Ohio

Ohio Environmental Protection Agency
1800 WaterMark Drive
P.O. Box 1049
Columbus, OH 43266-1049
(614) 481-7200

Ohio Technology Transfer Organization
65 East State Street, Suite 200
Columbus, OH 43266-0330
(614) 466-4286

Oregon

Oregon Hazardous Waste Reduction
 Program
Department of Environmental Quality
811 Southwest Sixth Avenue
Portland, OR 97204
(503) 229-5913

Pennsylvania

Pennsylvania Technical Assistance Program
501 F. Orvis Keller Building
University Park, PA 16802
(814) 865-0427

Center of Hazardous Material Research
320 William Pitt Way
Pittsburgh, PA 15238
(412) 826-5320

Bureau of Waste Management
Pennsylvania Department of Environmental
 Resources
Fulton Building
P.O. Box 2063
Harrisburg, PA 17120
(717) 787-6239

Rhode Island

Office of Environmental Coordination
Rhode Island Department of Environmental
 Management
83 Park Street
Providence, RI 02903
(401) 277-3434
(800) 253-2674 (Rhode island)

Ocean State Cleanup and Recycling
 Program
Rhode Island Department of Environmental
 Management
9 Hayes Street
Providence, RI 02908-5003
(401) 277-3434
(800) 253-2674 (Rhode Island)

Center for Environmental Studies
Brown University
135 Angell Street
P.O. Box 1943
Providence, RI 02912
(401) 863-3449

Tennessee

Center for Industrial Services
University of Tennessee
102 Alumni Hall
Knoxville, TN 37996
(615) 974-2456

Virginia

Office of Policy and Planning
Virginia Department of Waste Management
11th Floor, Monroe Building
101 North 14th Street
Richmond, VA 23219
(804) 225-2667

Washington

Hazardous Waste Section
Washington Department of Ecology
Mail Stop PV-11
Olympia, WA 98504-8711
(206) 459-6322

Wisconsin

**Bureau of Solid Waste Management
Wisconsin Department of Natural
Resources**
101 South Webster Street
P.O. Box 7921
Madison, WI 53707
(608) 267-3763

Wyoming

Solid Waste Management Program
Wyoming Department of Environmental
Quality
Herchler Building, 4th Floor, West Wing
122 West 25th Street
Cheyenne, WY 82002

Appendix H

Pollution Prevention Guides

The *Guides to Pollution Prevention* manuals describe waste minimization options for specific industries. This is a continuing series which currently includes the titles listed below. Titles may be ordered from:

EPA ORD Publications
CERI
26 West Martin Luther King Drive
Cincinnati, OH 45268
(513) 569-7562

Guides to Pollution Prevention: Paint Manufacturing Industry
EPA/625/7-90/005

Guides to Pollution Prevention: The Pesticide Formulating Industry
EPA/625/7-90/004

Guides to Pollution Prevention: The Commercial Printing Industry
EPA/625/7-90/008

Guides to Pollution Prevention: The Fabricated Metal Industry
EPA/625/7-90/006

Guides to Pollution Prevention For Selected Hospital Waste Streams
EPA/ 625/7-90/009

Guides to Pollution Prevention: Research and Educational Institutions
EPA/625/7-90/010

Guides to Pollution Prevention: The Printed Circuit Board Manufacturing Industry
EPA/625/7-90/007

Guides to Pollution Prevention: The Pharmaceutical Industry
EPA/625/7-91/017

Guides to Pollution Prevention: The Fiberglass Reinforced and Composite Plastic Industry
EPA/625/7-91/014

Guides to Pollution Prevention: The Automotive Repair Industry
EPA/ 625/7-91/013

Guides to Pollution Prevention: The Automotive Refinishing Industry
EPA/ 625/7-91/016

Guides to Pollution Prevention: The Marine Repair Industry
EPA/625/7-91/015

U.S. EPA Pollution Prevention Information Clearing House (PPIC): *Electronic Information Exchange System (EIES)-User Guide, Version 1.1.*
EPA/600/9-89/086

Footnotes

Chapter 1

1. SARA Title III provisions of CER-CLA ("Superfund" law).

2. Id.

3. Real Goods, Inc., Ukiah, CA.

4. Federal Noise Pollution Control Act.

Chapter 2

1. Retail prices compared at Office Depot, Home Club, and Costco. February 1993.

Chapter 3

1. Environmental Protection Agency, 1992.

2. Yard Waste Composting Program, Seattle, WA, 1992.

3. Environmental Protection Agency, 1990.

4. *Resource Recycling* (April 1991).

5. Arthur D. Little, Inc., Cambridge, MA

6. *Waste Characterization Study* (Portland, Oregon: Metropolitan Service District, 1987); *Waste Stream Composition Study Final Report 1988–89*, Volume I (Seattle, Washington); *Best Management Practices Analysis for Solid Waste* (Washington State Department of Ecology); *Proposed Comprehensive Solid Waste Management Plan* (Washington: King County Solid Waste Division, 1989).

Chapter 4

1. *Resource Recycling* (April, 1991).

Chapter 5

1. 40 CFR.

2. Deborah Hitchcock Lessup, *Guide to State Environmental Programs* (Washington, DC: Bureau of National Affairs, 1990).

Chapter 6

1. CERCLA Section 107.

2. RICO Title 18 USC 1961–68 and Title 18 USC 1956.

Chapter 7

1. Ross and Baruzzini. Energy Conservation Applied to Office Lighting, Federal Energy Administration. April, 1975

2. *The Alternative Energy Sourcebook*, 7th edition (Ukiah, CA: Real Goods).

Chapter 8

1. Rocky Mountain Institute, Snowmass, Colorado

2. Pequod Associates, Boston, MA

3. Phoenix, Arizona, and Los Angeles, California Water Districts

Chapter 9

1. *Statistical Abstract of U.S. 1992.*

2. CH2M Hill, Inc., *Snohomish County, Washington, Comprehensive Moderate Risk Waste Plan* (1992).

3. Shoup and Wilson, "Employer Paid Parking: The Influence of Parking Prices on Travel Demand" *Proceedings of the Commuter Parking Symposium* (Seattle, Washington, 1990. p.10).

4. Environmental Protection Agency, *EPA's Gas Mileage Guide.*

5. Jim Bald & Associates, trucking consultants, Houston, TX.

Appendix C

1. Guy Hodge, *Pocket Guide to The Humane Control of Wildlife in Cities & Towns.* The Humane Society of the United States, Washington, DC: 1990.

2. O'Donnell, Michael A. and Larry W. VanDruff, "Wildlife Conflicts in an Urban Area: Occurrence of Problems and Human Attitudes Toward Wildlife." State University of New York, College of Environmental Science and Forestry, Syracuse, NY: 1982.

Glossary

ASHRAE. American Society of Heating, Refrigeration, and Air Conditioning Engineers.

ASHRAE 90-75. ASHRAE standard for energy conservation in new building design.

Activated carbon. A form of carbon capable of absorbing odors and vapors.

Air changes. Expression of ventilation rate in terms of room or building volume. Usually air changes/hour.

Ambient. Surrounding (i.e., ambient temperature is the temperature in the surrounding space).

Ballast. A device used in a starting circuit for fluorescent and other types of gaseous discharge lamps. It limits the current drawn by the lamp.

Blow down. The discharge of water from a boiler or cooling tower sump that contains a high proportion of total dissolved solids.

Bobiology. The study of indoor diseases.

Boiler. The part of a generator in which water is converted into steam or hot water and which usually consists of metal shells and tubes.

British thermal unit (Btu). The basic unit used in most energy calculations. One Btu of energy is needed to heat one pound of water one degree Fahrenheit. One Btu equals 246 calories, and is equivalent to the energy released in a flaring kitchen match.

Building load. Expressed as heating load or cooling load, as explained below.

Heating load is the rate of heat loss from the building at steady state conditions when the indoor and outdoor temperatures are at their selected design levels (design criteria). The heating load always include ventilation loss and heat gain credits for lights and people.

Cooling load is the rate of heat gain to the building at a steady state condition when indoor and outdoor temperatures are at their selected design levels, solar gain is at its maximum for the building configuration and orientation, and heat gains due to infiltration, ventilation, lights, and people are present.

Coefficient of Performance (COP). Ratio of the tons of refrigeration produced to energy required to operate equipment.

Cogeneration. The use of the same fuel source to produce electricity and useful heat energy at the same time.

Cold Deck. The portion of the duct in an air conditioning system containing the chilled water coil or DX coil. Generally parallel with a bypass deck or hot deck.

Condensate. Water obtained by changing the state of water vapor (steam or moisture in the air) from a gas to a liquid usually by cooling.

Conductance, Thermal. A measure of the thermal conducting properties of a composite structure such as wall, roof, etc., including the insulating boundary layers of air.

Conductivity, Thermal. A measure of the thermal conducting properties of a single material expressed in units of Btu per inch thickness, sq. ft., hour, or degree F temperature difference.

Cooling Tower. Device that cools water directly by evaporation used in conjunction with an air conditioner.

Damper. A device used to vary the volume of air passing through an air outlet, inlet, or duct.

Degree Day (DD). The difference between the median temperature of any day and 65°F when the median temperature is higher or lower than 65° F. Degree day information is available from your local utility, the National Weather Service, and the National Oceanographic and Atmospheric Administration (NOAA).

Demand. The maximum rate at which power is used over a given time period; usually 15 or 30 minutes. Electricity cannot be stored in large quantities, so the utility must have the capacity to supply the combined electrical requirements of all its customers plus spare capacity for emergency loads at all times.

Demand Charge. The amount an individual customer pays a utility for keeping enough capacity in reserve to meet that customer's maximum demand.

Duel-Duct. A heating/cooling system in which heated and cooled air is ducted separately to the conditioned spaces and then mixed as needed in terminal mixing boxes.

Economizer. A mechanism that fits on an air conditioner and that uses outside air for cooling whenever possible rather than using mechanical cooling.

Economizer Cycle. A method of operating a ventilation system to reduce refrigeration load. Whenever the outdoor air conditions are more favorable (lower heat content) than return air conditions, outdoor air quantity is increased.

EER. Energy efficiency ratio at standard conditions.

Energy Management System (EMS). A central control system capable of controlling individual pieces of equipment by using a computer program.

Energy Utilization Index (EUI). A reference which expresses the total energy used by a building in a given period (month, year) per square foot of space.

Enthalpy. The total heat content of the air. For the purpose of air condition, enthalpy is the total heat content of air above a datum usually in units of Btu/lb. It is the sum of sensible and latent heat and ignores internal energy changes due to pressure change.

Envelope. All external surfaces which are subject to climatic impact. For example, walls, windows, roof, and floor.

Evaporative Cooler. A mechanism that uses the evaporation of water to cool the air.

Evaporator. A heat exchanger which adds latent heat to a liquid changing it to a gaseous state (in a refrigeration system, it is the component which absorbs heat).

Exfiltration. The outward flow of air through gaps, cracks, and other leaks in the building's structure.

Fixture. The socket-equipped accessory that holds a lamp.

Fluorescent Lamp. A lamp that produces light by passing electricity through mercury vapor which causes the fluorescent coating on the tube to glow.

Foot Candle. Unit of measure for lighting. One foot candle is the amount of light falling on a surface one foot from a standard sperm whale oil candle.

Hardness. The quantity of calcium and magnesium in water.

Hot Deck. The portion of the duct in a heating system containing the hot water coil.

HSPF. Heating seasonal performance factor. An efficiency measurement for heat pumps.

HVAC. Heating, ventilation, and air conditioning.

Incandescent Lamp. A lamp that produces light by electrically heating a filament so that it glows.

Infiltration. The uncontrolled inward air leakage through cracks and joints in any building element and around windows and doors of a building, caused by the pressure effects of wind and/or the effect of differences in the indoor and outdoor air density.

Kilowatt (kW). One thousand watts. See watts.

Kilowatt-Hour (kWh). The use of one kilowatt of electricity for one hour.

Lamp. The bulb, tube, or envelope that contains light-producing elements.

Life-cycle Cost. The cost of the equipment over its entire life including operating and maintenance costs.

Load. See Demand.

Load Shedding. The turning off of electrical loads to limit peak electrical demand.

Lumen. A measure of the intensity of the light source.

Luminaire. Light fixture designed to produce a specific effect.

Make-up. Water supplied to a system to replace that lost by blow down, leakage, evaporation, etc.

Mixing box. A box containing dampers in the hot and cold air stream, mixing the two and delivering the air to a space at a specified temperature.

Passive System. An energy conservation measure that requires no energy input but acts as a barrier to slow down heat gain or heat loss.

Peak Demand. The greatest rate of electrical consumption a user will have during the billing period.

Peak Load. The maximum electrical or thermal load reached during an arbitrary period of time.

Photovoltaic Cells. A solar cell in which electrons flow from one layer of material to the other when exposed to light, thereby converting sunlight directly to electricity.

Piggyback Operation. Arrangement of chilled water generation equipment whereby exhaust steam from a steam turbine driven centrifugal chiller is used as the heat source for an absorption chiller.

Recovered Energy. Energy utilization which would otherwise be wasted from an energy utilization system.

Scale. A chalky surface crust made of deposited calcium carbonate ($CaCO_3$), magnesium carbonate ($MgCO_3$), and silica dioxide (SiO_2) that settle out of passing water.

SEER. Seasonal energy efficiency ratio.

Therm. 100,000 Btus.

Thermograph. An infrared scan that can be used to detect heat loss due to poor insulation.

U-Value. The overall heat transmission coefficient, or quantity of heat in Btu transmitted per hour through one square foot of a building section (wall, roof, window, floor, etc,) for each degree F of temperature difference between the air on the warm side and the air on the cold side of the building section (inverse of "R" value).

Vapor Barrier. A moisture impervious layer designed to prevent moisture migration.

Variable Air Volume (VAV). A method used to cool or heat a space or zone by varying the amount of air delivered to that space as conditions change (versus holding the amount of air constant and changing the air temperature).

Waste Heat Recovery. The process that captures waste heat from equipment and puts it to useful work.

Watt (W). Basic unit of electricity, a current of one ampere under a pressure of one volt.

Zone. A space or group of spaces within a building with heating or cooling requirements sufficiently similar so that comfort conditions can be maintained throughout by a single controlling device.

Index

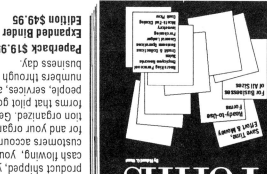

The book that will change for good the way you think about creating a business plan

We were impressed! In our world of business publishing, we sometimes see the unusual. A book so well conceived and well written that it gives you, the reader, value in ways you would never expect.

The Successful Business Plan by Rhonda M. Abrams is a great example. Frankly, it has more of what it now takes to get your idea or venture on paper in a way that sells.

More on marketing & sales. Better probe of target market. Tighter industry analysis. A new look at operations. Even a sharp new way for you to get the P&L and balance sheets on paper quickly. So simple it will bring sighs of relief. And there is something else here to make those reading your final plan sit up and take notice. It's the *look* of your plan. The logic of it. The way it presents itself clearly. *The Successful Business Plan* is strong on giving you ways to show your venture at its best. Proven ways. A needed aspect of business planning we found lacking until this book was written.

– The Editors at Oasis Press, PSI Research

1 You get expert help

Listen in, as Rhonda M. Abrams interviews some of today's most savvy business owners and venture financiers, Bill Walsh, Nancy E. Glaser, Eugene Kleiner and a dozen more. 159 tips from 15 experts reveal what works in business plans, and what doesn't. What they have to say will help you write a plan that responds best to what people are looking for now. Straight talk by those who read what business plans — about what plans should be in yours.

2 Worksheets to make it easy

You know plenty about your business. What you want now is your facts gathered and organized. You want the plan done fast, but complete, decisive. Get all that with the 72 worksheets in this book. They are packed with questions designed to draw out and organize all you know about your venture. The questions cover all the 11 critical plan sections and are clear on what to get and where it goes. You'll have the whole picture in front of you before you start writing the plan itself. No time wasted.

3 Sample plan to guide you

The sample plan is so interesting, you might forget it's there to guide you. Written in the actual wording and style used in plans already read and accepted. Section by section, the sample shows you how to put your facts & figures into a readable, compelling story. The story of your idea. To help present your idea there are specifics on retail, manufacturing, service and in-house corporate plans.

4 Get the binder and software combination

Give your plan a finished look. Use the 12 tabbed dividers to organize your final presentation. Also, a two-page planning checklist keeps you from missing even the smallest point. Extra copies of 28 critical worksheets give you plenty of room to work out details. IBM software includes a text editor program and prompts, as well as information taken directly from the book.

About Rhonda M. Abrams

Educated at both UCLA and Harvard, Ms. Abrams heads a west coast management consulting firm. Her common-sense approach to problem solving has made *The Successful Business Plan* as readable as it is powerful. Over 11 months of writing, two hundred hours of interviews, and Ms. Abrams' years of experience make this new book the best for business planning today.

Her comment? "No other work propels you as far forward in your enterprise as building your plan of action."

Proven tools and ideas to expand your business.

Marketing & Public Relations

Power Marketing
Book

A wealth of basic, how-to marketing information that easily takes a new or experienced business owner through the essentials of marketing and sales strategies, customer database marketing, advertising, public relations, budgeting, and follow-up marketing systems. Written in a friendly tone by a marketing educator, the book features worksheets with step-by-step instructions, a glossary of marketing terms, and a sample marketing plan.

How To Develop & Market Creative Business Ideas
Book

Step-by-step manual guides the inventor through all stages of new product development. Discusses patenting your invention, trademarks, copyrights, and how to construct your prototype. Gives information on financing, distribution, test marketing, and finding licensees. Plus, lists many useful sources for prototype resources, trade shows, funding, and more.

Marketing Your Products and Services Successfully
Book

Helps small businesses understand marketing concepts, then plan and follow through with the actions that will result in increased sales. Covers all aspects from identifying the target market, through market research, establishing pricing, creating a marketing plan, evaluating media alternatives, to launching a campaign. Discusses customer maintenance techniques and international marketing.

Customer Profile and Retrieval (CPR)
Software for IBM-PC & compatibles

Stores details of past activities plus future reminders on customers, clients, contacts, vendors, and employees, then gives instant access to that information when needed. "Tickler" fields keep reminders of dates for recontacts. "Type" fields categorize names for sorting as the user defines. "Other data" fields store information such as purchase and credit history, telephone call records, or interests.

Has massive storage capabilities. Holds up to 255 lines of comments for each name, plus unlimited time and date stamped notes. Features perpetual calendar, and automatic telephone dialing. Built-in word processing and merge gives the ability to pull in the information already keyed into the fields into form or individual letters. Prints mail labels, rotary file cards, and phone directories. *Requires a hard disk, 640K RAM and 80 column display. (Autodial feature requires modem.)*

Cost-Effective Market Analysis
Book

Workbook explains how a small business can conduct its own market research. Shows how to set objectives, determine which techniques to use, create a schedule, and then monitor expenses. Encompasses primary research (trade shows, telephone interviews, mail surveys), plus secondary research (using available information in print).

International Business

Export Now
Book

Prepares a business to enter the export market. Clearly explains the basics, then articulates specific requirements for export licensing, preparation of documents, payment methods, packaging, and shipping. Includes advice on evaluating foreign representatives, planning international marketing strategies, and discovering official U.S. policy for various countries and regions. Lists sources.

EXECARDS®
International Communication Cards

EXECARDS offer unique cards you can send to businesspeople of many nationalities to help build and maintain lasting relationships. One distinguished EXECARD choice is a richly textured and embossed white card of substantial quality that expresses thank you in thirteen languages: Japanese, Russian, French, Chinese, Arabic, German, Swahili, Italian, Polish, Spanish, Hebrew, and Swedish, as well as English. Another handsome option is an ivory card with thank you embossed in Russian and English. To each, you can add a personal note or order a custom printed message. *Please call for more information.*

Now – Find Out How Your Business Can Profit By Being Environmentally Aware

The Business Environmental Handbook
Book

Save your business while you are saving the planet. Here's your chance to learn about the hundreds of ways any business can help secure its future by starting to conserve resources now. This book reveals little-understood but simple techniques for recycling, precycling, and conservation that can save your business money now, and help preserve resources. Also gives tips on "green marketing" to customers.

Give yourself & your business every chance to succeed. Order the business tools you need today. Call 800-228-2275.

RR 3 06 3

Unique cards get you noticed. Books & software save you time.

Business Communications

Proposal Development: How to Respond and Win the Bid
Book
Orchestrates a successful proposal from preliminary planning to clinching the deal. Shows by explanation and example how to: determine what to include; create text, illustrations, tables, exhibits, and appendices; how to format (using either traditional methods or desktop publishing); meet the special requirements of government proposals; set up and follow a schedule.

Write Your Own Business Contracts
Book
Explains the "do's"and "don'ts" of contract writing so any person in business can do the preparatory work in drafting contracts before hiring an attorney for final review. Gives a working knowledge of the various types of business agreements, plus tips on how to prepare for the unexpected.

Complete Book of Business Forms
Book
Over 200 reproducible forms for all types of business needs: personnel, employment, finance, production flow, operations, sales, marketing, order entry, and general administration. Time-saving, uniform, coordinated way to record and locate important business information.

EXECARDS®
Communication Tools
EXECARDS, business-to-business message cards, are an effective vehicle for maintaining personal contacts in this era of rushed, highly-technical communications. A card takes only seconds and a few cents to send, but can memorably tell customers, clients, prospects, or co-workers that their relationship is valued. Many styles and messages to choose from for thanking, acknowledging, inviting, reminding, prospecting, following up, etc. Please call for complete catalog.

PlanningTools™
Paper pads, 3-hole punched
Handsome PlanningTools help organize thoughts and record notes, actions, plans, and deadlines, so important information and responsibilities do not get lost or forgotten. Specific PlanningTools organize different needs, such as Calendar Notes, Progress/Activity Record, Project Plan/Record, Week's Priority Planner, Make-A-Month Calendar, and Milestone Chart. Please call for catalog.

Customer Profile & Retrieval (CPR)
Software for IBM-PC & compatibles

Easy computer database management program streamlines the process of communicating with clients, customers, vendors, contacts, and employees. While talking to your contact on the phone (or at any time), all notes of past activities and conversations can be viewed instantly, and new notes can be added at that time. Please see description under "Marketing & Public Relations" section on previous page.

Business Relocation

Company Relocation Handbook: Making the Right Move
Book
Comprehensive guide to moving a business. Begins with defining objectives for moving and evaluating whether relocating will actually solve more problems than it creates. Worksheets compare prospective locations, using rating scales for physical plant, equipment, personnel, and geographic considerations. Sets up a schedule for dealing with logistics.

Retirement Planning

Retirement & Estate Planning Handbook
Book
Do-it-yourself workbook for setting up a retirement plan that can easily be maintained and followed. Covers establishing net worth, retirement goals, budgets, and a plan for asset acquisition, preservation, and growth. Discusses realistic expectations for Social Security, Medicare, and health care alternatives. Features special sections for business owners.

Mail Order

Mail Order Legal Guide
Book

For companies that use the mail to market their products or services, as well as for mail order businesses, this book clarifies complex regulations so penalties can be avoided. Gives state-by-state legal requirements, plus information on Federal Trade Commission guidelines and rules covering delivery dates, advertising, sales taxes, unfair trade practices, and consumer protection.

Need it tomorrow? In most cases that's possible if you order before noon, PST. Just give us a call at 800-228-2275.

RR 3 06 3

Step-by-step techniques for generating more profit.

Financial Management

Financial Management Techniques for Small Business
Book and software for IBM

Clearly reveals the essential ingredients of sound financial management in detail. By monitoring trends in your financial activities, you will be able to uncover potential problems before they become crises. You'll understand why you can be making a profit and still not have the cash to meet expenses, and you'll learn the steps to change your business' cash behavior to get more return for your effort. Software makes your business' financial picture graphically clear, and lets you look at "what if" scenarios.

Risk Analysis: How to Reduce Insurance Costs
Book

Straightforward advice on shopping for insurance, understanding types of coverage, comparing proposals and premium rates. Worksheets help identify and weigh the risks a particular business is likely to face, then determine if any of those might be safely self-insured or eliminated. Request for proposal form helps businesses avoid over-paying for protection.

Debt Collection: Strategies for the Small Business
Book

Practical tips on how to turn receivables into cash. Worksheets and checklists help businesses establish credit policies, track accounts, and flag when it is necessary to bring in a collection agency, attorney, or go to court. This book advises how to deal with disputes, negotiate settlements, win in small claims court, and collect on judgments. Gives examples of telephone collection techniques and collection letters.

Negotiating the Purchase or Sale of a Business
Book

Prepares a business buyer or seller for negotiations that will achieve win-win results. Shows how to determine the real worth of a business, including intangible assets such as "goodwill." Over 36 checklists and worksheets on topics such as tax impact on buyers and sellers, escrow checklist, cash flow projections, evaluating potential buyers, financing options, and many others.

Business Owner's Guide to Accounting & Bookkeeping
Book

Makes understanding the economics of business simple. Explains the basic accounting principles that relate to any business. Step-by-step instructions for generating accounting statements and interpreting them, spotting errors, and recognizing warning signs. Discusses how banks and other creditors view financial statements.

Controlling Your Company's Freight Costs
Book

Shows how to increase company profits by trimming freight costs. Provides tips for comparing alternative methods and shippers, then negotiating contracts to receive the most favorable discounts. Tells how to package shipments for safe transport. Discusses freight insurance and dealing with claims for loss or damage. Appendices include directory of U.S. ports, shipper's guide, and sample bill of lading.

Accounting Software Analysis
Book

Presents successful step-by-step procedure for choosing the most appropriate software to handle the accounting for your business. Evaluation forms and worksheets create a custom software "shopping list" to match against features of various products, so facts, not sales hype, can determine the best fit for your company.

Financial Templates
Software for IBM-PC & Macintosh

Calculates and graphs many business "what-if" scenarios and financial reports. Forty financial templates such as income statements, cash flow, and balance sheet comparisons, break-even analyses, product contribution comparisons, market share, net present value, sales model, pro formas, loan payment projections, etc. Requires 512K RAM hard disk or two floppy drives, plus Lotus 1-2-3 or compatible spreadsheet program.

Get business tips from over 157 seasoned experts.

Business Formation and Planning

The Successful Business Plan: Secrets & Strategies
Book and optional kit

Start-to-finish guide to creating a successful business plan. Includes tips from venture capitalists, bankers, and successful CEOs. Features worksheets for ease in planning and budgeting with the Abrams Method of Flow-Through Financials. Gives a sample business plan, plus specialized help for retailers, service companies, manufacturers, and in-house corporate plans. Also tells how to find funding sources.

Starting and Operating a Business in... series
Book available for each state in the United States, plus District of Columbia

One-stop resource to current federal and state laws and regulations that affect businesses. Clear "human language" explanations of complex issues, plus samples of government forms, and sources for additional help or information. Helps seasoned business owners keep up with changing legislation, and guides new entrepreneurs step-by-step to start and run the business. Includes many checklists and worksheets to organize ideas, create action plans, and project financial scenarios.

Starting and Operating a Business: U.S. Edition
Set of eleven binders

The complete encyclopedia of how to do business in the U.S. Describes laws and regulations for each state, plus Washington, D.C., as well as the federal government. Includes lists of sources of help, plus post cards for requesting materials from government agencies. This set is valuable for businesses with locations or marketing activities in several states, plus franchisors, attorneys, and other consultants.

The Essential Corporation Handbook
Book

This comprehensive reference for small business corporations in all 50 states and Washington, D.C. explains the legal requirements for maintaining a corporation in good standing. Features many sample corporate documents which are annotated by the author to show what to look for and what to look out for. Tells how to avoid personal liability as an officer, director, or shareholder.

Surviving and Prospering in a Business Partnership
Book

From evaluation of potential partners, through the drafting of agreements, to day-to-day management of working relationships, this book helps avoid classic partnership catastrophes. Discusses how to set up the partnership to reduce the financial and emotional consequences of unanticipated disputes, dishonesty, divorce, disability, or death of a partner.

California Corporation Formation Package and Minute Book
Book and software for IBM & Mac

Provides forms required for incorporating and maintaining closely held corporations, including: articles of incorporation; bylaws; stock certificates, stock transfer record sheets; bill of sale agreement; minutes form; plus many others. Addresses questions on fees, timing, notices, regulations, election of directors and other critical factors. Software has minutes, bylaws, and articles of incorporation already for you to edit and customize (using your own word processor).

Franchise Bible: A Comprehensive Guide
Book

Complete guide to franchising for prospective franchisees or for business owners considering franchising their business. Includes actual sample documents, such as a complete offering circular, plus worksheets for evaluating franchise companies, locations, and organizing information before seeing an attorney. This book is helpful for lawyers as well as their clients.

Home Business Made Easy
Book

Thinking of starting a business at home? This book is the easiest road to starting a home business. Shows you how to select and start a home business that fits your interests, lifestyle, and pocketbook. Walks you through 153 different businesses you could operate from home full or part time. Author David Hanania has boiled the process down to simple steps so you can get started now to realize your dreams.

The Small Business Expert
Software for IBM-PC & compatibles

Generates comprehensive custom checklist of the state and federal laws and regulations based on your type and size of business. Allows comparison of doing business in each of the 50 states. Built-in worksheets create outlines for personnel policies, marketing feasibility studies, and a business plan draft. Requires 256K RAM and hard disk.

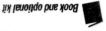

Related Resources

Gain the power of increased knowledge — Oasis is your source.

Acquiring Outside Capital

Financing Your Small Business
Book

Essential techniques to successfully identify, approach, attract, and manage sources of financing. Shows how to gain the full benefits of debt financing while minimizing its risks. Outlines all types of financing and walks you step by step through the process, from evaluating short-term credit options, through negotiating a long-term loan, to deciding whether to go public.

The Loan Package
Book

Preparatory package for a business loan proposal. Worksheets help analyze cash needs and articulate business focus. Includes sample forms for balance sheets, income statements, projections, and budget reports. Screening sheets rank potential lenders to shorten the time involved in getting the loan.

The Successful Business Plan: Secrets & Strategies
Book and software for IBM-PC

Now you can find out what venture capitalists and bankers really want to see before they will fund a company. This book gives you their personal tips and insights. The Abrams Method of Flow-Through Financials breaks down the chore into easy to manage steps, so you can end up with a fundable proposal. Requires a hard drive.

Financial Templates
Software for IBM-PC & Macintosh

Software speeds business calculations including those in PSI's workbooks, *The Loan Package*, *Venture Capital Proposal Package*, *Negotiating the Purchase or Sale of a Business*, *The Successful Business Plan: Secrets & Strategies*. Includes 40 financial templates including various projections, ratios, histories, amortizations, and cash flows. *Requires Lotus 1-2-3, Microsoft Excel 2.0 or higher*

Business Planning System
Software for IBM-PC

Complete your business plan quickly and easily using this StandAlone program. Enjoy the flexibility of writing segments of the plan as you collect the information or as time allows. Examples of wording are included. Questions lead you through the development process.

Managing Employees

A Company Policy and Personnel Workbook
Book

Saves costly consultant or staff hours in creating company personnel policies. Provides model policies on topics such as employee safety, leave of absence, flextime, smoking, substance abuse, sexual harassment, performance improvement, grievance procedure. For each subject, practical and legal ramifications are explained, then a choice of alternate policies presented.

A Company Policy and Personnel Workbook
Software for IBM-PC & Macintosh

The policies in *A Company Policy and Personnel Workbook* are on disk so the company's name, specific information, and any desired changes or rewrites can be incorporated using your own word processor to tailor the model policies to suit your company's specific needs before printing out a complete manual for distribution to employees. *Requires a word processor and hard disk and floppy drive.*

Managing People: A Practical Guide
Book

Focuses on developing the art of working with people to maximize the productivity and satisfaction of both manager and employees. Discussions, exercises, and self-tests boost skills in communicating, delegating, motivating, developing teams, goal-setting, adapting to change, and coping with stress.

Safety Law Compliance Manual for California Businesses
Book
Plus optional binder for your company's safety program

Now every California employer must have an Injury and Illness Prevention Program that meets the specific requirements of Senate Bill 198. Already, thousands of citations have been issued to companies who did not comply with all seven components of the complicated new law. Avoid fines by using this guide to set up a program that will meet Cal/OSHA standards. Includes forms. **Also available — Company Injury and Illness Prevention Program Binder —** Pre-organized and ready-to-use with forms, tabs, logs and sample documents. Saves your company time, work, and worry.

People Investment
Book

Written for the business owner or manager who is not a personnel specialist. Explains what you must know to make your hiring decisions pay off for everyone. Learn more about the Americans With Disabilities Act (ADA), Medical and Family Leave, and more.

BOOKS FROM THE OASIS PRESS® Please check the edition (binder or paperback) of your choice

TITLE	BINDER	PAPERBACK	QUANTITY COST
Accounting Software Analysis	☐ $39.95		
The Business Environmental Handbook		☐ $19.95	
Business Owner's Guide to Accounting & Bookkeeping		☐ $19.95	
California Corporation Formation Package and Minute Book	☐ $39.95	☐ $29.95	
A Company Policy and Personnel Workbook	☐ $49.95	☐ $29.95	
Company Relocation Handbook	☐ $49.95	☐ $19.95	
Complete Book of Business Forms	☐ $49.95	☐ $19.95	
Controlling Your Company's Freight Costs	☐ $39.95		
Cost-Effective Market Analysis	☐ $39.95		
Debt Collection: Strategies for the Small Business	☐ $39.95	☐ $17.95	
The Essential Corporation Handbook		☐ $19.95	
Export Now	☐ $39.95	☐ $19.95	
Financial Management Techniques For Small Business	☐ $39.95	☐ $19.95	
Financing Your Small Business		☐ $19.95	
Franchise Bible: A Comprehensive Guide	☐ $49.95	☐ $19.95	
Home Business Made Easy		☐ $19.95	
How to Develop & Market Creative Business Ideas		☐ $14.95	
The Loan Package	☐ $39.95		
Mail Order Legal Guide	☐ $45.00	☐ $29.95	
Managing People: A Practical Guide	☐ $49.95	☐ $19.95	
Marketing Your Products and Services Successfully	☐ $39.95	☐ $18.95	
Negotiating the Purchase or Sale of a Business	☐ $39.95	☐ $18.95	
People Investment	☐ $39.95	☐ $19.95	
Power Marketing for Small Business	☐ $39.95	☐ $19.95	
Proposal Development: How to Respond and Win the Bid (HARDBACK BOOK)	☐ $39.95	☐ $19.95	
Retirement & Estate Planning Handbook	☐ $49.95	☐ $19.95	
Risk Analysis: How To Reduce Insurance Costs	☐ $39.95	☐ $18.95	
Safety Law Compliance Manual for California Businesses		☐ $24.95	
Company Illness & Injury Prevention Program Binder (OR GET KIT WITH BOOK AND BINDER $49.95)	☐ $34.95	☐ $49.95	BOOK & BINDER KIT
Starting and Operating A Business in... BOOK INCLUDES FEDERAL SECTION PLUS ONE STATE SECTION —	☐ $29.95	☐ $21.95	
PLEASE SPECIFY WHICH STATE(S) YOU WANT:			
STATE SECTION ONLY (BINDER NOT INCLUDED) — SPECIFY STATES.	☐ $8.95		
U.S. EDITION (FEDERAL SECTION — 50 STATES AND WASHINGTON, D.C. IN 11-BINDER SET)	☐ $295.00		
Successful Business Plan: Secrets & Strategies (GET THE BINDER...IT'S A BUSINESS PLAN KIT)	☐ $49.95	☐ $21.95	
Surviving and Prospering in a Business Partnership	☐ $39.95	☐ $19.95	
Write Your Own Business Contracts (HARDBACK BOOK)	☐ $39.95	☐ $19.95	

BOOK TOTAL (Please enter on other side also for grand total)

SOFTWARE Please check whether you use Macintosh or 5-1/4" or 3-1/2" Disk for IBM-PC & Compatibles

TITLE	5-1/4" IBM DISK	3-1/2" IBM DISK	MAC	PRICE	QUANTITY COST
Business Planning System		☐	☐	☐ $129.95	
California Corporation Formation Package Software	☐	☐	☐	☐ $39.95	
★ California Corporation Formation Binderbook & Software	☐	☐	☐	☐ $69.95	
Company Policy & Personnel Software	☐	☐	☐	☐ $49.95	
★ Company Policy Binderbook & Software	☐	☐	☐	☐ $89.95	
Customer Profile & Retrieval: Professional		☐	☐	☐ $119.95	
Financial Management Techniques		☐		☐ $99.95	
★ Financial Management Techniques Binderbook & Software		☐		☐ $129.95	
Financial Templates	☐	☐	☐	☐ $69.95	
The Small Business Expert		☐	☐	☐ $34.95	
Successful Business Plan		☐		☐ $69.95	
★ Successful Business Plan Binderbook & Software		☐	☐	☐ $109.95	

SOFTWARE TOTAL (Please enter on other side also for grand total)

Please add above totals on other side to complete your order. Thanks!

PSI Successful Business Library / Tools for Business Success Order Form (please see other side also)
Call, Mail or Fax to: PSI Research, 300 North Valley Drive, Grants Pass, OR 97526 USA
Order Phone USA (800) 228-2275   Inquiries and International Orders (503) 479-9464   FAX (503) 476-1479

Sold to: PLEASE GIVE STREET ADDRESS NOT P.O. BOX FOR SHIPPING

Name _____   Title: _____

Company _____   Daytime Telephone: _____

Street Address _____

City/State/Zip _____

❑   *YES, I want to receive the PREMIERE ISSUE of the PSI 1993 NEWSLETTER.*
   Be sure to include: Name, address, and telephone number above.

Ship to: (if different)   **PLEASE GIVE STREET ADDRESS NOT P.O. BOX FOR SHIPPING**

Name _____

Title _____

Company _____

Street Address _____

City/State/Zip _____

Daytime Telephone _____

Payment Information:

☐ Check enclosed payable to PSI Research (When you enclose a check, UPS ground shipping is free within the Continental U.S.A.)

Charge - ☐ VISA ☐ MASTERCARD ☐ AMEX ☐ DISCOVER Card Number: _____ Expires _____

Signature: _____   Name on card: _____

ITEM	PRICE EACH	QUANTITY	COST
EXECARDS Thank You Assortment (12 assorted thank you cards)	$ 12.95		
EXECARDS Recognition Assortment (12 assorted appreciation cards)	$ 12.95		
EXECARDS Marketing Assortment (12 assorted marketing cards)	$ 12.95		
EXECARDS TOTAL (Please enter below also for grand total)			$

Many additional options available, including custom imprinting of your company's name, logo or message. Please request a complete catalog.

PLANNING TOOLS — Action Tracking Note Pads

ITEM	NUMBER OF PADS
Calendar Note Pad ☐ 1993	
☐ 93/94	
☐ 1994	
Total number of pads	
Multiply by unit price:	x
PLANNING TOOLS TOTAL	$

UNIT PRICE FOR ANY COMBINATION OF PLANNING TOOLS
1-9 pads $3.95 each
10-49 pads $3.49 each
50 or more pads $2.98 each

SAFETY PROGRAM FORMS

ITEM	PRICE EACH	QUANTITY
Employee Warning Notification (Package of 20)	$4.95	
Request for Safety Orientation (Package of 20)	$4.95	
Report of Potential Hazard (Package of 20)	$4.95	
SAFETY PROGRAM FORMS TOTAL	$	

YOUR GRAND TOTAL

BOOK TOTAL (from other side)	$
SOFTWARE TOTAL (from other side)	$
EXECARDS TOTAL	$
PLANNING TOOLS TOTAL	$
SAFETY PROGRAM FORMS TOTAL	$
TOTAL ORDER	$

Rush service is available. Please call us for details.

Please send me:

_____ **EXECARDS Catalog**

_____ **Oasis Press Software Information**

_____ **Oasis Press Book Information**

Use this form to register for advance notification of updates, new books and software releases, plus special customer discounts!

Please answer these questions to let us know how our products are working for you, and what we could do to serve you better.

Title of book or software purchased from us:_____

It is a:
- ☐ Binder book
- ☐ Paperback book
- ☐ Book/software combination
- ☐ Software only

Rate this product's overall quality of information:
- ☐ Excellent
- ☐ Good
- ☐ Fair
- ☐ Poor

Rate the quality of printed materials:
- ☐ Excellent
- ☐ Good
- ☐ Fair
- ☐ Poor

Rate the format:
- ☐ Excellent
- ☐ Good
- ☐ Fair
- ☐ Poor

Did the product provide what you needed?
- ☐ Yes ☐ No

If not, what should be added?_____
_____
_____
_____
_____

This product is:
- ☐ Clear and easy to follow
- ☐ Too complicated
- ☐ Too elementary

Were the worksheets (if any) easy to use?
- ☐ Yes ☐ No ☐ N/A

Should we include:
- ☐ More worksheets
- ☐ Fewer worksheets
- ☐ No worksheets

How do you feel about the price?
- ☐ Lower than expected
- ☐ About right
- ☐ Too expensive

How many employees are in your company?
- ☐ Under 10 employees
- ☐ 10 – 50 employees
- ☐ 51 – 99 employees
- ☐ 100 – 250 employees
- ☐ Over 250 employees

How many people in the city your company is in?
- ☐ 50,000 – 100,000
- ☐ 100,000 – 500,000
- ☐ 500,000 – 1,000,000
- ☐ Over 1,000,000
- ☐ Rural (under 50,000)

What is your type of business?
- ☐ Retail
- ☐ Service
- ☐ Government
- ☐ Manufacturing
- ☐ Distributor
- ☐ Education

What types of products or services do you sell?
_____
_____
_____
_____

What is your position in the company?
(please check one)
- ☐ Owner
- ☐ Administration
- ☐ Sales/marketing
- ☐ Finance
- ☐ Human resources
- ☐ Production
- ☐ Operations
- ☐ Computer/MIS

How did you learn about this product?
- ☐ Recommended by a friend
- ☐ Used in a seminar or class
- ☐ Have used other PSI products
- ☐ Received a mailing
- ☐ Saw in bookstore
- ☐ Saw in library
- ☐ Saw review in:
  - ☐ Newspaper
  - ☐ Magazine
  - ☐ TV/Radio

Where did you buy this product?
- ☐ Catalog
- ☐ Bookstore
- ☐ Office supply
- ☐ Consultant
- ☐ Other_____

Would you purchase other business tools from us?
- ☐ Yes ☐ No

If so, which products interest you?
- ☐ EXECARDS® Communication Tools
- ☐ Books for business
- ☐ Software

Would you recommend this product to a friend?
- ☐ Yes ☐ No

If you'd like us to send associates or friends a catalog, just list names and addresses on back.

Do you use a personal computer for business?
- ☐ Yes ☐ No

If yes, which?
- ☐ IBM/compatible
- ☐ Macintosh

Check all the ways you use computers:
- ☐ Word processing
- ☐ Accounting
- ☐ Spreadsheet
- ☐ Inventory
- ☐ Order processing
- ☐ Design/graphics
- ☐ General data base
- ☐ Customer information
- ☐ Scheduling

May we call you to follow up on your comments?
- ☐ Yes ☐ No

May we add your name to our mailing list?
- ☐ Yes ☐ No

If there is anything you think we should do to improve this product, please describe:_____
_____
_____
_____

Thank you for your patience in answering the above questions. Just fill in your name and address here, fold (see back) and mail.

Name_____
Title_____
Company_____
Phone_____
Address_____
City/State/Zip_____

PSI Research creates this family of fine products to help you more easily and effectively manage your business activities:

The Oasis Press®
PSI Successful Business Library

PSI Successful Business Software
EXECARDS® Communication Tools

FOLD HERE SECOND, THEN TAPE TOGETHER

I¹¹ıı¹¹ıı¹¹ıı¹ıı¹ı¹ı¹¹ı¹¹ıı¹ı¹¹ıı¹¹ı¹ıl

PSI Research
PO BOX 1414
Merlin OR 97532-9900

POSTAGE WILL BE PAID BY ADDRESSEE

FIRST CLASS MAIL PERMIT NO. 002 MERLIN, OREGON

BUSINESS REPLY MAIL

NO POSTAGE
NECESSARY
IF MAILED
IN THE
UNITED STATES

FOLD HERE FIRST

Name	Name
Title	Title
Company	Company
Phone	Phone
Address	Address
City/State/Zip	City/State/Zip

If you have friends or associates who might appreciate receiving our catalogs, please list here. Thanks!

GREYSCALE

BIN TRAVELER FORM

Cut By _Smith_ Qty 14 Date 03-13-25

Scanned By _____ Qty _____ Date _____

Scanned Batch IDs

_____   _____   _____

Notes / Exception

_____

_____

_____

_____

_____